UNIVERSAL HYPNOSIS:

Universal Hypnosis:

Fantastical & Mind Bending Tales from the Untamed Cosmos

WILLIAM WAELCHLI JR

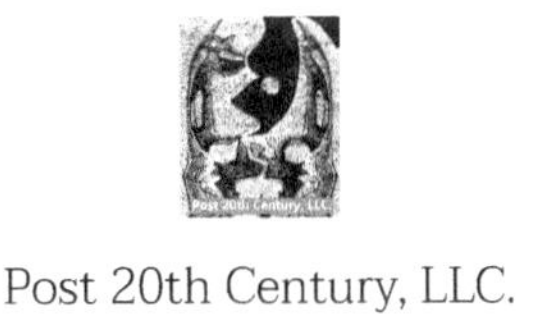

Post 20th Century, LLC.

Contents

Special Note Concerning The "Untamed Cosmos Companion Saga"   xi
Thoughtful Thank You's   xiii
A Short Dedication To Those Who Have Influenced Me During My
Journey Along My Cosmic Path: xvii
Preface: An Ode to the Future   xxi
Summaries About This Book: xxvii

1   "A Man's Journey to the Edge of the Planet...and his Mind"   1

2   "Sub Atomic Power Source: A Complicated Road to
Heaven" – or – "Who Controls Our Soul's Cosmic Path?"   9

3   "Thirst Comes First -or- H2O My Gosh!"   22

4   "First Contact: Noirian Style!"   31

5   "I Sure Wish I Could Play Galactic Pinball" - or – "Planeta
Extinctor and the Famished Insects"   39

6   "How To Traverse the Universe" -or "Circumnavigating the
Evolution of The Cosmos"   47

7   "Experiencing the Inconceivable & Incredible Seismic
Activity of the Unavoidable Creation Of Terraunus, While
Recalling the Supercontinent Pangæa"   55

8   "The Mysteries Surrounding the Discovery of the White Meteor" –or- "What's On The Menu This Evening? Spaghetti or Spaghettification?"   66

9   "Peering Through the Looking Glass at a Strange "Hole of Fire," While Imagining What Exists Beyond" - or – "Space Trippin' During A Psilocybinge"   78

10   "Careful With That Laser, Eugene" -or- "Galactic Laser Tag"   90

11   "A Crash Course In Cosmic Hitchhiking"   98

12   "Diamonds Aren't Forever...Even Though Bling is the in Thing" -or- "An Indecisive Future Concerning Scintillam and its Near Infinite Volatility..."   107

13   "An Uncertainty Regarding Orbital Acceleration" -or- "Who Caused Infinite Flames of Unfathomable Destruction to Tear Across the Universe?"   117

14   "Homage to Mr. King: The Sworn Swarm" -or- "Cosmic Carnivores"   124

15   "Please Don't Transpose Even a Single Letter as this Could Endanger the Planet Causing a Possible Planetary Genocide" -or- "I Love the Smell of Extinction Early in the Morning"   135

16   "Be Careful What You Think As Someone May Be Listening..."– or - "The Remote Control Aerial Laser May Just Delete the Space Junk Halo"   150

17   "Synchronized Sky Climb: 1,000,001 Nightmares At 50,000+ Feet...Skyrocketing Toward Space and Losing Fuel by the Second"   164

18   "Dark Energy & Dark Matter: Best Friends or Best Foes?" - or - "Anticipating the Completion of the Cosmic Ring of Accelerated Evolution"   173

19   "An Ethical & Moral Dilemma Concerning the Creation of a Mirror Universe and Its Future Implications Concerning Potential Universal Genocide" - or - "A Scientific Nemesis of Sorts..."   190

20   "Cosmic Collisions & Other Chaos from Them' Crazy Cosmos" - or – "Tonight Everyone Will Witness "Gamma Ray Charles"   201

21   "A Mind Traveler and the Trauma Machine's Malicious Intentions Regarding the Hyperinsane" – or - "Did Humanity Create Insanity or Did Insanity Create Humanity?"   214

22   "Close Encounters of the Mind Kind" - or – "Cerebral Manipulation: The Birth of the Renowned Collective Conscience"   228

23   "Has Egypt's Best Technology Just Been Discovered in an Ancient Tomb?" - or - "The 150 Billion Supernovae Explosions Extravaganza!"   239

24   "An Inquiry Concerning the Possible Abolishment of Aging" - or - "Cosmically Condemned"   253

25   "Evacuation from the Center of the Mind"– or -"Over Population Earth: Could You Live a Fulfilling Life Knowing the Exact Day You Will Die?"   265

26   "Electrickery" -or- "Post Conceptualization of Atomic Manipulation"   277

27   "Chainsaws & Robots"- or – "The Realest Reality TV Show Ever Seen: 'To Free A Killer'"   288

28   "Invasion of the Resource Snatchers!" -or- "Trippin' Earth" -or- "The Only Good Purploh Is A Dead Purploh!"   298

29   "How to Colonize the Moon: A Treaty to Conquer Space, Finally" - or - "Civilization or Colonization: The Choice May Not Be Yours"   314

30   My Pet Black Hole   324

31   "Planetary Evolution 101" -or- "Surfing A Magma Wave Beyond The Barriers of Infinity"   332

Biography of an Artistic Author   340
Information About The Illustrations & How To Purchase The Author's Art   344
One Last Thing...   363

ISBN: 979-8-88525-657-5

Library of Congress Control Number: 2022900836

Book One in the "Untamed Cosmos Companion Saga"

First Printing, 2022

Special Note Concerning The "Untamed Cosmos Companion Saga"

PLEASE NOTE THAT THIS FIRST BOOK IN THE "UNTAMED COSMOS COMPANION SAGA" HAS PARTIALLY BEEN CULMINATED FROM THE AUTHOR'S PREVIOUS BOOK "COSMIC APOCALYPTIC PHENOMENA: MORALITY TALES FROM THE UNTAMED COSMOS" AND INCLUDES A CULMINATION OF STORIES FROM THAT BOOK AND NEWLY WRITTEN VERY SHORT STORIES. THE NEWLY WRITTEN STORIES FOR THIS PUBLICATION IS MUCH MORE ROBUST AND MAKE YOU THINK HARDER WITH STORIES/CHAPTERS THAT I HOPE YOU, THE READER, WILL FIND COSMICALLY FASCINATING. TAKE A CHAPTER/STORY A NIGHT FOR A MONTH, AND YOU WILL BE ENTERTAINED FOR AN ENTIRE MONTH. WELCOME TO THE "UNTAMED COSMOS."

Thoughtful Thank You's

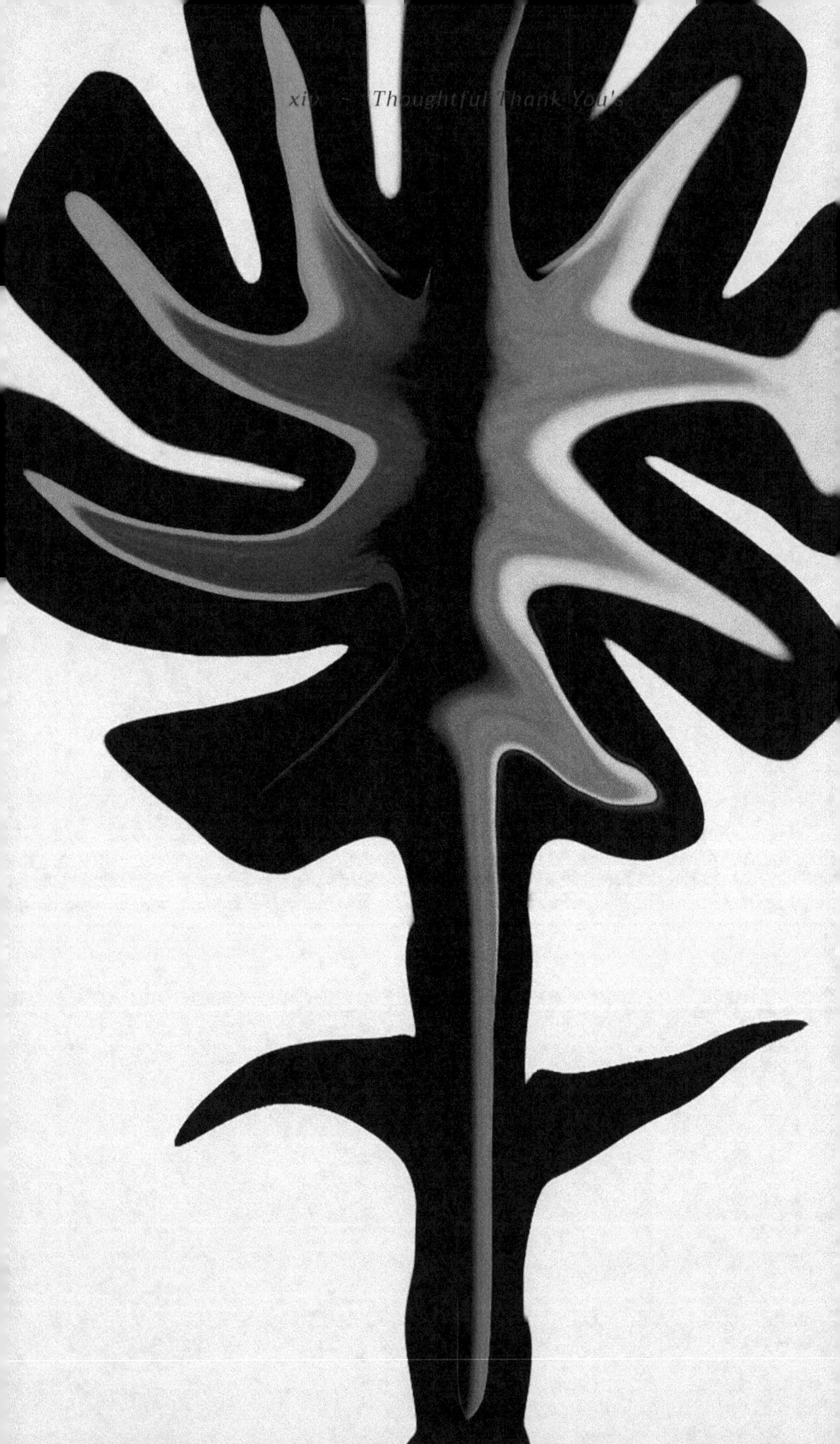

<u>Deepest gratitude to the following persons who have supported me</u>
<u>through this grueling endeavor of bringing the "Hypnotized Universe"</u>
<u>to you:</u>

First and Foremost, my immediate Family:
Father, Bill Waelchli
Mother, Karen Waelchli
Sister, Lisa Waelchli
Sister, Jana Waelchli
Nephew, Owen Frey
Niece, Annie Frey
Dog, Chopper Waelchli

My Friends:
Dave Frey
Chip Solomon
Kylie Solomon
Alexis Solomon
George Schlegel
Glen Martin
Peter Dunski
George Aloia
Austin Gualazzi
Bill Mekel
Riley Radoszek
Arto Grassler
Bob Trigg
Dave Thibeault
Niki Zink
Wesley McHugh
Shannon Spinoza
Joe Lentine
David Stamps
Steven Ospina
Lisa A. Krick-Leindecker
The Clubhouse of Allentown and its Members
John Vagenas (Bassist for the Greek Band "NAXATRAS")

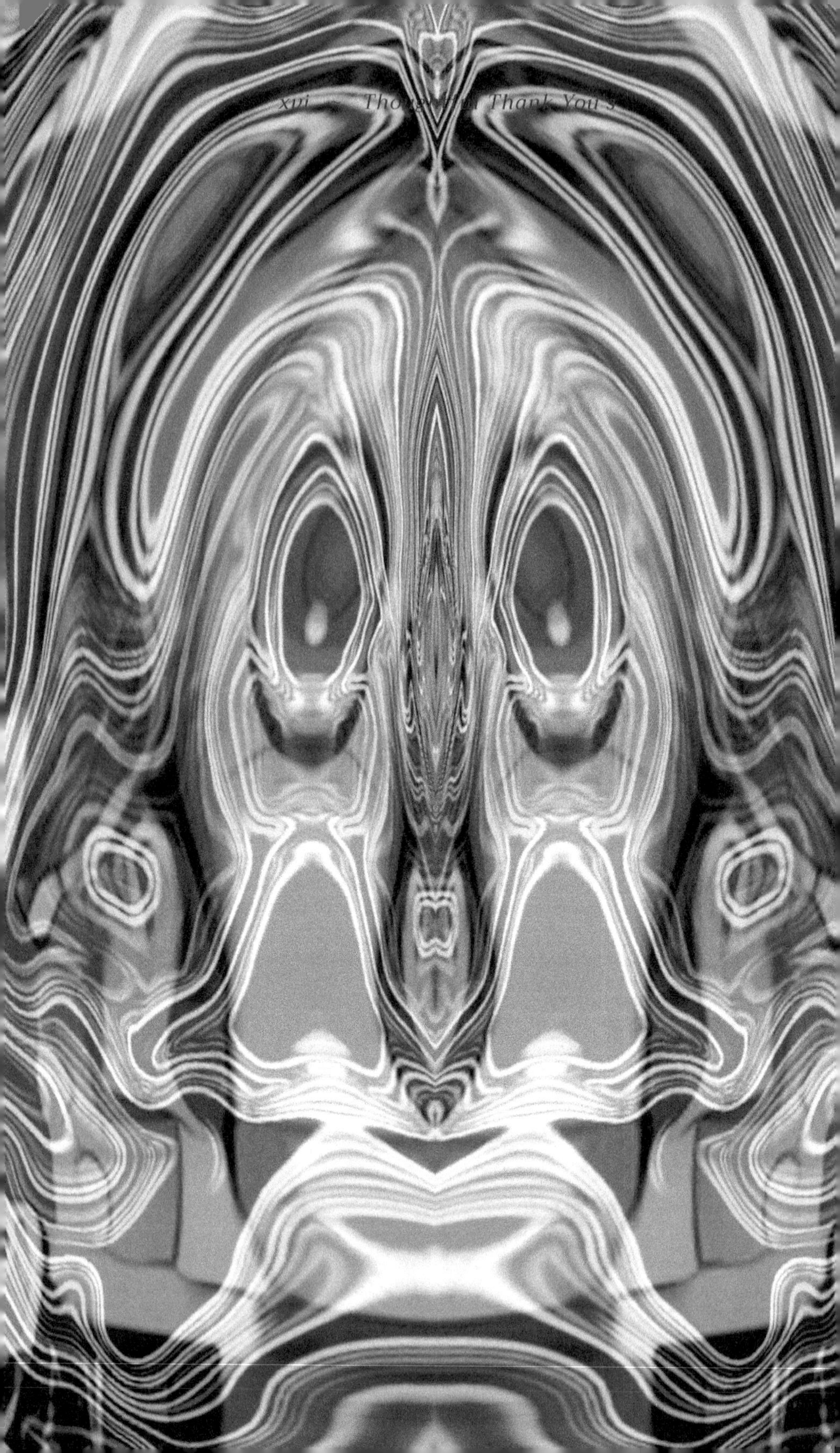

A Short Dedication To Those Who Have Influenced Me During My Journey Along My Cosmic Path:

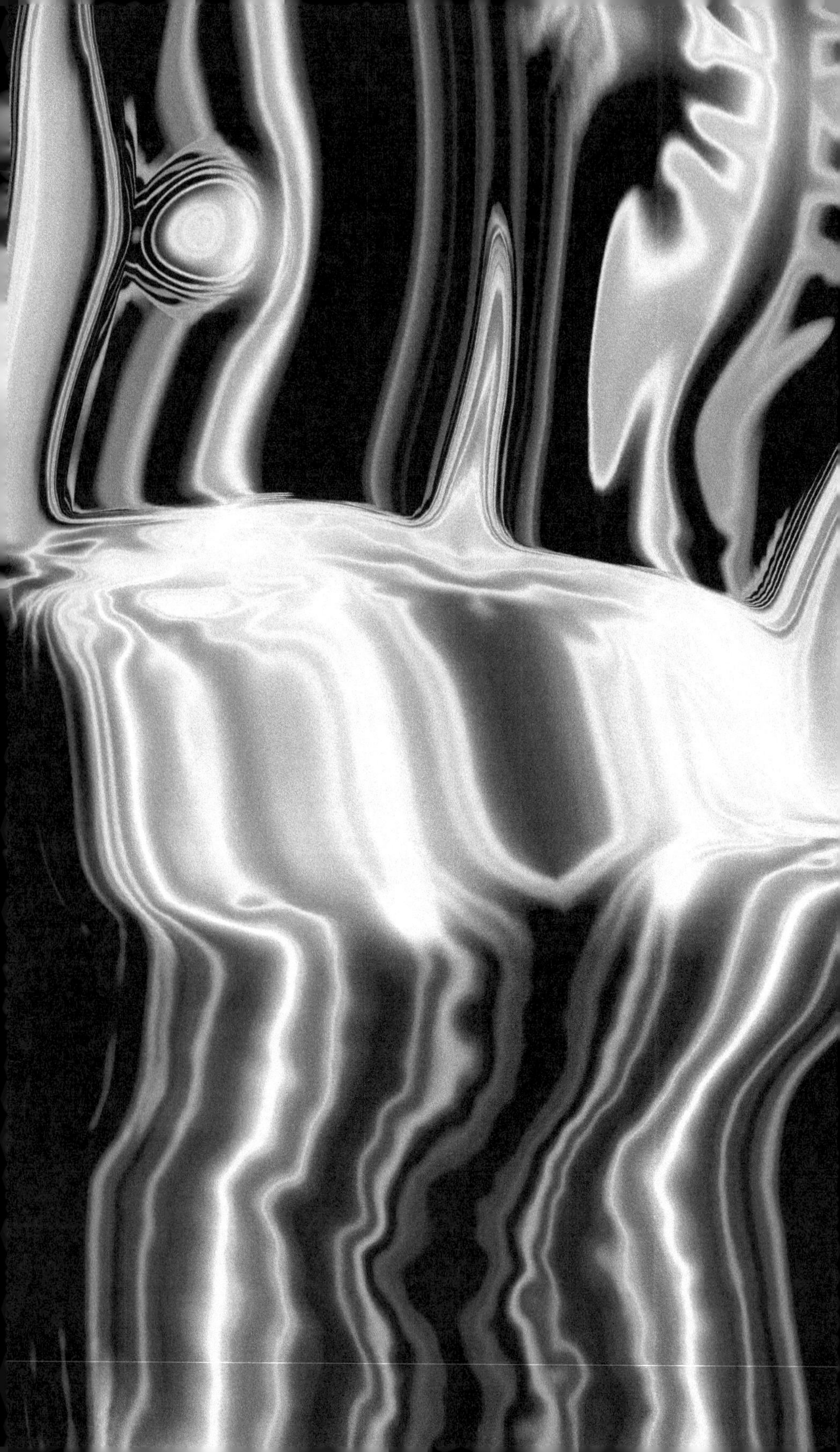

These ominous and sometimes "tongue in cheek" tales of planetary and cosmic disturbances gone very awry are told in a narrator's "play by play tone."

This "Untamed Cosmos Companion Saga" was conceived partly due to the persons mentioned below:

Firstly to Rod Serling, for his innovative work in television, including the classic "Twilight Zone" and "Night Gallery" series. Mr. Sterling's work further exemplified the psychological horror genre, which still scares people to this day, decades and decades later. The first incarnation of "The Twilight Zone" started many decades ago in 1959 and is still relevant today.

My mother even mentioned the Twilight Zone episode "It's A Good Life" and how it scared her from ever having a jack in the box ever again. Now that is good writing!

This collection of very short stories is also dedicated to Mr. Stanley Kubrick and Sir Arthur C. Clarke, who conceived the immortal film "2001: A Space Odyssey" in 1968. It is considered one of the finest films of all time among critics and fans alike. Without this groundbreaking film, the science fiction genre may not have evolved to what it is today.

Now I extend a warm welcome and invite you to read this chaotically calamitous 'untamed' collection of 31 very short stories, which may take you beyond infinity and back again, It cannot be guaranteed that you will be in one piece upon your return from your Trip.

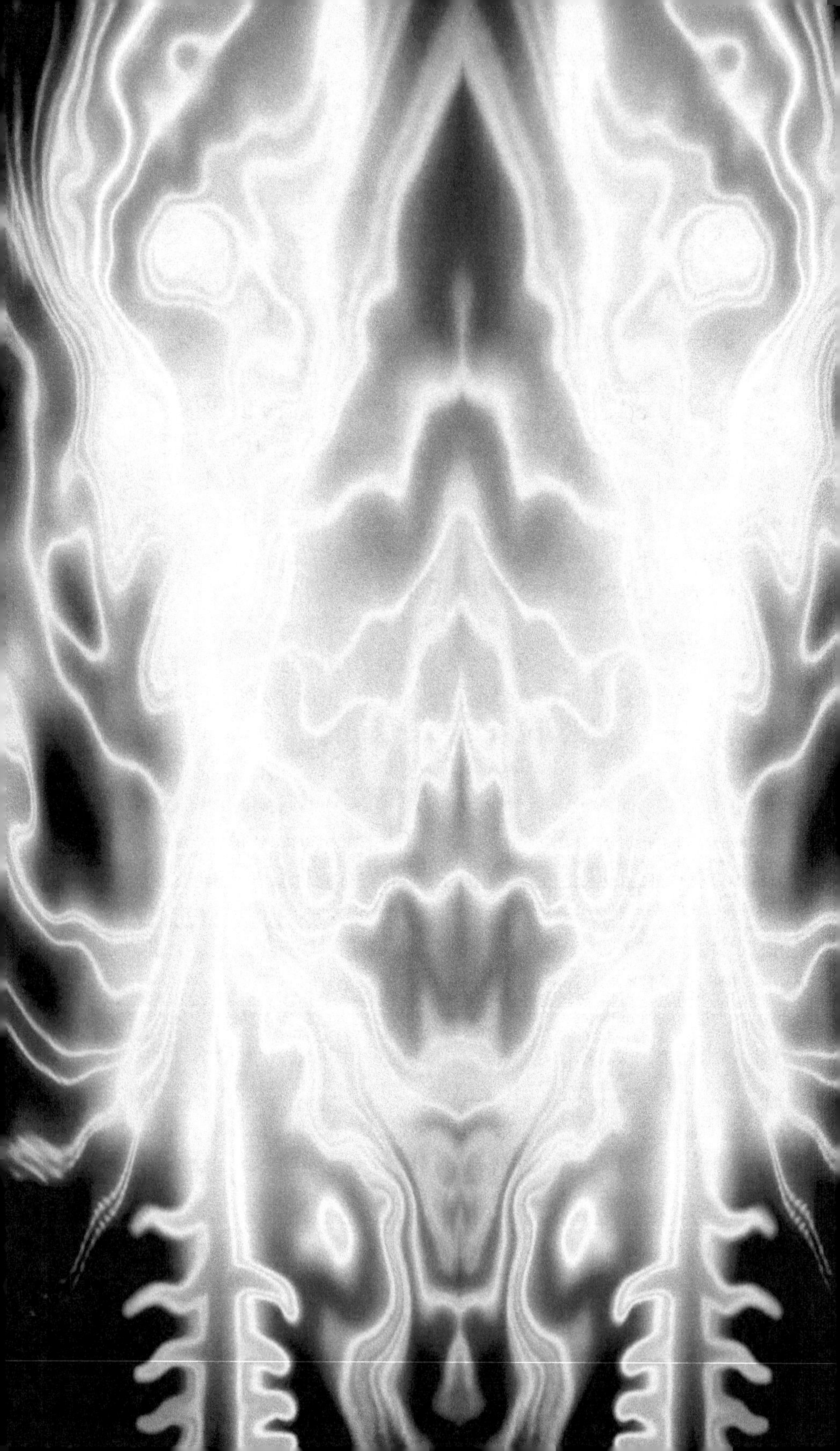

Preface: An Ode to the Future

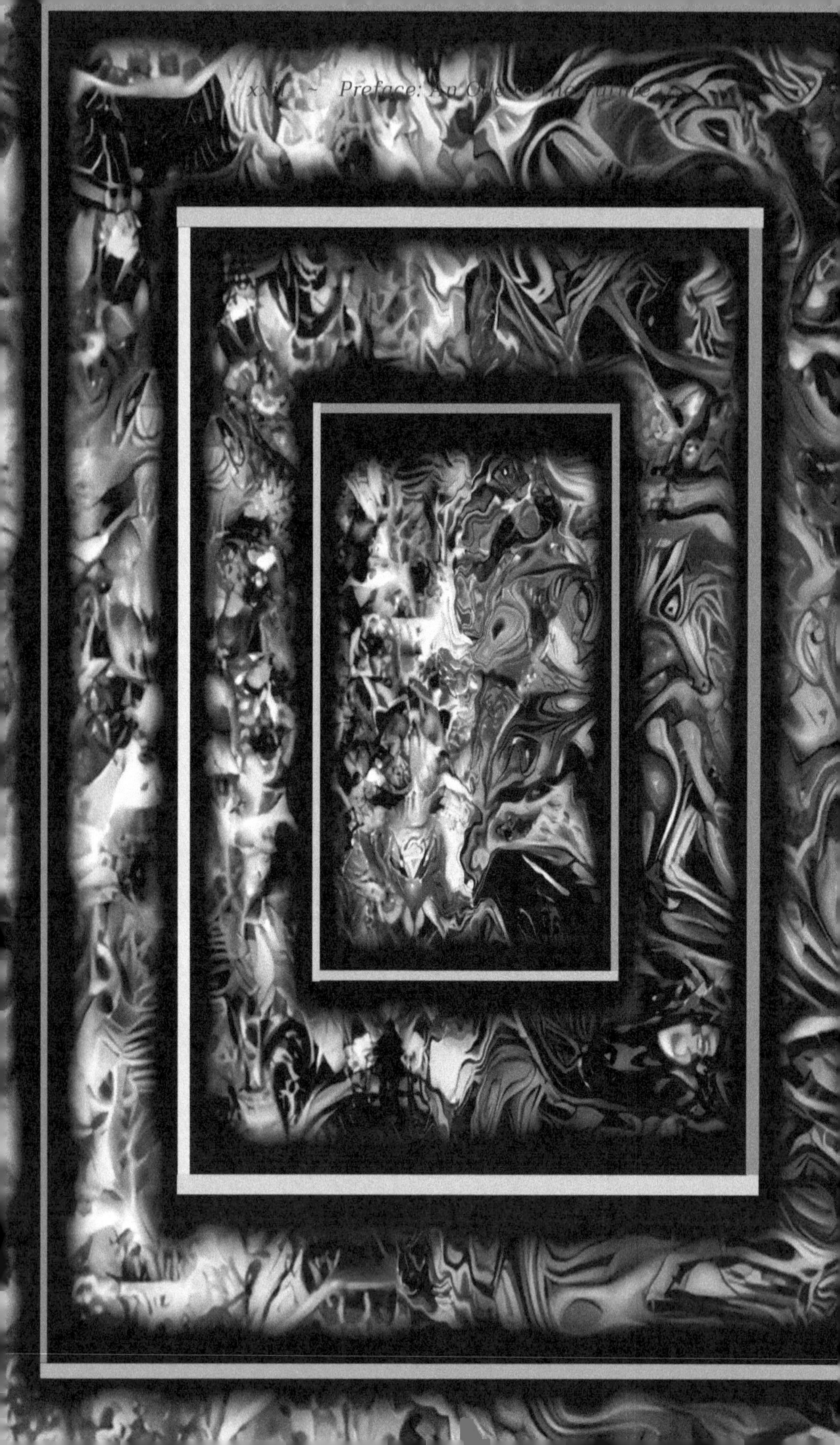

The entire Human Race is in utter turmoil, and overcome by fears of a possible cosmic cataclysm, or is it just the 'aliens' again? All the while, the cosmos, being silently violent and magnificently malevolent, plans its next strategy regarding a possible decimation of Earth or perhaps the entire universe , or perhaps nothing at all will happen.

These 31 very short stories/chapters assembled into this compact book of cosmic catastrophes should pique any cosmos-loving Human's interest. There are also many stories of hope and overcoming opposing odds, like when those darned Noirians came to Earth... Rest assured, the terror is balanced out by the hopeful endings of planetary love and peace & happiness dotted throughout this collection of very short stories.

The 31 chapters are not by accident. This book is designed where a chapter may be read each day for a month, and not a single chapter will repeat. Then repeat accordingly... Of course you could just read it out-right, which I hope will be an enjoyable experience for all readers.

Within the blink of an eye, everything could go black and stay that way forever. Of course, this may happen at the "hands" of rogue black holes, hypervelocity planets, tearing holes through the very fabric of space-time, and any other matter of planetary or possible universal ending scenarios.

There is possible "mind erasure" on the horizon, and it will not be known until it is way too late to retrieve the contents of what was once your mind. Also, did everybody forget about the "Cataclysmic Pole Shift Hypothesis?"

Ever had a splitting headache? So does the Earth, and the "splitting" is happening right in the middle of the planet. What chaos will this scenario breed? Like a head crash to a hard drive, Humanity may be rendered completely inoperable due to cosmic corruption.

Perhaps you may witness the discoverer of a stray space object that leads to a newer and more accurate way to define something important in the universe, thus changing everything we once knew about the cosmos or maybe we will learn nothing at all.

Also included in this Untamed Cosmos Companion Saga book may be the cosmological location of Heaven. Although going to "Heaven" may prove more than worrisome for the astronauts chosen to make the trip out into the cosmos where they will meet The Supreme Leader.

A peculiar rock is found deep underground that shocks the miners present... Did you ever receive an electric shock? How about a shock with so many volts they cannot be counted? Me neither...

Following this Preface will be a list of summaries for chapters in this untamed companion book. They will offer no chapter designations, as it should be fun to match up the summaries with the chapters.

In the 'Untamed Cosmos Companion Saga,' this book was written over a 19-month period during 2020 – 2021. After 1000s of hours and experiencing stressors never thought possible, I bring this untamed book to you.

This book was designed with 31 very short stories across 31 chapters. It is designed for reading a single chapter a day for a month. This way, you may receive the maximum effect by giving your brain a 24-hour rest between stories because you may need that.

From my imagination to yours: Let's read!!

William Waelchli Jr,
4 January 2022

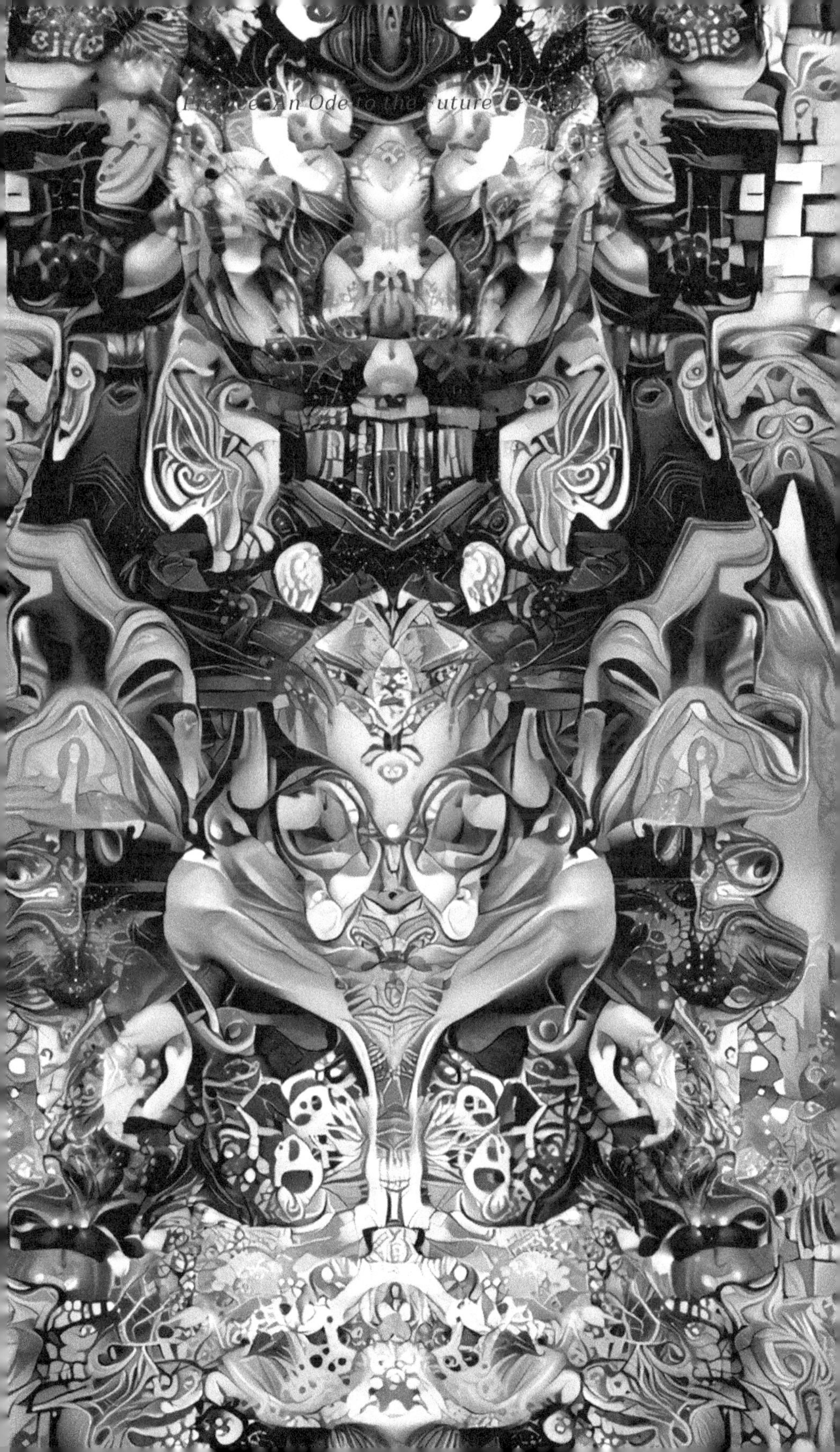
Prelude: An Ode to the Future Present

Summaries About This Book:

...sacrificing the planet or a generation of your children? Let your mind decide as your thoughts are being recorded...

Ten thousand airplanes in the sky have lost control...Nobody knows if they can break free of their hellish sky prisons. Do we have a autopilot in the house?

A man takes a not-so-mellow drive when the road's center line starts to smoke like a campfire. Was it stated he is all alone with nobody else in sight.

A menacing psychological time bomb plummeting towards an unimaginable outcome... does anybody know the definition for a cranial supernova?

A new Space Race ensues as the journey towards Mars has begun. Be careful when packing for your trip as you may need more than you packed...

A strange technology is found in the Egyptian desert, enabling Humanity to see "everything." Perhaps it is not such a good day for such adventures?

A war of elements is waged where the losers (if any) will take an all-expenses-paid trip to our Sun.

A white meteor causes a chase to locate a new home in the Cosmos. But, Humanity can only run so far from its problems.

A window to a new universe is discovered. What lurks in the darkness, yearning for your blood? Perhaps mushroom hunting is in order?

'Aliens' touch down on Earth... Why so many strange disappearances now? And why am I unable to think?

An ever-changing landscape of cosmic madness comes to Earth with possible dire consequences. Read on if you dare.

An inconceivable jolt of electricity of near-infinite volts may ravage Earth, or maybe a black hole will collide with it or maybe nothing.

Any time of day is a good day for an Ice Age. Just crank the heat, and you should be ok... As long as those darned insects stay at bay.

Anyone a fan of unfathomable body count numbers? I'm not either... Just don't light that cigar during a gasoline storm...

Dark energy is harnessed, giving us godlike control of the cosmos. Did anybody verify this is a good idea? Or safe? Or legal?

Despite your thoughts on the subject, you are ill-advised never to create a computer version of the solar system...

Earth is rich in rare undiscovered elements. It's a shame the Noirian's knew this first...

Do eyes that see beyond the Cosmos seem pretty cutting-edge? Not until you see what is beyond our normal way of observing the cosmos.

Feeling paradoxical? Take a trip through a psychological prison and notify me when you are stripped of your mind.

Human expiration dates? Male pregnancy? An electric planet? It's time to hand over that conscience as it no longer belongs to you.

Purplohs (?) invade Earth... Did I mention the entire planet is under the influence of lady Lucy? No, we do not have any resources...

Seven serial killers apprehended in seven days? Let's put them on reality TV...just make sure that one escapes Robot Island with their life if that is possible.

Take in a breathtaking view of the Electric Sky while it falls on your head.

The soul has been atomically located! Now maybe the particles will lead us to Heaven, or will they?

Do you want to lose all of your negativity? The Collective Conscience will do this for you! Just look to the skies before consuming the nerve agent.

Chapter 1

"A Man's Journey to the Edge of the Planet...and his Mind"

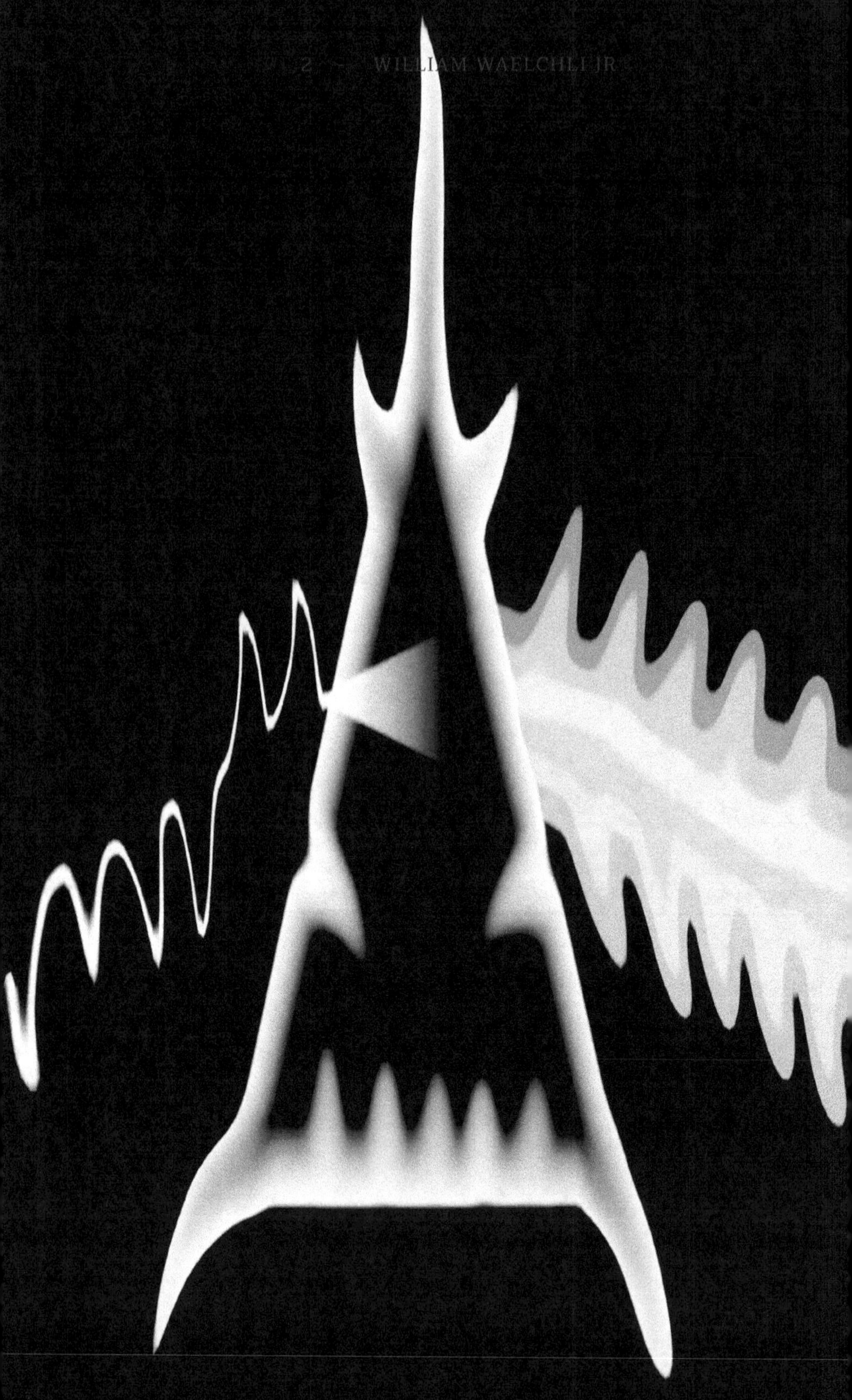

George Fortem was cruising down the interstate in his cherry-red 1965 Ford Thunderbird at 2 pm local time. He just received good news and was very happy today. He was going through many issues in his personal life, making this drive well worth it. This helped his mental state as well, had it not been for his eerie surroundings...

For some odd reason, George was the only person outside at an unusually busy time of day, being it was mid-afternoon. Fear enveloped George, and he felt an uneasy feeling in his stomach. He took this as something was very wrong, and George was alone and scared...

George drove down the road. He was enjoying the crisp air coming in the windows of his "T-Bird." Without warning, a black line appeared in the space between the double yellow lines and was breaking the road apart very slowly.

This was complete, with smoke billowing out of the mini earthquake in the road appearing before him. For the life of him, he could not figure out how the line appeared and what may transpire from the mysterious smoke line billowing up from the road as he drove.

Most strange of all was the heat that George could feel on his side of his car while driving near the smoke line. He was having second thoughts about driving on the road.

George pulled his car over to sit on a park bench near an empty park that should be teeming with people since it was summer. But alas, there was nobody there. It was as if everyone had just vanished, except for George. His fear was mounting.

As he was sitting on the park bench (while facing the road), a wall of smoke about 15 feet (4.5 meters) high shot up from the road.

When the dust settled, and the smoke wall vanished, George took note that the smoke wall, somehow, caused a line on the ground as far as his eyes could see in every direction.

George stared in disbelief as the smoke line started to grow higher; he looked up at the sky, noting that the smoke line was in the sky as well.

George became even more scared because he did not know the smoke line, why it was getting wider, and why it appeared near where he was on the bench.

There was no evading the growing line of smoke, as it was obvious from the sky as to what had happened, although George was terrified to admit it.

He looked at his phone a moment to see the time but was rather abruptly caught off guard when an online article he read stated a brief, nearly blinding flash had happened in Japan as the Japanese people slept last night. It was so bright it was daytime for an instant. More reports of countries reporting the flash everywhere it was dark, about twelve hours ago.

George noted that the smoke line, on the ground and in the sky, was now a good three feet wide and widening more and more as time ticked by.

Suddenly, a loud rumbling rang out that was so loud that George had to cover his ears. He made a good decision by getting back in his antique Thunderbird and drove next to the menacing line of smoke that continued to grow wider and wider.

George had quite a difficult time driving since the smoke line was in the middle of the road. All at once, the smoke line shifted, and all of a sudden, the entire line of smoke (that encircled the Earth) fell 56 feet, during a global Earthquake measuring an astonishing 17.5 and instantly breaking every Richter scale that was taking a reading at the time.

What was odd was that at the smoke line, the Earth jutted upwards, showing that, worst-case scenario, that George's side of the Earth may give way.

Scientists always surmised that there could never be an Earthquake over the 10.0 reading on the Richter scale. It looks like they were wrong, although Humanity did not expect that a planet-wide earthquake would ever happen.

As George drove back to his house, he turned off the treacherous road and towards his home. Unfortunately for George, the smoke line went through his house, destroying it in the process.

George surveyed the situation as he looked at the jagged edge to see how far everything had fallen. Suddenly, the Earth's incision fell 212 feet (64.6 meters), making it 268 feet (81.7 meters) down. George just looked on in a confused fashion at a blank dirt wall.

Elsewhere, scientists finally figured out that some rogue laser beam from an extraterrestrial civilization must have shot through the Earth. That corroborated the flashes seen by all persons in Eurasia, Australia, and Oceania.

George was still at his home. The growing wall of dirt in front of him kept on growing taller and taller as the Earth's two halves were drifting apart, rather quickly, breaking apart from one another. The drifting apart of both halves of Earth overwhelmed George as he conjured up a way to escape this possibly inescapable mess.

All George could do was stare at the huge wall of dirt, knowing that it would eventually fall out of orbit and both halves would drift in space forever. Of course, that was not if they collided with anything else out there in the cosmos.

All at once, the wall of dirt grew another staggering 3333 feet (1016 meters), and now rock and debris were starting to rain down near George, so he got back in his 65' Thunderbird and drove as far as he could away from this frightening planetquake, which had destroyed his home and everything he owned.

As soon as he pressed the gas, George looked in his window and witnessed something that was beyond terrifying. The half of Earth that George was on "released" the other half of the Earth, now dire consequences will be dealt.

He saw darkness where the other half of Earth should have been. It seemed that the Earth's halves finally broke apart where the core rained down like it was a punctured water pipe.

As the raining lava poured down around the street George was driving on, he saw a purple gate or portal up ahead on his side of the road. As the halve of Earth George was on started to freefall, he felt very uneasy. As George's stomach felt like going down a tall roller coaster hill times 1000, he drove into the gate, hoping it would take him to a safe and habitable place.

He became so blinded by the light that he just hoped he would not hit something while driving. Before he knew it, he exited the time gate and found himself driving down the road near his home. Earth was also in one piece, and there was no menacing magma rain.

He drove back to his home and noted that it was intact. It seemed that George had found a rare time portal that enabled him to go back one day before the laser even hit the sky.

George seemed happy at first to be back at his home since it was in one piece. Will the smoke line return in one day? If it does, would George be able to find another time gate? Even then, that only buys him another day at the most before impending doom repeats.

THE END

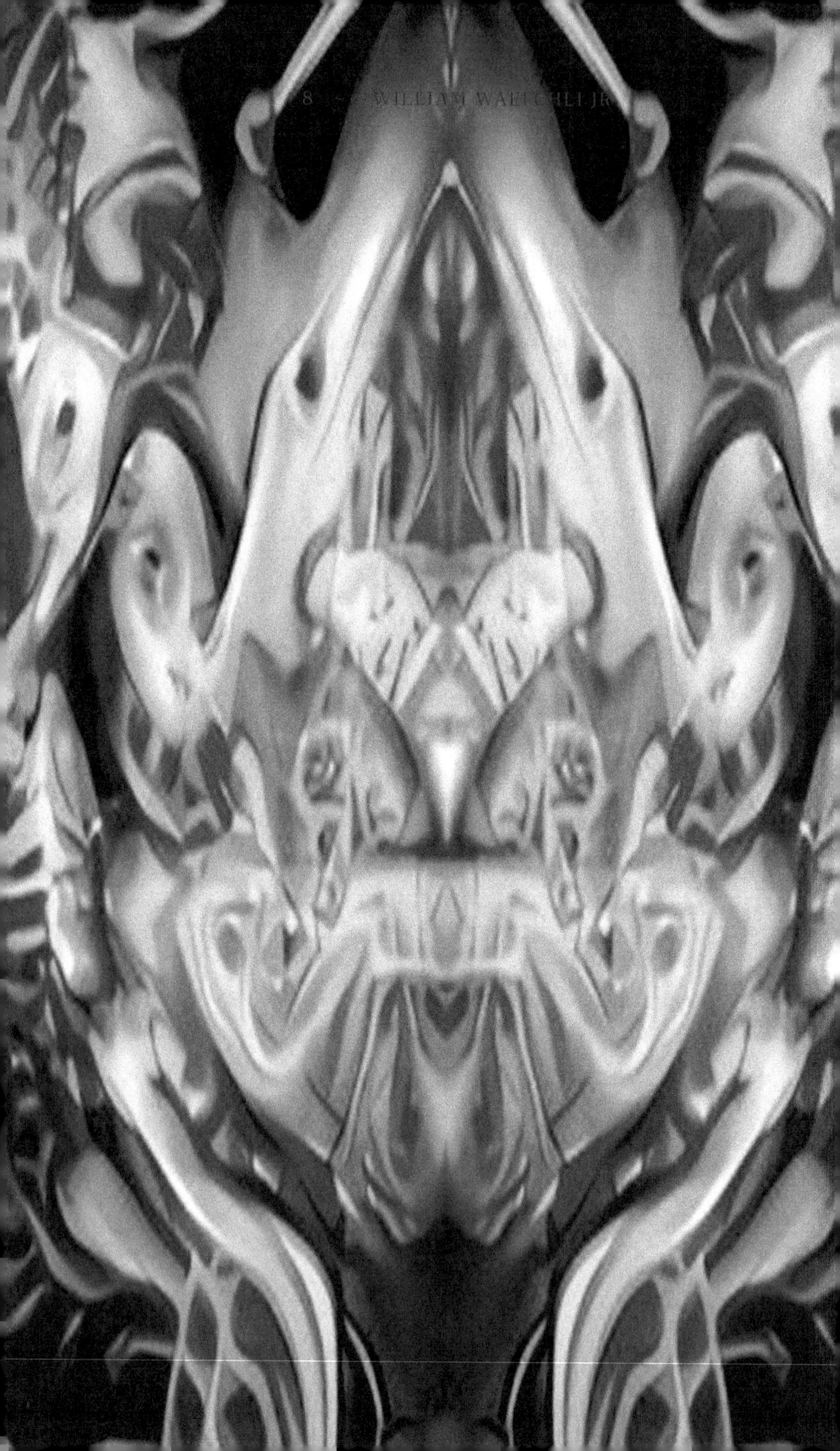

"Sub Atomic Power Source: A Complicated Road to Heaven" – or – "Who Controls Our Soul's Cosmic Path?"

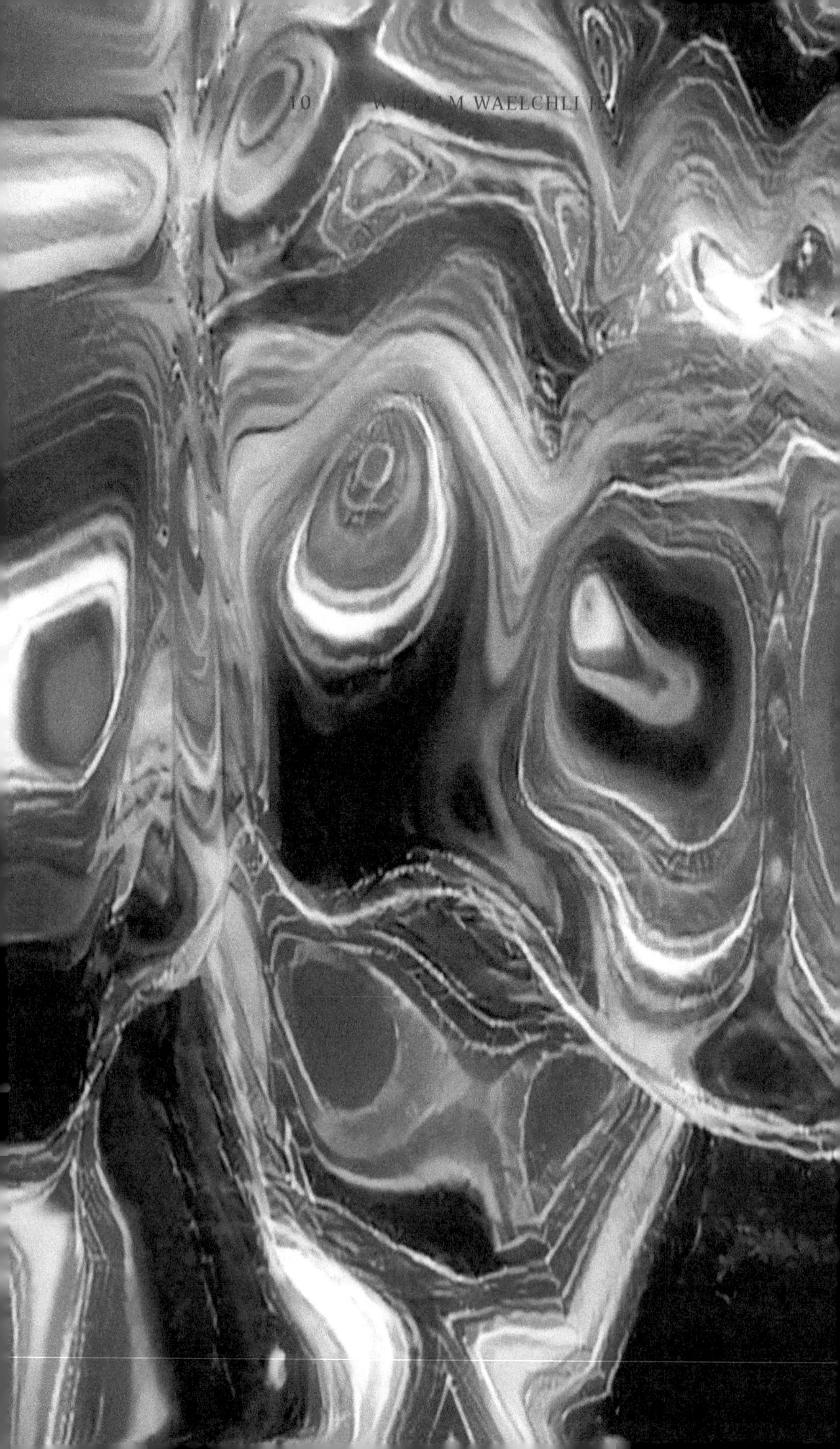

Earth was in a state of confusion about where we eventually go once we exit our bodies and go to our final resting place of eternity.

Humanity had asked many people in the scientific community questions to get results on where we go once we pass on and become postorganic. In a way to find an answer to the question about "Where do we go after we die," scientists started microscopically looking at passed person's atoms who were about to pass away.

It seemed so elementary at the time, but no one ever looked at a person's atomic structure during the transition from life to death. What the scientists found was "life" changing.

A gluon is the mind of the atom and makes decisions that caused the atom to operate. It is a subatomic part of each atom. Each adult has around 7^{27} atoms. That is a seven with 27 zeros or around an octillion atoms in each adult body.

Upon closer examination, the gluons "disconnected" and spiraled out of the deceased's bodies and through the ceiling. Scientists were baffled at this revelation and knew they were on to something special.

The scientists needed to track the gluons' movement to see where they went as it was hypothesized that the gluons were, in fact, the soul and held our visual and auditory record and consciousness from the cradle to the grave. This was all hypothesized and may or may not be accurate.

We held on to this belief and hoped that it was correct, and then by that rationale, we took "everything we have ever felt through any sense" with us to Heaven.

The next item of business for the scientists was to follow the gluons and see where they go and, maybe just maybe, we could locate Heaven out in the cosmos.

It took some time, but engineers invented a "gluon detection system," or GDS for short, to track the deceased's gluons' movement anywhere in the Universe.

The machine identified any gluons having exited humans' bodies anywhere on Earth and tracked them throughout their journey out in space. They could not see the gluons. Instead, their coordinates showed up on a screen showing every gluon's trajectory.

They tracked the GDS for just over a month before they made an astonishing discovery: every gluon went to the same coordinate. It seemed almost too good to be true but somewhat plausible...

Once the scientists located the universal coordinate that kept on showing up out in space, they noted that it was only 222,333 miles away. Scientists were immediately excited as this place is reachable with modern spacecraft. We especially wanted to know what this place was as we needed to understand why all of the "Dead" were going there and staying there.

The Search for Extraterrestrial Intelligence (SETI) sent out a friendly message to "Heaven" and hoped the Earth would receive a message back. After months of waiting, nothing was received from the newly discovered planet, so it was deemed appropriate to send a team of astronauts to the "gluon planet."

Scientists noted an Earth-like atmosphere on the planet, and we were sure it had intelligent life because we could see buildings, houses, etc., on the surface.

We noted what appeared to be substantial circular vents at the top and bottom of the North Pole and the South Pole. These vents were 1000 square miles around. It was believed that the planet was hollow in its center and contained inside its central cylinder must have been the hijacked gluons of the Dead that may be used as the strange planet's power source.

Scientists were not 100% positive whether this was the case or not, but we ran with it once scientists made a particular discovery: The gluon detection system picked up the gluons or souls of the Earth's Dead. They were all contained in the very central cylinder, and their heat must have given those no good extraterrestrials all the power they would ever need.

This did not bode well with Humanity, who wanted the souls set free to follow their cosmic path to Heaven. Some people wanted the planet, after gluon removal, to be destroyed. Surprisingly, this was not meant much resistance, although a more sinister "punishment" may be in store.

Humanity will send five astronauts to the strange planet to verify if the hypothesis was correct. With modern-day space-craft, the astronauts will make it to the planet, now named "Vitafur" (meaning Life Thief in Latin), in around a week since the planet is somewhat near Earth.

The mission was to land on Vitafur, approach the leaders, and tell them that they must immediately release the central cylinder's Souls'/gluons'. They had tried a diplomatic approach rather than having gone in guns blazing.

If they reach resistance, the astronauts will leave immediately, at which point a secret plan will be executed to guarantee the release of the Dead souls from the central cylinder of Vitafur at any cost.

No matter what obstacles stood in Humanity's way, they were determined to release every soul, which was held in a prison that allegedly had no way of escaping. Although we Humanity will see how accurate this was.

On launch day, the five astronauts boarded the spacecraft and set out towards Vitafur. The spacecraft started its way towards the strange planet. After some time, it honed in on the mysterious planet as the planet fast approached.

It must have been twice the Earth's size and had purple oceans, and the land was light blue. The leaves on the trees were a deep crimson color, and this made the astronauts laugh: The sky was urine-colored yellow and must have showered Vitafur in that golden color when it rained that only a yellow sky could bring.

The spacecraft entered Vitafur's airspace and got to admire the brilliant architecture and cleanliness of the planet. The astronauts took note of the massive circular vents at the North and South poles.

They saw a great city ahead and knew that this would be an excellent place to land. The astronauts were hoping that the extraterrestrials were welcoming and not hostile.

They landed the spacecraft on a side street in the center of the great city.

All five astronauts exited the spacecraft after an air analysis was done, having checked if it was breathable. After a few moments, the air analysis displayed to the astronauts that the air was breathable.

They were awestruck by the serene beauty and the serenity of the area surrounding them. The city seemed quite empty until a group of what the astronauts deemed "female Reptilian-like creatures" were seen in the distance. They had bright purple skin and claws that could rip anybody to shreds.

The three reptilians caught sight of the astronauts, and they had nowhere to run if things got ugly. As the reptilians approached them, the lead astronaut announced, "We are humans from Earth. We come in peace." The reptilians had a robotic attachment to their arm, which they spoke through.

The computer attachment translated any language into their native tongue. It also translated the extraterrestrials' language back and played through the speaker in English for the astronauts to hear. The one reptilian lady walked forward, and the robotic arm started to emit her voice.

"Welcome to our wonderful planet. You are in the city of "Necevadere." This is the capitol city of the planet. Let us take you to our supreme leader as he is near." The astronauts knew what Necevadere meant in Latin, and it was not such a great thing or heartwarming at that.

Translated as "no escape," the astronauts were dealt a fear-like blow causing them to feel trapped...but the show had to go on as the astronauts would meet the supreme leader and hopefully convince them to free all of their souls.

The reptilian group led them to a grand white marble palace. That must have been near the size of a football field. Even more friendly reptilians greeted the five astronauts. They were told that the reptilians would retrieve Zoth, their supreme leader.

After a few minutes, Zoth greeted the astronauts and shook their hands. "You certainly must be uncomfortable in those suits. Let us get you, nice people, something more comfortable to wear during your stay with us." Zoth stated. He had a very warm and welcoming demeanor that eased the fear factor of the astronauts.

What was failed to mention earlier was that the astronauts would strategically place cameras in the palace, which will beam back live video to mission control, giving them a front seat-like view of all that transpires in the grand palace. No more than two inches across, the cameras should be easy to hide.

The astronauts changed into some strange red and white, form-fitting suits. Hey, it was better than wearing their space gear the whole time. This was even if they looked like Santa Claus' elves.

As they were finishing up getting dressed, one of the palace guards entered the room and told them that a special dinner was being prepared. The Palace guard said that they could reconvene in the grand dining room in five minutes.

As the astronauts walked to the luxurious dining room, they covertly placed cameras where mission control could spy on everything that was happening. The astronauts were very anxious about what they would be served on this reptilian planet.

Some other dignitary types joined the astronauts for dinner, including Zoth. The soup served was some sort of blue, cream soup with some small green meatballs, or at least that is what it looked like. But hey, at least they were not served monkey brains... As they dug into their soup, the astronauts noted that the strange colored meatballs were better than any they had on Earth.

Zoth spoke, "Now that I have your attention, Earthlings, let me explain how things operate around here." "This planet has a gluon detecting radar that pulls in the gluon stream and "harvests" the souls of all of the Dead by using them as a permanent power source, found in the planets center." "Don't feel so bad. Your pitiful Earth is not the only planet we harvest from."

One of the astronauts spoke up, "How long have you been stealing souls from our planet and other galactic neighbors?" He appeared to pass clean out before he could receive an answer, where his head banged off the soup bowl, spilling it all over the place. The other astronauts now felt mounting panic and hoped their lives would not end on this strange planet.

Zoth spoke again, "The only way you will ever free all of the gluons is to penetrate the great vent at the North Pole. But now that you are "frozen" here, you will not be destroying our only power source." "Nice try, Earthlings..."

The astronauts got up to run, but the red suits Zoth gave the astronauts earlier froze them in place, making any move-ment impossible. Before too long, the four other astronauts succumbed to the immense poisons that tainted their soup.

With the astronauts gone, Zoth was sure to find the cameras, which will give him the inclination that Humanity will most likely send in more astronauts from the Space Force to rectify this horrible situation and release the Dead from their captors.

Back on Earth at mission control, all craziness had ensued with witnessing the deaths of all five astronauts.

As sad as this was, the World Space Project had to prepare more astronauts to return to Necevadere, although they will not be stepping foot on that revolting planet...

Their mission was to destroy the northern vent and release the souls of everyone who ever lived in the reptilians' stellar neighborhood, including Earth. Having a spacecraft outfitted with a front-mounted "molecular" laser that would quickly remove the massive vent at the North Pole of the enemy's planet will be utilized. This allowed all of Earth's and the planetary neighbors' souls to escape and travel to their final destination of Heaven.

The launch day arrived, and everything went as planned, including the astronaut's trip through space & time, which had arrived at Necevadere. The radar-avoiding spacecraft secretly hovered near the vent. The laser quickly cut the roof of the clean vent clean off with the special mounted laser.

As luck would have it, it seemed Zoth and company had the same technology as we had for detecting gluons/souls. Removing the vent would release the souls and prevent the reptilians from stealing or harvesting more souls since the temperature on Necevadere would plummet like the stock market in 1929.

The astronauts positioned the molecular laser around the vent and started to make a surgical incision around the top of the vent. Without delay, rainbows of millions of colors shot out of the top of the planet, reflecting light in all directions.

It was the most beautiful thing anyone in the spacecraft had ever seen. At the least, it instilled a profound amount of faith in all who witnessed this grand death spectacle courtesy of the souls escaping their captors.

As previously stated, all of the colored light headed straight for the Cosmic Core or Universal Light as it was known. This gave them passage outside of the Universe to Heaven.

Oh yeah, Necevadere...It will quietly and quickly iced over the entire planet, and froze everyone alive through and through over the next couple of months until all that was left are frozen extraterrestrials of every reptilian who lived on their planet or popsicles, whatever way you want to think of it.

At the lavish palace, Zoth was jolted from his sleep and received the unfortunate news that the Earthlings had destroyed the northern vent and caused the countless souls to escape.

He asked a member of his entourage why it was so bitter cold in the room. To which the guard answered that "the heat source is now gone." Zoth thought a bit and then went back to bed, knowing he had been defeated.

As the days and weeks passed on by, it was realized that the irony of the planet's name being Necevadere meant "no escape," it became damn clear that the joke was definitely on Zoth and his people. Neither they nor anyone else survived the next couple of months as the extreme cold froze the planet solid, rendering it an enormous iceberg.

Humanity collectively wondered what it must have been like in Heaven since who knows how many souls just arrived there tonight. They also instilled more hope, knowing that their souls will take the right path upon their souls' planetary exit through the Universal Light, guaranteeing passage to where they should rightfully belong, in Heaven.

THE END

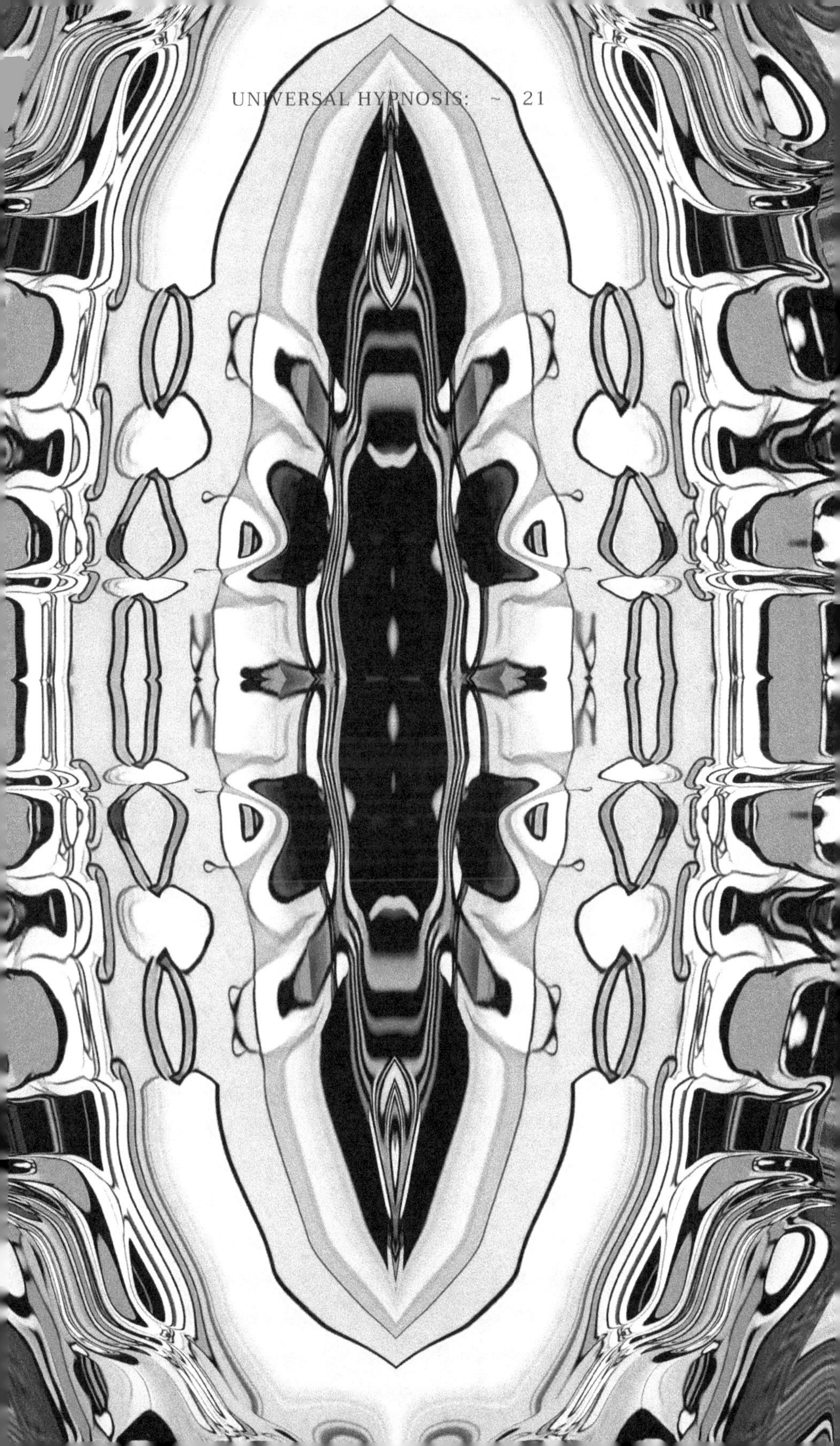

Chapter 3

"Thirst Comes First
-or- H2O My Gosh!"

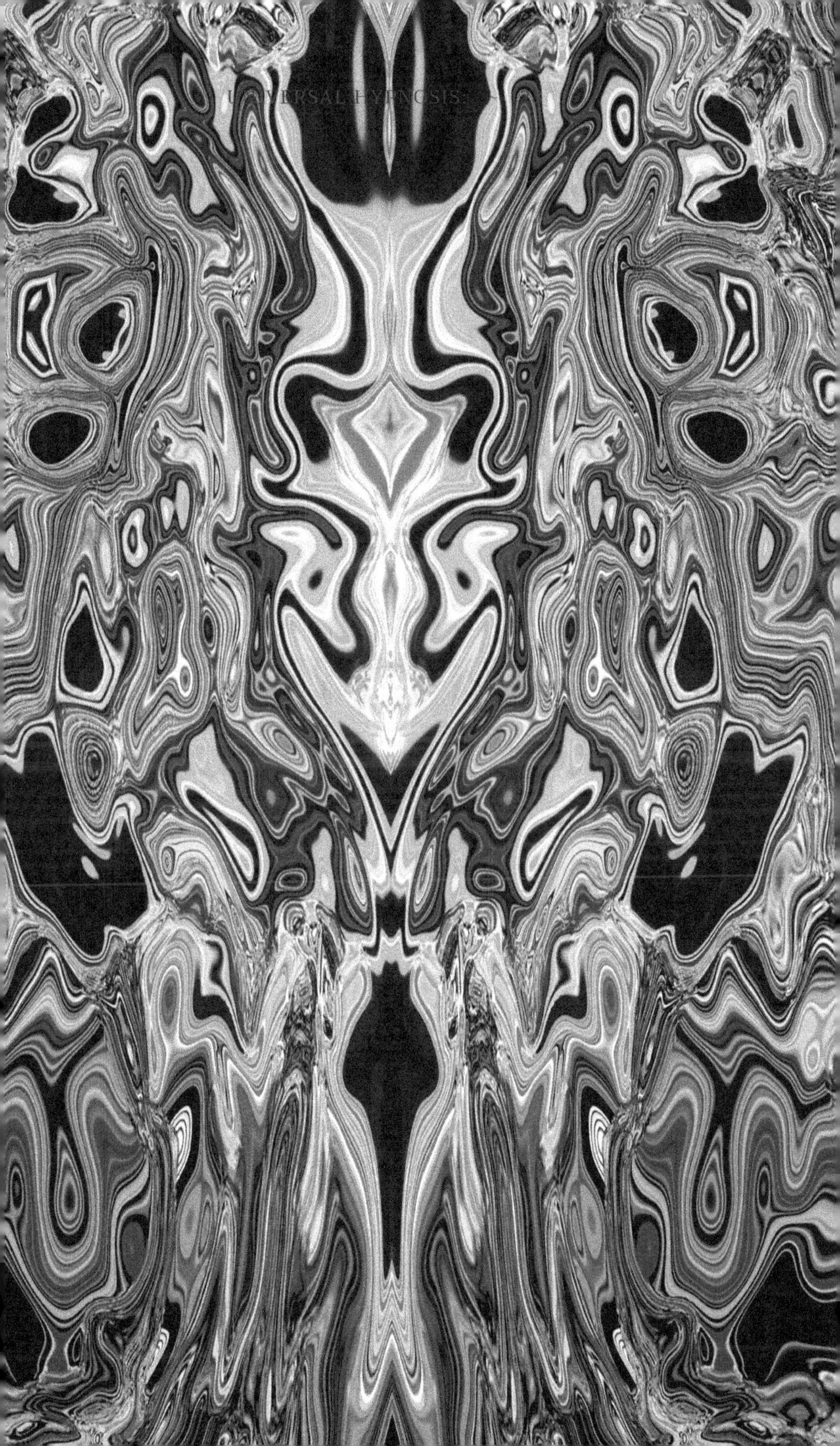
UNIVERSAL HYPNOSIS

The engineering of technologies related to the conquest of Mars had created a new Space Race to see what country would make it to Mars first as the cosmological stakes had never been higher.

Many countries across the world started to create technologies in stride that will eventually get astronauts to Mars. This would be Humanity's most significant cosmological achievement since the Moon landing in 1969.

The Space Race caused friendly competition worldwide to see who would send Humans to Mars first.

Countless governmental contracts were given out all over the world. It was said that there were more contracts given out in six months than there were for than the preceding ten years.

The astronauts understood whoever bravely traveled to Mars could not return to Earth, and their survival was not guaranteed.

This hindered many persons from signing up to be "Marsbound." Then there was the other side who wanted to leave Earth and never return, even though it seemed hard to stomach that even a single person would want to leave our Mother Earth's majestic nature.

Whoever touched down on Mars first would make all future governmental decisions regarding its terraforming (ability to change Mars to be Earth-like) and other items to how the incredible Red Planet will evolve once colonized.

It can be imagined how technology accelerated over the next several years due to the friendly competition across Earth.

To put it differently, Mother Earth had Father Mars on her mind, literally since it is rumored that Earth has a consciousness. Which raises the obvious question: What does She think about Humanity?

Most countries got in on the action and hoped to be the first to colonize the red planet and make all decisions regarding its future.

A lot was riding on this new Space Race since the outcome would enable a country to first travel to the red planet and claim "dibs."

Several countries looked like they were nearing completion and being one step closer to inhabiting Mars.

The latest technology that Russia had to engineer was a way to propel the spacecraft. It took over a year, but Russia created a spacecraft whose power source was electromagnetism, so no fuel was needed to propel the craft.

A little while later, the cosmonauts were launched into orbit, with their destination being Mars.

Shortly after that, Japan, India, Brazil, America, and several other countries launched spacecraft. These included approximately 50 astronauts on each ship as mandated by the World Space Project as to how many total astronauts could go on the first trip to Father Mars.

It was the World Space Project's (or WSP was the governing body over all Earth's 72 total space agencies including NASA) belief that we should not send, for instance, 10,000 astronauts for the maiden voyage to the red planet in case something catastrophic happened.

Eight months later, Russia landed first, claiming Mars for themselves.

Parades through Moscow's Red Square were some of the most festive times in Russia's history. This allowed Russia to flex its cosmic muscles.

Shortly after, nineteen other countries touched down safely.

Upon arrival, it was mission critical to desalinate or clean the water because all water supplies were exhausted en route to the desolate place.

All 1000 astronauts/cosmonauts were all dehydrated and needed to drink water as soon as possible.

The first item of business for all of the astronauts from each country and cosmonauts was to desalinate the Martian water, making it "clean" enough for everyone to drink.

The astronauts were so ecstatic about surviving the trip that they decided to plan a party for later that night.

The astronauts set up their desalination machines built by the same Chinese company to create clean Martian water. After some time, the first amounts of freshwater were ready for consumption.

After the desalination process concluded, astronauts gave Martian water the first drinks to select astronauts/cosmonauts.

Almost immediately, the astronauts and cosmonauts all fell to the ground clutching their stomachs, and a tar-like liquid seeped from their mouths, ending their lives too soon.

An eerie sight caused a fearful feeling for all the remaining astronauts and cosmonauts on the barren and unforgivable planet.

After witnessing the deaths of many astronauts and cosmonauts, the fact that they were nearly 36 million miles from home tore their minds to pieces.

A wave of uneasiness spread over the desolate planet, making everyone wonder what exactly was wrong with the desalination process.

The Martian water contained too much acidity that none of the desalination machines were designed to remove. Did the Chinese company whom the Chinese emperor knew sabotage the machines to not clean the water, or was this just bad luck?

The astronauts became terror-stricken, knowing that they would eventually perish, alone on the Martian landscape, without leaving a trace. All they would leave was their name...

In retrospect, it would have been better had the technology for the mission not been accelerated, and had Humanity just taken their time, we may have avoided this colossal calamity.

It was either that, or you cannot desalinate Martian water to be drinkable or even terrorism.

It caused a solemn mood on Mars since no fresh drinkable water would ever be a reality there.

It is such a shame that the poorly engineered desalination machines had led to the demise of all 500 plus astronauts and cosmonauts. It was a dear shame that haunted Humanity for generations to come.

It looked like Mars' colonization was a pipe dream that Humanity could only fantasize about anymore because it may never be a reality.

America took a stance on the catastrophe and built a grand memorial in Washington DC, listing all 1000 or so names of all now deceased astronauts and cosmonauts.

This was the least Humanity could have done to show their respect for all of the fallen.

As previously mentioned, China's emperor had a contact that owned the company that built the now-infamous desalination stations and caused a monopoly for making them for all countries that went to Mars.

After an investigation into the desalination debacle, it was proven that the machines could not remove Mars' levels of acid in the water and that no terrorism had occurred.

Earth kept on moving forward even if we may never attempt another trip to Mars ever again.

At least we got to keep all of the cool technologies that were developed.

THE END

[Author's Note: Please read chapter 27,"Marstropolis," in the second companion book saga to this one entitled "?Universal Extinction¿ More Utopian & Dystopian Tales from the Untamed Cosmos" where Humanity attempts, once again, to "make it" on The Red Planet by building a great city].

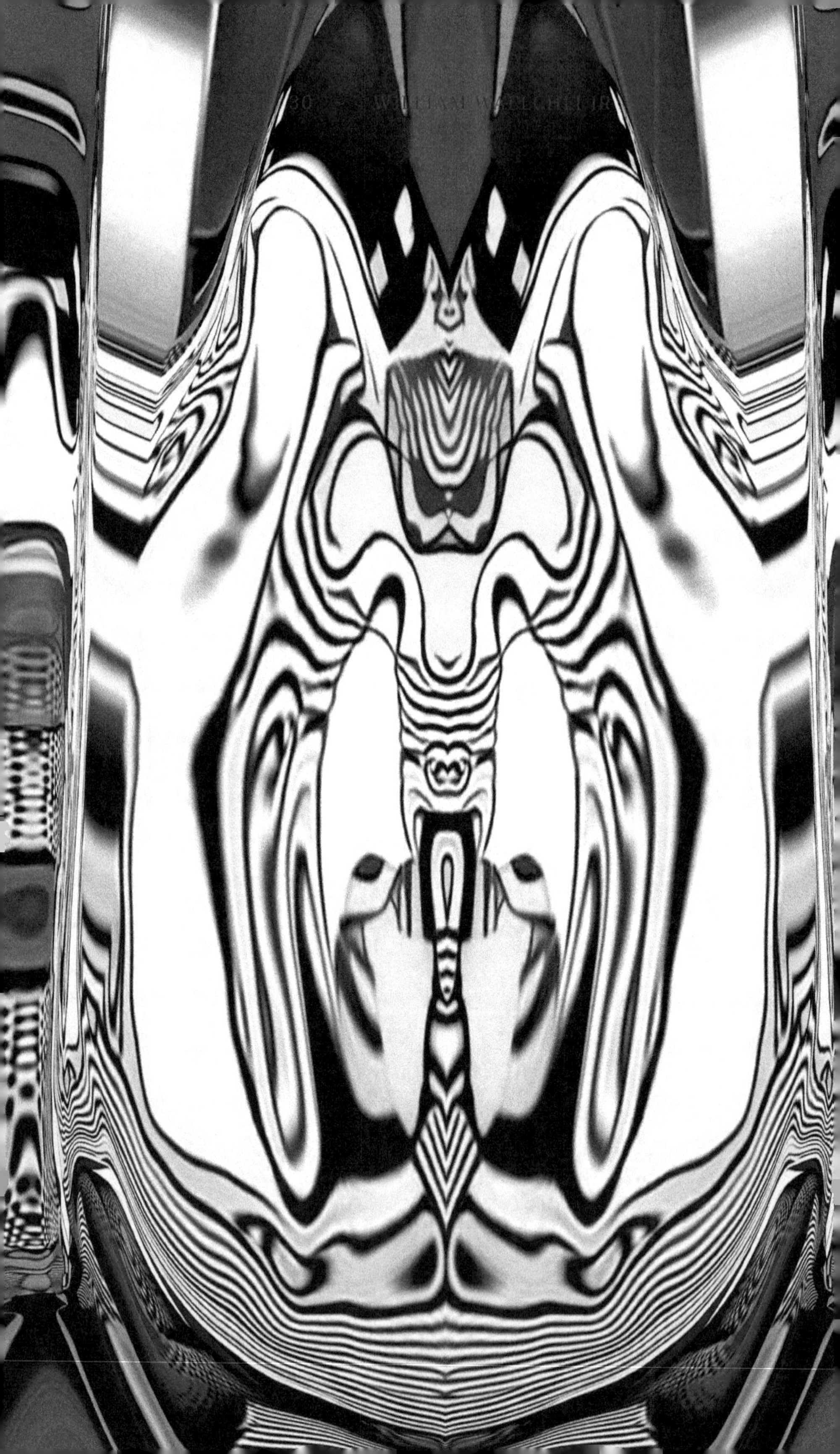

Chapter 4

"First Contact: Noirian Style!"

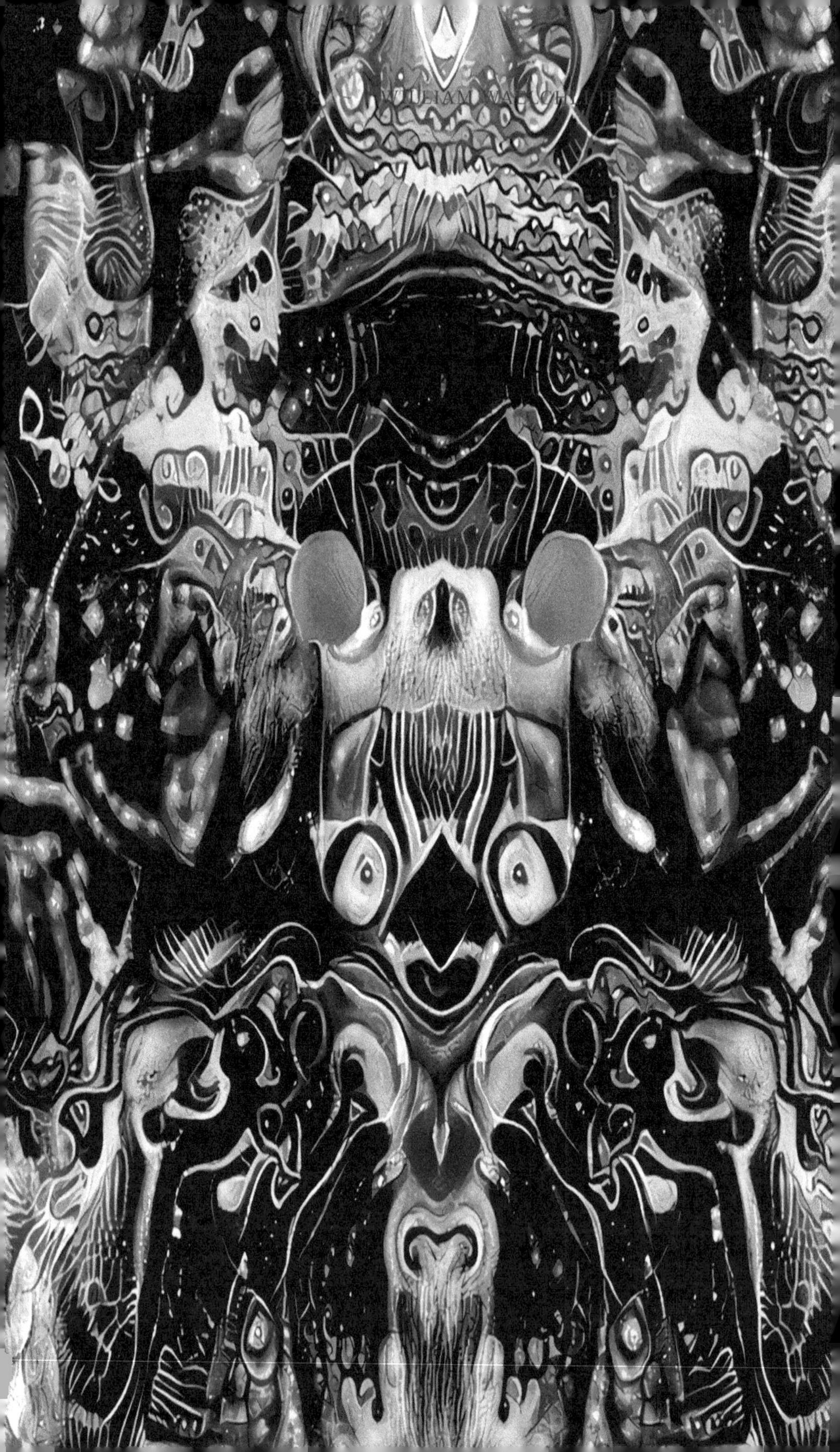
WILLIAM WALLACE

It was the year 2131, and the Earth was a happening place. Morale was high, and depression and even debt were low. Science was advancing at a steady rate, but we had yet to make first contact with any type of intelligent extraterrestrial Life.

Humanity had a very small (the size of a match head) microchip inserted into their right hips. This chip was connected to the massive "Collective Conscience," a computer that held all of Humanity's minds. This will be important later...

An artist suggested that scientists "temporarily change Earth's color to make it more visible in space." The scientists thought that was a great idea. Scientists researched the most visible color in space, and they learned it was green. They devised a plan to make the Earth more visible to would-be visitors.

The scientists came up with a system of lasers that made the Earth appear completely neon green. As long as the lasers were running, the Earth appeared bright neon green from space without compromising the planet's beauty. The lasers shot into the Exosphere (highest point of the atmosphere) and did not show any neon green color on Earth.

The artist's idea was spot on because two large, damaged, extraterrestrial spaceships were headed on a trajectory straight for Earth. The scientists erupted in excitement, as they were the first persons to know that we may, in fact, receive first contact very, very soon.

The world's governments were told of the possible extraterrestrial visitation from the two incoming spaceships. The public was not informed about our incoming visitors to keep the craziness to an absolute minimum. Scientists only hoped that not telling the public would not backfire on them.

Scientists and world leaders wanted to meet the extraterrestrials and see what they were like, then there would be breaking news sent to news outlets worldwide that would give the public the information they needed to know about the incoming spaceships and the extraterrestrials contained in them.

The Search for Extraterrestrial Intelligence (SETI) was responsible for communication with whatever was out there in the cosmos. SETI beamed a friendly message towards the spaceships in hopes of the extraterrestrials returning some kind of communication.

Within minutes, a message from the extraterrestrials was received. It simply stated, "Please help us!" This puzzled the SETI employees about what they would possibly need help with on Earth.

Days later, the twin extraterrestrial spaceships approached. One spaceship landed at the direct top of the planet, and the other landed at the bottom of the planet in Antarctica.

Somehow, the extraterrestrials, which were located at inhospitable and unreachable locations, hijacked the Internet, and suddenly, the public knew about the two spaceships.

The extraterrestrials were black as tar and had different striped vertical lines all over their bodies. Think of them as appearing like psychedelic zebras. They had ten yellow eyes encircling their head, enabling them to see in all directions.

They did not give off an evil, ominous, or diabolical nature whatsoever. If anything, they seemed shy when broadcasting over the Internet, reaching every corner of the Earth.

The extraterrestrials appeared on the screen in front of billions of people, and one of them spoke: "We are the Noirians (NWAR-E-INS) of Tenebrism. We live in the local galactic neighborhood and are here to ask for your help.

We are in dire need of a special element named "Krystilio (CRY-STILL-E-O)." This specific element is needed for us to fuel our spaceships all of the way back to Tenebrism, where we can fully fuel our spaceships."

She continued, "Our spaceships are positioned at the top and bottom of your planet where we will cast a laser where it will liquefy and bring all of the Krystilio to the surface where my fellow Noirians' will be able to harvest it.

"We will do this by sending strong lasers over the entire planet, then we will zap the Krystilio aboard ships and get home safely to Tenebrism." With that stated, a sustained red flash engulfed all of Earth. While the red covered Earth, rumbling could be heard before the Krystilio came to the surface.

When the intense red light had gone away, a bright blue light enveloped Earth, and during this light, all of the Krystilio was atomically broken down and beamed onto the two extra-terrestrial spaceships.

The light went back to normal, although the light would most likely appear to be the only thing that was normal now. Unfortunately, something bad had happened planetwide, and

Humanity knew what happened, although no one wanted to admit it.

Something had been overlooked by the extraterrestrials. They never checked or even cared to check what a suitable amount of radiation Human beings can withstand before they start to behave in ways they wished they hadn't behaved.

Due to the more than toxic amounts of radiation that Humanity had been exposed to and the fact that the Earth's green hue also emitted radiation, and when both came in contact with each other, it released enough radiation to end the lives of 100 billion people.

While Humanity's flesh started to melt off their bones, it was noted that there were thousands of the same spaceships that the Noirians were piloting that were headed straight toward Earth. As they drew closer, it became more evident that Humanity had just lost the planet to the mysterious extraterrestrials known as the Noirians.

If Humanity were still alive to ponder what just happened, they would simply ask, "Why?" Humanity would be hardpressed to find an answer, other than Tenebrism becoming overpopulated?

Remember the great computer known as the Collective Conscience that maintained the minds of Humanity? The computer, working completely on artificial intelligence, shot out a laser of its own that interacted with the neon green lasers above the atmosphere and changed the planet back to blue. This made it way more difficult, if even possible, for the Noirians to see Earth.

If they existed yet, Humanity would hope that there was some way that the Collective Conscience could somehow alleviate the current dilemma. The melted scientists would have somehow patiently waited for something to happen...and they hoped the wait would not be long.

All of a sudden, a pure white light covered the entire Earth. This light originated from the Collective Conscience. Enveloped in white light, something spectacular happened: As the healing light engulfed the Earth, the artificial intelligence was working overtime to make things possibly work out, although there were no guarantees.

Once the light faded, you could hear voices again, cars driving, people going to get coffee. No one had melted, and nothing negative had been bestowed upon Humanity.

Why were the scientists not sweating their possible demise? They knew that the Collective Conscience, as a fail-safe, was pre-programmed to "rewind" time in case of any Humanity ending disasters.

THE END

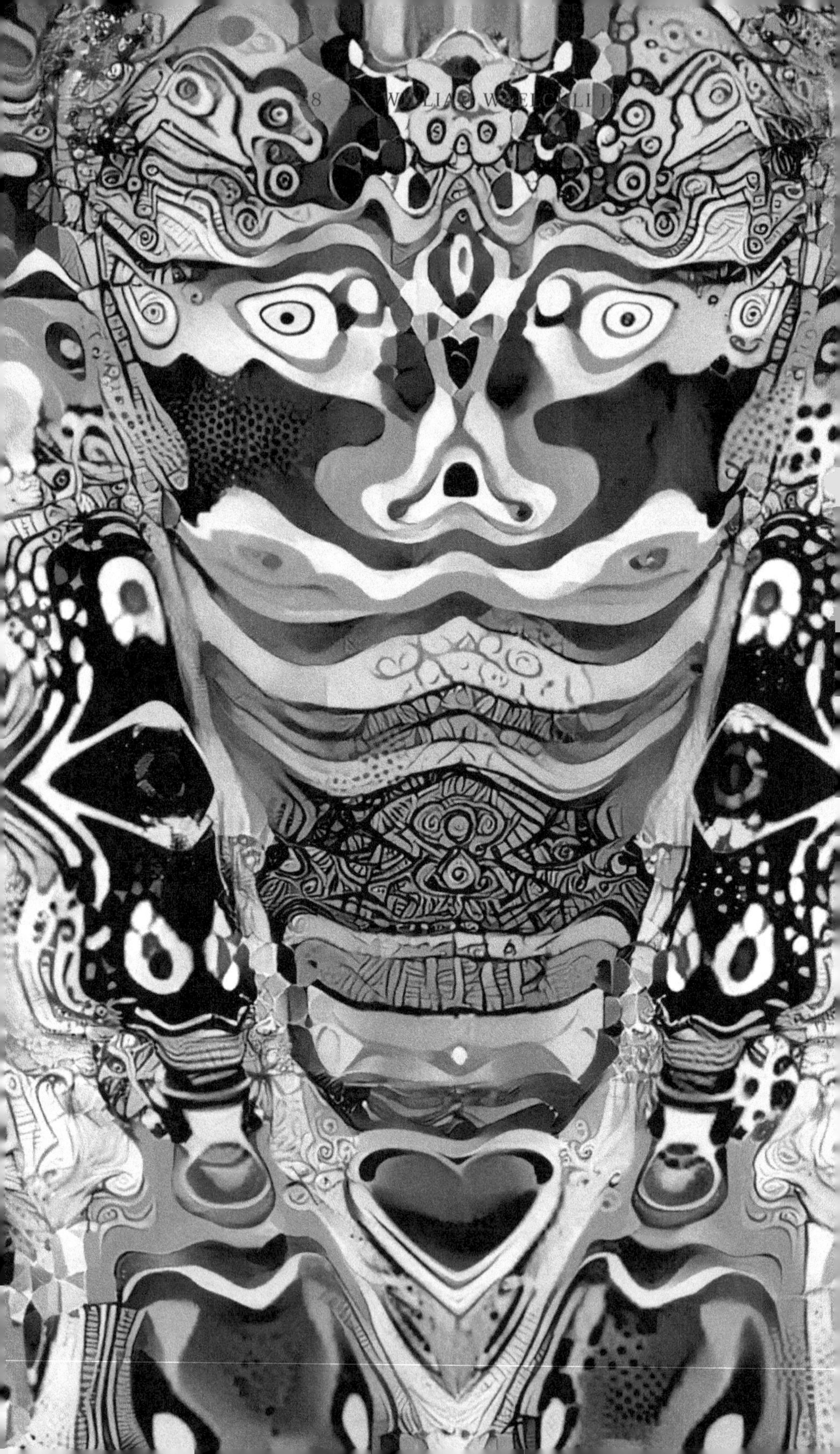

Chapter 5

39

"I Sure Wish I Could Play Galactic Pinball" - or –
"Planeta Extinctor and the Famished Insects"

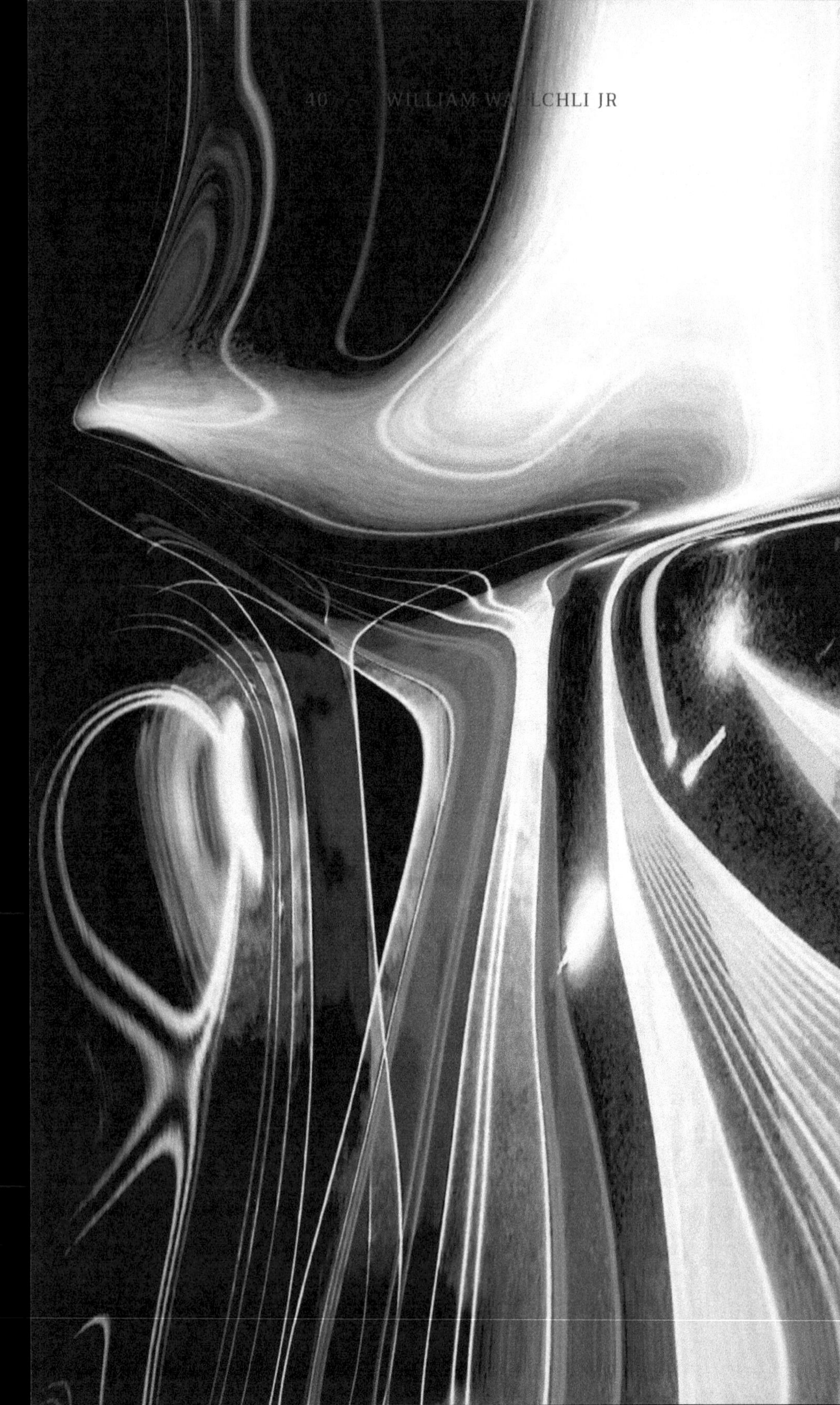

Since Humanity had solved global warming, the planet had been healthier than ever before. It was the year 2200, and morale was high. Humanity wondered how the brand new century would progress.

After surviving an asteroid collision a century ago, Humanity, with its rapidly evolving technologies, was able to keep the sky clear of smoke using controlled wind. Thus prevented the atmosphere from being consumed by acrid black smoke, conflicting life on Earth.

It utilized great fans built all over Earth, which "pushed" the black smoke out through the atmosphere and into space. Life continued and flourished further and further beyond anyone's wildest dreams.

Most of Humanity thought we were doomed like the dinosaurs, but they were humans, and they would be damned if anyone would ruin their prestigious planet. Needless to say, a great number of persons in the population were cynical as it related to the great fans.

They thought that controlled wind would never clear the possible planet-destroying smoke from the atmosphere. But alas, controlling the wind was the key to controlling the eventual clearing of the sky.

Some persons, as horrible as it sounded, joked around that the meteorologists had the easiest job: "Today it will be mostly cloudy all day and night with a possible chance of acid rain...."

It was a memorable time for Humanity. Who would have thought we would have survived an asteroid strike? Obviously, not many people thought we could and were pleasantly surprised.

Previously, it was the year 2100 (or 1000 years ago), and out of nowhere, an asteroid struck Russia, and Humanity feared the worst. We knew that eventually, the sky would become engulfed in smoke, quickly destroying life as we knew it.

Back to present day, while doing a routine survey of the sky, astronomers noted that our closest star, Alpha Centauri A, was no longer present out in space. Previously, this was the closest star within proximity to Earth, but not any longer.

This baffled scientists and made them question where the star went and if any other stars had vanished. The hypothesis stated that Alpha Centauri A must have been swallowed by a rogue black hole, although the scientists did not know for sure as it was all speculation at this point.

Upon examining Sagittarius A*, scientists noted that the black hole at the galactic center was "vomiting" up objects it swallowed in the past.

This concerned scientists who had the grim news of telling the public, unaware that any of this was going on, that the Earth might not exist in the future if the black hole's aim was as good as its reputation of being a cosmic glutton.

Everyone's first question was always, "Are there any objects that will collide with our planet?" Fortunately, it was a re-sounding no. There was absolutely nothing headed towards us at the present moment.

Upon closer examination, the black hole had a bright white

color within the "ring of fire" that a black hole had around its event horizon or the black hole's entrance.

Evidentially, black holes in the galaxy had evolved to become quasi-white holes. Scientists could not explain why such evolution happened so quickly and why it happened at all.

This means that rogue planetary objects can now enter the Universe at any given moment at any given time from the black holes. After much debate, it was determined that Alpha Centauri A was hit by one of the objects shot out during a black hole ejection.

Then the day came when scientists made an important discovery. There was some sort of heavy object headed towards Earth. Perhaps it might be a star impact that may collide with Earth. As the object approached Earth, it was determined to be made of solid carbon or diamond.

The trajectory was hard to pinpoint since the star was spinning erratically. Week's later, scientists made a mind-numbing discovery: The star was about to enter our solar system. They were able to get an accurate weight of the star.

The number was so astronomical it could only be explained like this: The rogue star weighed 125 times that of the Sun! This showed how the Earth would not stand a chance against such a colossal foe.

There were no existing deflection methods that could be implemented since such technologies did not yet exist and may never be invented. Telling the rest of Humanity the bad news was no easy feat, and the solemn news was not taken lightly.

Scientists predicted that the star would impact Earth within a week. With the possible impending doom approaching, we held ourselves close and hoped for the best. The star was nicknamed "Planeta Extinctor," which translates to "Planet Extinguisher" in Latin.

It was 1:11 pm in the Eastern Standard Time on a Tuesday afternoon when the lights went "out." It was not a star collision at all. The star shot passed us, missing us by only 10,000 miles. And like that, darkness enveloped the entire planet.

It was one heck of a sight to see. No one knew what happened...except the scientists, who noted that the rogue star had obliterated the Sun, and daytime was a thing of the past. Was it mentioned how the rogue star affected Earth's gravity and orbit?

The orbit was completely erratic, moving in a wobbly line rather than its original orbit around what was the Sun. This will have significant implications since the Earth was no longer in the regular orbit and receiving nourishment from the Sun, which had been annihilated.

It also did not help that the Earth's rotation had sped up to 20,000 miles per hour. This was ten times faster than the speed of the original rotation. Sadly for Humanity, the temperature plummeted across Earth, rendering it a near-dead and freezing planet within a couple of short months after the sun "left."

Humanity made many boreholes underground, where it remained warm due to the heat from the core. For the first time, Humanity pulled together and made a bad thing into a good thing.

It's good until ice crept from the Arctic down to Antarctica, covering all of the Americas and other entire continents as well. Within a year, the relentless ice covered the whole planet for however many years to come. "Iceball Earth" would've been the right name for our freezing planet since it is a rogue cosmic iceberg hurtling through the cosmos at who knows how fast.

Look at it on the bright side, Humanity would have perfectly preserved themselves for when the ice melts, and the next intelligent species discovers us and will have billions of perfectly preserved humans to examine.

That is if the insects do not get to them first.

THE END

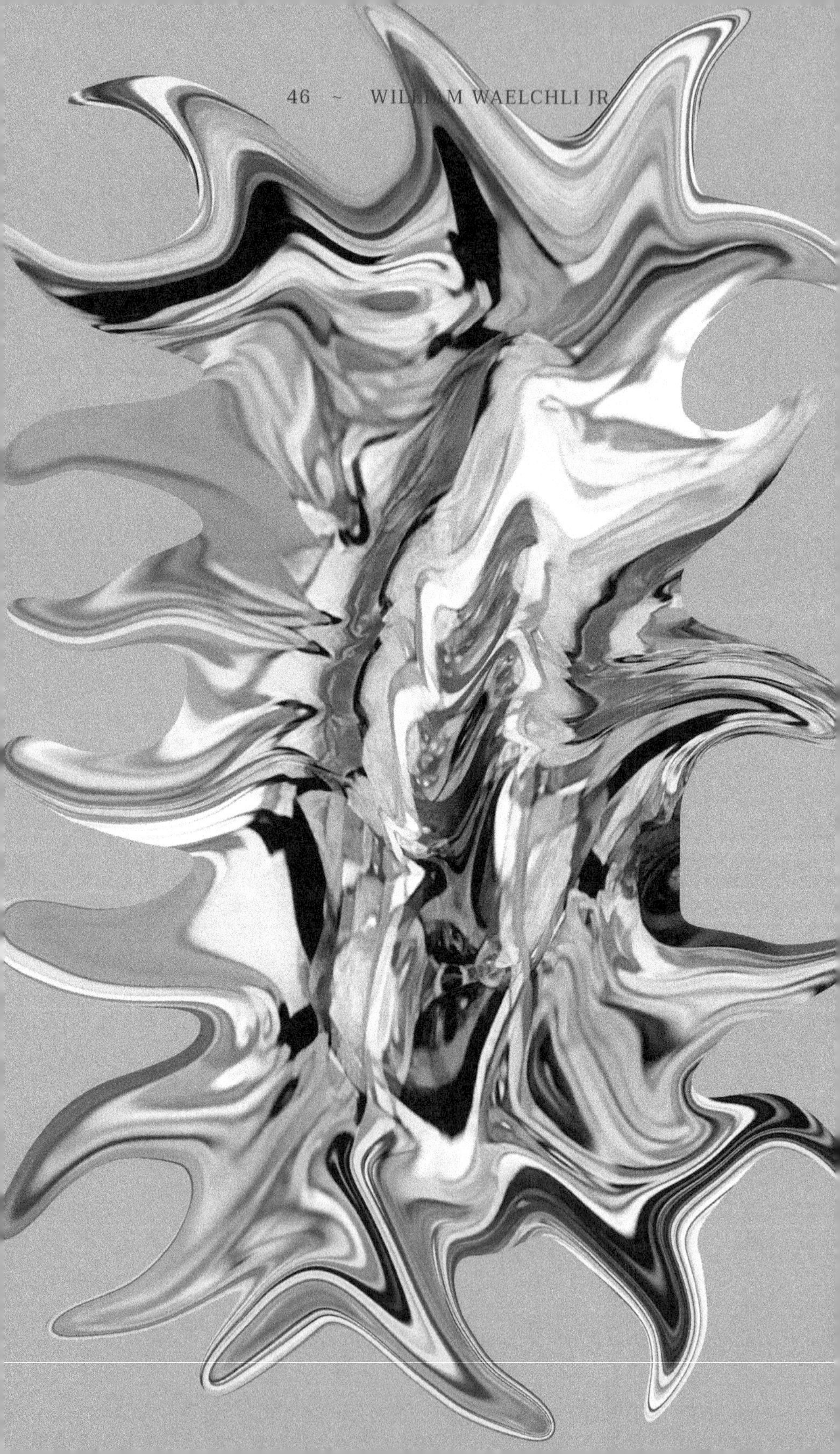

Chapter 6

"How To Traverse the Universe" -or "Circumnavigating the Evolution of The Cosmos"

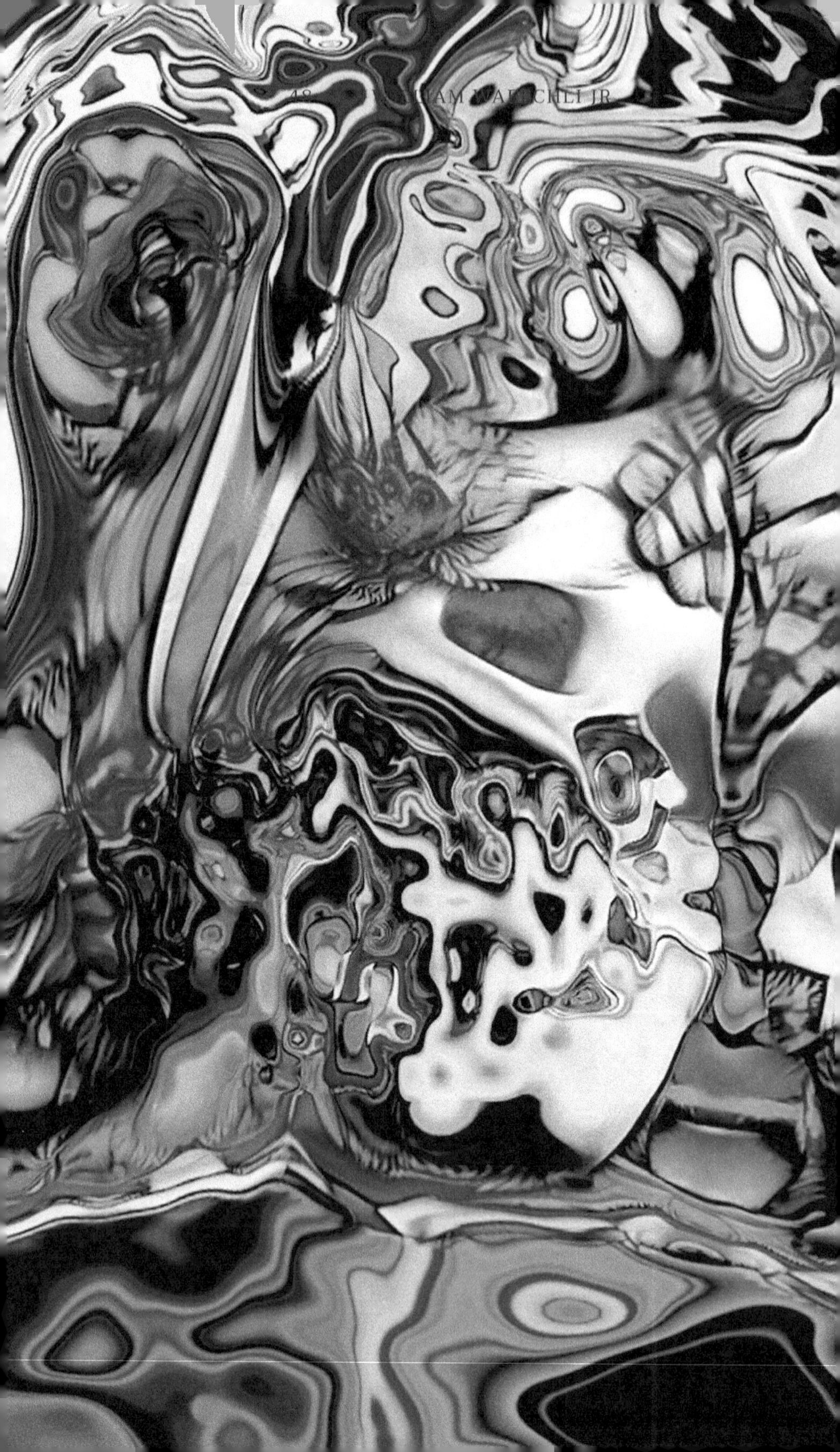

Little did Humanity know that a future archaeological find would change history forever. Will it be for better or for worse? Only the future knows for sure.

In Egypt, near the Sudan border, an important archaeological dig was taking place. The Egyptologists and Archeologists at the dig were ecstatic to find a tomb buried beneath the desert for many millennia.

As they entered the tomb, they made a fascinating discovery. The tomb contained but a single item: A large clay tablet. The tablet was 3 feet by 6 feet with paragraph after paragraph engraved on it, stating something unknown at the time.

As the months progressed, it would be a planet-changing find rewriting history as Humanity knew it.

Back in the present, after carefully removing the large ancient tablet, it was hand-delivered to a select group of top Egyptologists in Cairo to decipher the lengthy inscription on the tablet.

It took some time and a lot of trial and error to decipher the tablet due to the immense amount of inscribed letters carved into it. The Egyptologists pressed on towards a solution as to what the large tablet said.

With some painstaking work, Egyptologists finally deciphered the tablet. Humanity patiently waited for what the tablet's inscription read.

Shockingly, it explained how to create a "gravity gate" in great detail. It states at the end that it can transport people back in time by going through a large enough gate.

This may prove useful now that we inch towards the era of the Sun becoming a red giant and consuming Mercury, Venus, and even Earth.

The gravity gate's discovery came at the right time in the history of our famed Mother Earth. Scientists thought about making a gate a bit larger than Earth out in space and placing the whole planet through it.

This was seen as the best method of saving the planet from being cosmically consumed.

The tablet was very vague about where the gravity gates led. This made scientists a bit uneasy, although they all pushed ahead with small-scale experiments.

Scientists built a small example of the gate, and once the pieces were connected, the gate turned black as a moonless night.

Upon closer examination, scientists noted that they could see stars thru the gate. Evidently, the gravity gate will send us somewhere out in the Cosmos, but where was anyone's guess. We were desperate to save our planet and would do nearly anything to do so.

They started to create the gravity gate out in space. Several months later, the planet-wide gravity gate was built per the tablet's instructions in space ahead of Earth's orbital path.

When astronauts placed the last block, the gravity gate turned white with a special sheen in its color, proving that the gate would lead us somewhere else in the mad cosmos. This gave verification that the gate was now operational. It was a risk, but it's either that or be burned alive by the expanding Sun.

The Earth headed towards the gravity gate. Humanity collectively held their breath as Earth entered the gate.

The Earth passed safely through the gravity gate and entered an unknown time in the Cosmos. Humanity let out a sigh knowing that they survived the trip thru the gate. As the gate closed up behind them, the last bit of light shone through and then disappeared behind them.

The Earth saw a star up ahead that shined like our mother star, the sun.

Earth was able to see outside the planet because there was always a view of space. Evidently, the gate sent us back in time to experience the big bang occurring right next to our planet.

Now we could view the evolution of our incredible cosmos and learn everything about it in stunning first-person detail, expanding scientists' minds planetwide.

This was fine and dandy, but what will happen when Earth reaches the present day? This was Humanity's burning question.

As it happened, the scientists had no explanation. Other than the Earth colliding with the past Earth in a universal billiards game, although no one could tell for sure.

They also had no way of controlling the planet. It naturally drifted along, showing us the evolutionary path the cosmos had taken to get us back when we exited the gate.

Stars, planets, black holes, and every other celestial body formed right in front of our planet, blowing open the doors to new knowledge we thought we would never gain about how the cosmos evolved until we went thru the gate.

Humanity had undoubtedly got more than they had bargained for by going through the gravity gate. Earth's telescopes picked up an extremely bright object in the distance.

Humanity was excited about the news. Perhaps this strange journey was nearing an end, and Humanity could settle back down in its original place and focus on everything learned from the trip.

It was invaluable information now knowing how the cosmos evolved, showing us everything that came before us.

As Earth entered the solar system, the scientists could see that there was no duplicate Earth, so all were safe from that possible collision mentioned earlier.

When Earth settled in its final spot in the Solar System, scientists got to work on what they learned.

There was a tremendous amount of information learned that would eventually change the standard model of physics.

Now that Humanity was shown the cosmos' evolution, we could write the entire universal evolution, unlocking all of its secrets.

It was not mentioned that the Earth went back to 100,000 B.C., causing Earth to dodge the expanding Sun. It was a breath-taking moment in the prestigious Earth and all of Humanity's history as the new day beckoned a new beginning.

THE END

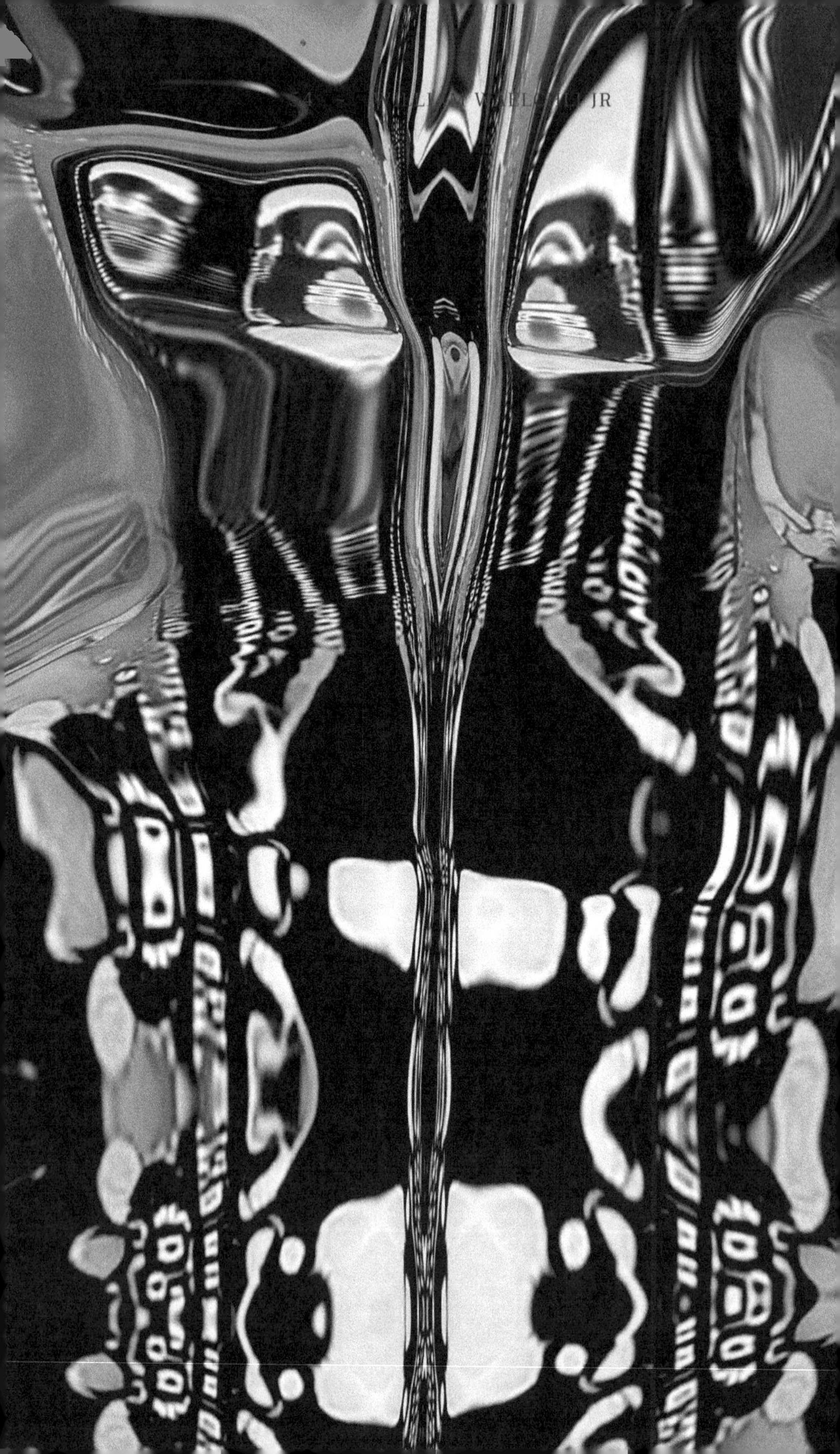

Chapter 7

"Experiencing the Inconceivable & Incredible Seismic Activity of the Unavoidable Creation Of Terraunus, While Recalling the Supercontinent Pangæa"

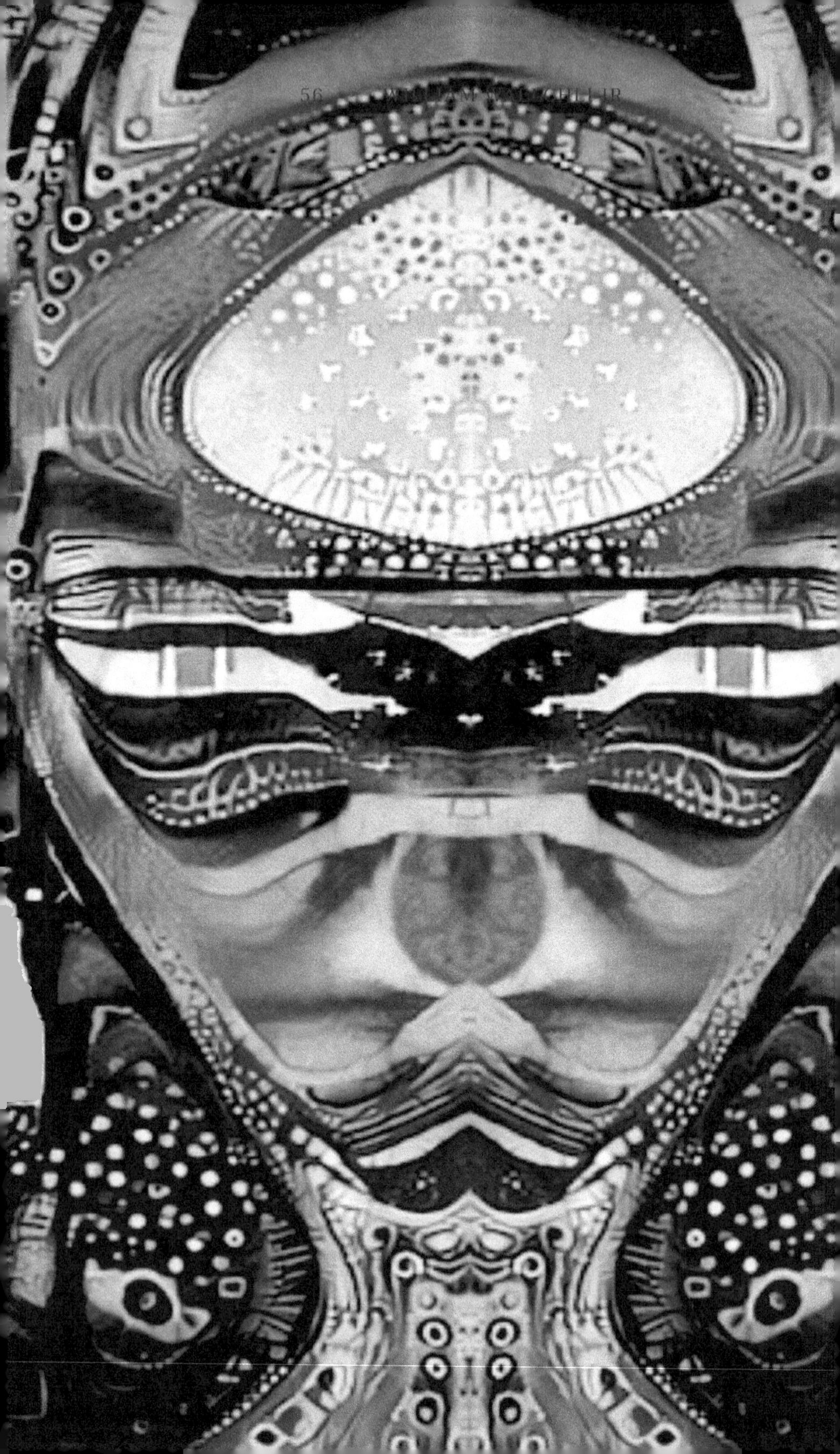

It is the year 2091, and Humanity is chugging along, living their hopefully glamorous lives.

The burning question was: "When will the Earth's magnetic poles complete their shifts?"

This one question had kept scientists busy for years.

Humanity had the belief that global cataclysms would happen when our planet's magnetic poles flipped. They must have conjured this up after seeing fake news on the Internet...or maybe they are exactly right. Only time will tell.

When the North Pole goes down south, and the South Pole goes north, it is stated that all continents will stagger in one direction or the other, causing severely fatal earthquakes, accelerated climate change, and extinction of many species, possibly our own.

There had been much action with the North Pole inching south lately, but not without a complete shift...yet...

The morning news stated that the South Pole had "awakened" and had moved 200 feet in the last 24 hours.

Humanity was concerned, but it was only 200 feet. This was not so bad, right...

"Cataclysmic Pole Shift Hypothesis" was what scientists named the scientific reasoning behind the poles' movement, actively shifting with possible dire environmental consequences.

The name of the hypothesis accurately described the phenomena that the planet was experiencing now and what it will continue to go through when the poles do their steady climb, eventually reversing.

To put things simply, when pole shift completes, all compasses will show north as south and south as north. We can only hope that the geocaching community would be able to find hidden stashes of loot without their trusty compasses. This all assumes that Humanity exists after the major pole shift that is occurring now,

Scientists kept a constant close eye on the poles to monitor when or if they moved.

Then, like that, the South Pole shifted 1/4 of the way around the globe. Causing 470 6.2 or higher earthquakes across the world, crippling the infrastructures of many countries.

Many cities were ravaged, and casualties were too high to get a proper count. Scientists believed that the death toll was possibly in the millions.

It was not looking good for team Humanity.

Within 36 hours, the North Pole shifted to the 1/4 position matching, where the South Pole was only on the opposite side of the planet.

The North Pole movement caused another 364 earthquakes of 6.4 and above, claiming scores of human lives worldwide and bringing many countries to their proverbial knees. Many cities fell in the wake of the poles slowly shifting.

The earthquakes left many cities in ruins, caused trillions of dollars in damages, and also loss of life all across the planet. There was a sense of total terror in the minds of the surviving population.

There was no locale anywhere that wasn't somewhat affected by the recent barrage of severe earthquakes.

Scientists theorized that once the poles completely shift, the continents will crash into each other making mountain ranges higher than Olympus Mons, which is part of the Martian landscape.

To put this into perspective, Olympus Mons is 2.5 times higher than Mount Everest being an astonishing 72000 feet or 13.6 miles (22 km) above sea level. At the same time, Mount Everest, in comparison, is a measly 29000 feet or around 5.5 miles (8.8 km) above sea level.

To the surprise of the scientists, the poles had not budged for months. Some scientists convinced s the population that we were in the clear, denying scientists warnings that they would eventually shift completely.

The rest of Humanity braced themselves for the following days and months, having expected the worst and yearning for the very best. Some days, the poles moved hundreds of miles, disrupting the power grids and knocking out power in hundreds of thousands of homes worldwide.

More earthquakes occurred. Although this time, the earthquakes were near coastal areas causing extremely powerful tsunamis that washed away homes and people alike. It violently dragged scores of persons into the sea, never to be seen or heard from again.

Luckily, the poles' movement did not trigger volcanic eruptions, especially from the 20 supervolcanoes dotted throughout the world.

The North and South poles shifted right past the equator and went to 3/4 shifts or, more importantly, only 1/4 movement until both poles made a complete shift.

Humanity could now feel the continental movement since the landmasses moved more quickly since the magnetic poles were about to flip.

There was a 9.2 magnitude earthquake under the ocean and ripped a 1000 mile wide gash in the seafloor. This is how the ocean water drained into the inner core and cooled off the core.

It probably happened because the ocean water that went through the crack disabled it from closing, but no one was sure.

We did know that with the core "cooled off," it could spell doom for Humanity from another culprit besides the infamous pole shifting.

We did not know what would happen to Earth now that the molten core had been cooled off and is no longer in a molten state.

Before too long, it finally happened. The poles shifted completely, and now north is south and south is north and rendered all compasses obsolete. If Humanity is not careful, they may become obsolete as well.

The continents violently and quickly collided, causing at most 10.1 magnitude earthquakes worldwide that were too numerous to count. This caused a new supercontinent to form again, given the proper name "Terraunus," which means "One Earth" in Latin.

The impact of the continents colliding caused incredible seismic activity and the destruction of countless miles of coastline from the barrage of tsunamis that repeatedly occurred, ravaging almost every coastline on Earth.

Most of Humanity was very busy caring for the injured. They had known deep inside that they were thrilled to still draw breath after how badly battered the Earth became.

On a lighter note, Earth started to experience significant magnetic interference and a mightier magnetic force. Scientists discovered that the magnetosphere was growing.

Scientists could not explain the magnetic anomaly and how suddenly there was an almost "new" magnetic presence on Earth, which was not the result of the poles' complete shift.

It seemed that something beyond Humanity was at work, and only time would reveal what that is. Trust assured, Humanity will know what it is when it happens.

After checking the records, it was determined that this is the most magnetism that ever existed on Earth. All of a sudden and without warning, the Earth's axis started to straighten out.

The axis became even straighter (up and down), changing the planet's angle. Instead of Earth being tilted to one direction, it stood straight up without an angle.

No more seasons for Earth now...

The planet's angle was such that it became impossible to walk without falling off the surface and plummeting into space. After a few weeks, the Earth flipped 180 degrees, perfectly flipping the planet upside down. This was something that Humanity did not expect.

It's kind of hard to process the fact that the oceans fell into space, never to be seen again. Scientists were unsure whether the pole shift completion or the dead core caused the Earth's axis to switch positions.

Everyone must permanently stay in their homes as the planet has made a complete shift with Antarctica on top and the Arctic at the bottom.

And before the question is asked, there was no "dancing on the ceiling" going on.

Imagine a world where you have to walk on the ceilings. Survivors of the "Spacefall" must turn off all ceiling fans because who wants to deal with a bruised leg, which you can't have looked at by a doctor? To leave the house would cause an unintentional plunge through the atmosphere and out into space.

The sheer and utter terror of knowing that you can never leave home again and knowing that you could tumble off into the sky by simply opening the front door was enough to scare people shitless.

This was enough to drive some people to an altered state of insanity with no one to help them.

The planet flipped not because of its recent pole shift but because of the Universe's poles shifting. As stated earlier, Universal North and Universal South flipped out of the blue, rendering the entire Universe upside down.

Humanity, what was left, remained holed up in their homes living off of whatever rations they had to keep them alive because the supermarket is kind of out of reach now.

Humanity's scientists could tell when the Earth will flip back around the real way based on historical data: 300,000 years!

It would be hard-pressed to find any trace of Humanity still existing in 300,000 years, although they might. The planet was in bad shape since it had flipped around, causing everything unhinged to freefall into space.

It was also not a plus that the core was now cooled and will have dire consequences on Earth as the months and years pass. When the universal pole shift was completed, persons outside took a fatal plunge off the Earth and got a taste of the sky before being cast into space.

They burned up from the freefall because of the bone marrow having boiled, causing all the bones of everyone who plummeted off the surface to explode. This is from the built-up pressure inside the bone marrow, further resulting in bloated sacks of skin floating in space forever.

Hungry micro black holes might consume them if such "atrocities" exist...This fate awaited anybody who accidentally fell off the surface.

Unfortunately, the Universal poles decided to shift now...maybe it did not even matter since Earth is mostly dead without its molten core, and it did not help that the universe flipped the planet upside down for at least the next 300,000 years.

THE END

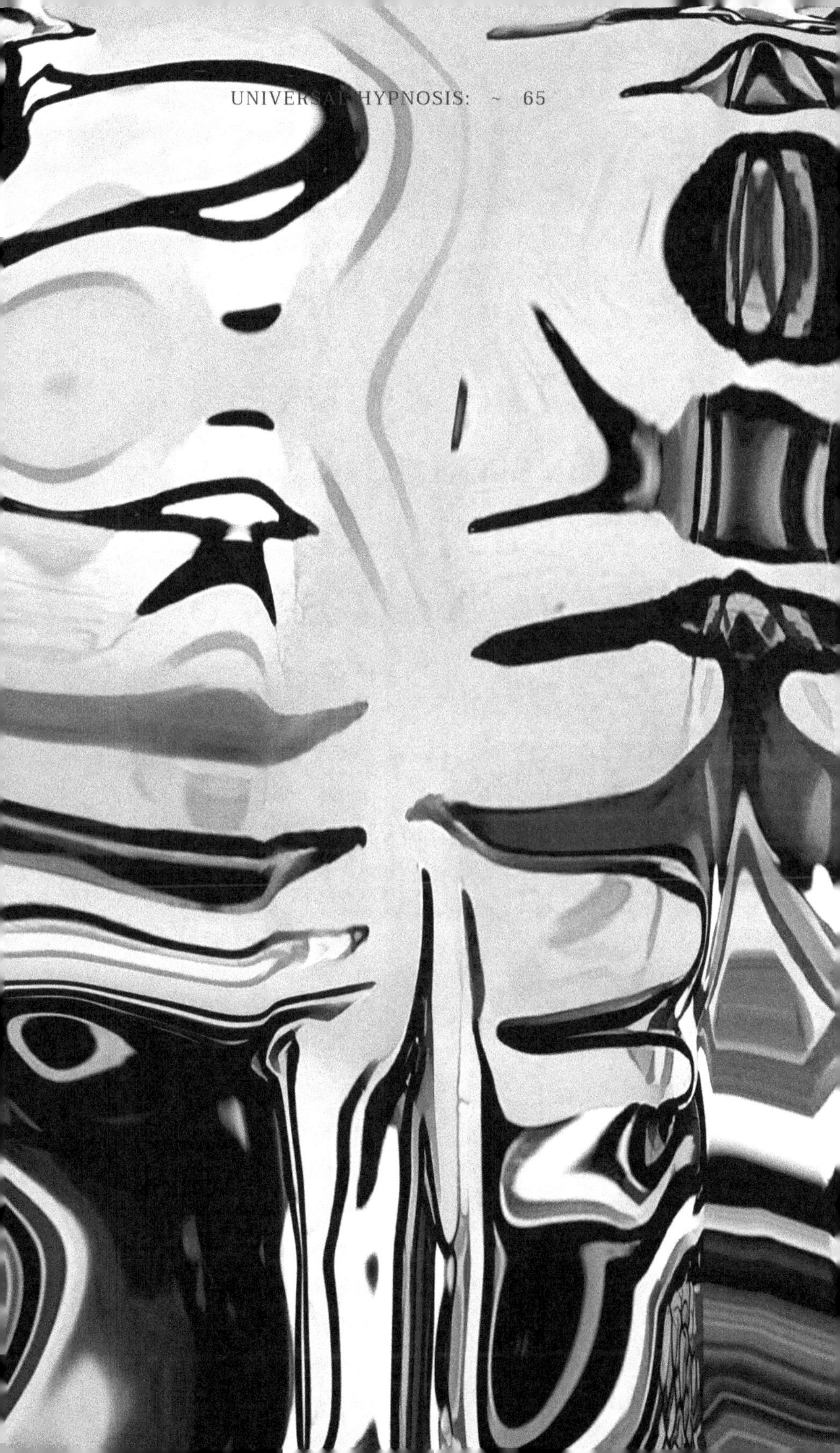

"The Mysteries Surrounding the Discovery of the White Meteor" –or- "What's On The Menu This Evening? Spaghetti or Spaghettification?"

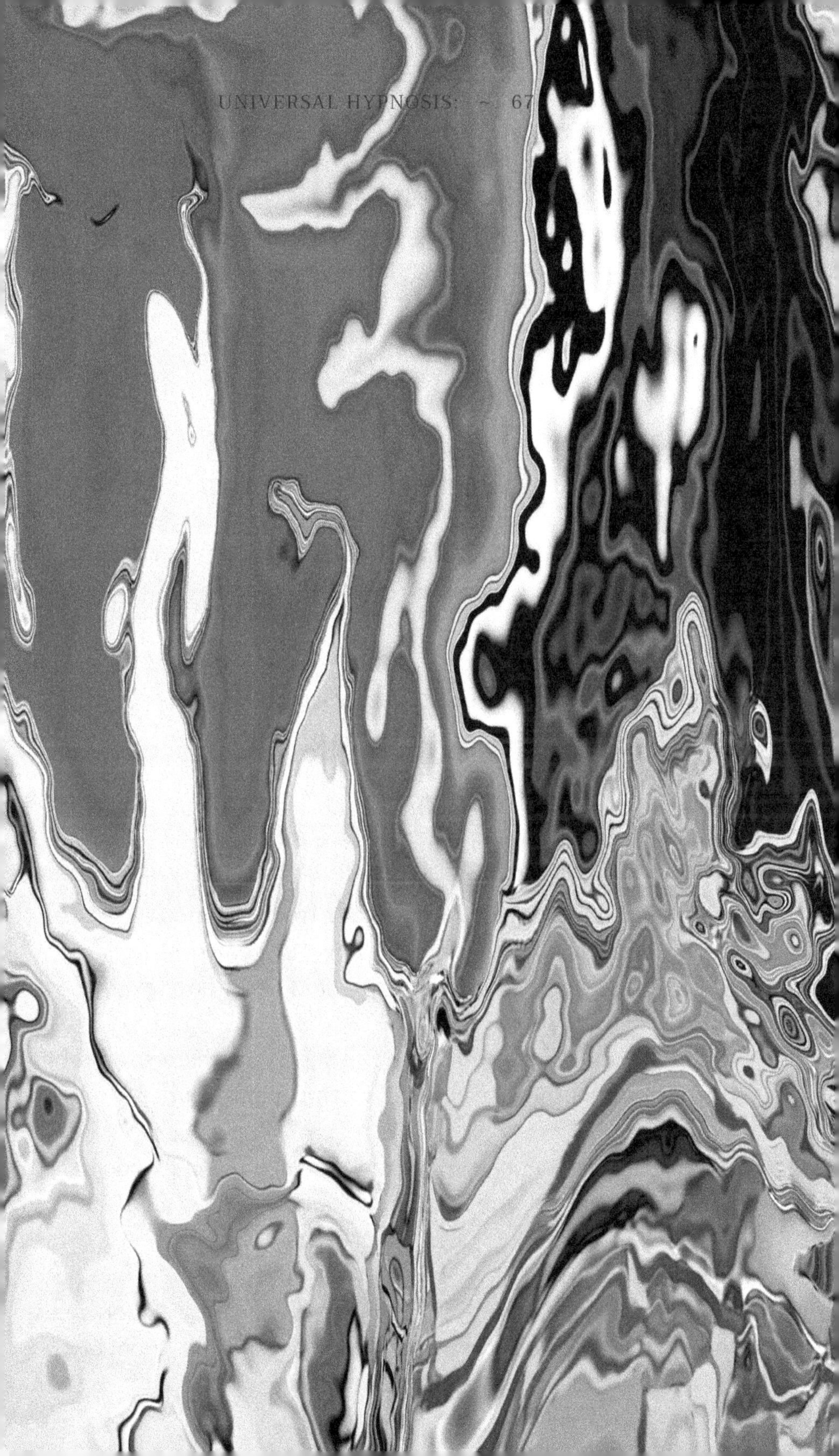

[Author's Note: As a refresher, spaghettification results from being thrust into stationary and lurking black holes. Bodies' stretch in every direction, like spaghetti noodles, apparently, was where the spaghettification term had arisen and has become part of scientists' lexicon].

Two centuries ago, Humanity was still thriving on their only planet, Earth.

It was not too long ago when a meteor touched down near the town of Emerald, Pennsylvania. This baffled everyone present: It was pure white, which was impossible in our cosmos, or so it was thought by the discovery of the white meteor.

This cosmic problem led scientists to speculate that it may have originated in a different universe altogether, causing all branches of the universal sciences to be tested.

A study of the composition of the materials in the meteor caused more questions than answers.

It seemed that the meteor was made from common metals, except they were all white. Unbelievable, it seemed, although this set in motion a future Humanity would never have expected.

Then it came time to calculate the age of the meteor, and that was when the universe at large became a lot "weirder."

Scientists were shocked to discover that they had made major miscalculations in the aging of the universe and all objects it contained.

The age of the meteor was determined to be 22.2 billion years old, making it older than the universe's age. We thought the universe currently was at 13.77 billion years, which was an accurate number/age, or so scientists thought.

Over time, the scientists came up with formulas that could re-establish the age of everything in the universe.

Scientists did not expect the Sun to enter its red giant phase, which meant it would consume Earth over time. Something had to be done to save our wonderful planet. Scientists united and committed themselves to have had created a way to escape the expanding star of doom.

All said and done. The universe was determined to be an astonishing 13.77 TRILLION years old or more properly written as 13.77 TYA.

There was some error in the calculations of the universe's age where the last three zeroes were discarded. We can only hope that this was not a fateful decision for Humanity.

After this revelation, priority number one was saving the solar system and all the planets & moons included within it.

Due to mega-advanced technologies being developed related to teleportation, it was hypothesized that scientists could teleport the entire solar system to another spot in the universe away from our ailing Sun.

Each heavenly body in the solar system had to be electronically connected to Earth to make this happen.

The way this was done was by placing numerous obelisks on each planet & moon, then placing an electromagnetic bomb on each planet and "lighting" the obelisks with electricity and enveloping every planet and moon, causing "Electrospheres." These will occur on every rock and ball of gas in our solar system or cosmic hood'. The Electrosphere was a thin layer of electricity that encased the planet like an eggshell.

As it was now a race against the clock before the Sun consumed us, the obelisks were neatly placed on each heavenly body throughout the solar system. Before too long, scientists had created an Electro-sphere that enveloped each heavenly body and was now ready to be teleported elsewhere in the cosmos.

Throughout the electrification of the solar system, scientists were hard at work determining a Sun-like star that could support our solar system and its orbital patterns. The entire solar system will be teleported and cast into orbit around our new Sun.

Scientists found a star almost identical to ours with some cosmic luck. The new star was only 1 billion years old. Also, scientists used the new aging formula to age the star, so the scientists had the most accurate data possible.

The day came when the solar system was about to be teleported to its new home in the cosmos. Before that could happen, scientists had a brazen idea that may change the future of not only everyone on Earth but anything residing in the solar system.

It came time to teleport, and everything and everyone was in place when a certain scientist had a brilliant (?) idea: "Before we get to our final resting place in the cosmos, why don't we make a pit stop near a black hole. We will then understand what they are and what their purpose is."

It was understood that the entire solar system would teleport to a safe distance to view the black hole and take some quick measurements before the solar system was teleported to where it will stay near its new Sun.

So the scientists put in what they thought were the correct coordinates, and the button was pressed, which will teleport everything that ever existed, including the entire solar system.

Within the blink of an eye, it went dark outside, and what was witnessed next floored every living being on Earth and in the solar system, assuming anything lived elsewhere in the solar system.

It was noted that the solar system had been teleported to the black hole. Only to the horror of every scientist present, the coordinates were entered into the computer wrong with two transposed numbers. This may prove infinitely lethal for not just Earth but all Her neighbors in the solar system.

To have placed the solar system properly outside the black hole, the coordinates had to have been placed further away to compensate for the time it takes to move the solar system to the black hole. This was ignored or forgotten when the coordinates were placed into the computer.

When people outside looked up in the sky, they could see a distinct ring of fire across the entire sky that could be viewed by everybody on Earth, in every hemisphere, even in other parts of the world where it was daytime.

They did not know that this infamous ring on fire was, in fact, the event horizon or entrance to the black hole.

The scientists were worried, knowing that the solar system was now inside the event horizon and was about to become the next meal of the allegedly famished black hole, Sagittarius A*.

There was no time to think before gravitational disturbances were felt throughout the entire solar system. Regretfully, or not, the entire solar system started to get pulled inwards towards the singularity or center of the black hole. Within minutes, the solar system was pulled through the black hole.

No one knew if we would be spaghettified or not. To explain this phenomenon, non-rotating black holes cause everything that enters them to stretch and stretch until nothing was left.

Luckily for Humanity, no one stretched, as the solar system penetrated a light wall and popped out on the other side of the black hole in what appeared to be a different universe or for all anyone knew, it could be the same universe, but of course, that pesky white meteor may have come from here.

The teleportation no longer worked because no coordinates were known in this foreign universe. This told Humanity that we were now sitting ducks in an unforgiving cosmos that nothing was known about.

Most astonishing of all was a planet very near to ours, which appeared to be an Earth, or so it seemed.

The only thing we could do to possibly find a way back to our universe was to land on the Earth-like planet and find out how to go back to our home universe.

Luckily, a sun-like star near the solar system gave ample heat and light, so we did not freeze in the vastness of space.

The World Space Project immediately set up a human-crewed mission to the Earth-like planet. The mission was to land at Cape Canaveral (if such a place existed) and see what we could find out about this alien place and see if they could provide instructions on how we could go back.

It was obvious that the solar system could go back towards the black hole, but Humanity had no idea as to whether the black hole upon reentry would destroy them,

The astronauts took off towards the different Earth and touched down on what they thought was this planet's version of Cape Canaveral. The astronauts proceeded to walk into the hangar, not knowing who or what to expect. To their surprise, there were human-looking people tending to the various computers inside the hangar.

Someone spotted the astronauts and said, "Hello fellow humans, my name was Fatumachina (FAY-TUM-OCK-IN-A)." In your language, my name translates to "Fate Machine." "We require a new galactic home as our parent star, the Sun, has reached the end of its lifecycle and will soon consume Earth, lighting it ablaze like an unattended campfire destroying the planet in the process." The lead astronaut told Fatumachina.

"Time is of the essence, and you must make haste." Take this computer with you. It is called a "Vitacyclum" and is used to control the life cycles of stars, mainly their ages. and then sets the age to whatever you find feasible." Fatumachina explained.

"As for exiting our universe, you may exit out the black hole you entered from as our astronomers have picked up where your solar system was placed," Fatumachina said. However, the astronauts noted that Fatumachina held back laughter when he stated how to exit their universe.

This cast doubt on what exactly the astronauts had been told, and if the black hole exit works...or maybe the entire solar system will become a meal for said black hole...

Nonetheless, the astronauts launched off of this strange Earth-like planet and ventured back to the real Earth, where the astronauts shared the Vitacyclum with the head of the World Space Project (WSP).

Kelly Maitis, the head of the WSP, was astounded at this new technology and was excited to get our Sun back as it was determined that the solar system would go back to its original position near our Sun...pending the trip through the black hole.

So everyone on Earth held their breath as the solar system entered the black hole, not knowing what would happen. Everything will either be spaghettified or pass through as it did previously.

Everyone on Earth braced themselves while the solar system entered the famed black hole... The solar system survived its journey through the black hole by magic or whatever else.

It ended up on the opposite side of the event horizon, and under great gravitational tension, the solar system was now able to teleport again.

The first business that had to happen was having the solar system teleported to its former position in orbit around the

Sun.

Immediately, we were back where we originally were. There was only one problem, the sunlight was not bright, and in fact, it looked like perpetual dawn all over Earth. Humanity needed to find out why the Sun was so dim.

We understood that the Sun was ailing (for now), but we knew it would still cast that same brightness of light, at least in the interim...

Scientists were not very happy to report something strange encasing the Sun, and we could also see the culprits regarding who was dimming OUR Sun.

From the scientist's viewpoint from Earth, they observed that some extraterrestrials were building a Dyson sphere encasement around our Sun. A Dyson sphere is a way of pulling energy from stars, in this case, our Sun. This was not a huge deal as Humanity could teleport out of the area and go to the original Sun-like star they were headed towards when they ended up black hole bound.

As the solar system was about to teleport to its final destination, the Vitacyclum was utilized. Setting our Sun's age to billions of years in the future, it exploded or went supernova, destroying any trace of the extraterrestrials that were most likely harvesting its energy.

As a new day started in Humanity's new position within the cosmos, every person on Earth was damn lucky to have survived the entire cosmic onslaught thrust upon them of a black hole and energy harvesting extraterrestrials and whatever else...

Now it was time to enjoy Humanity's new view of all neighboring planets and get friendly with the new "neighbors."

THE END

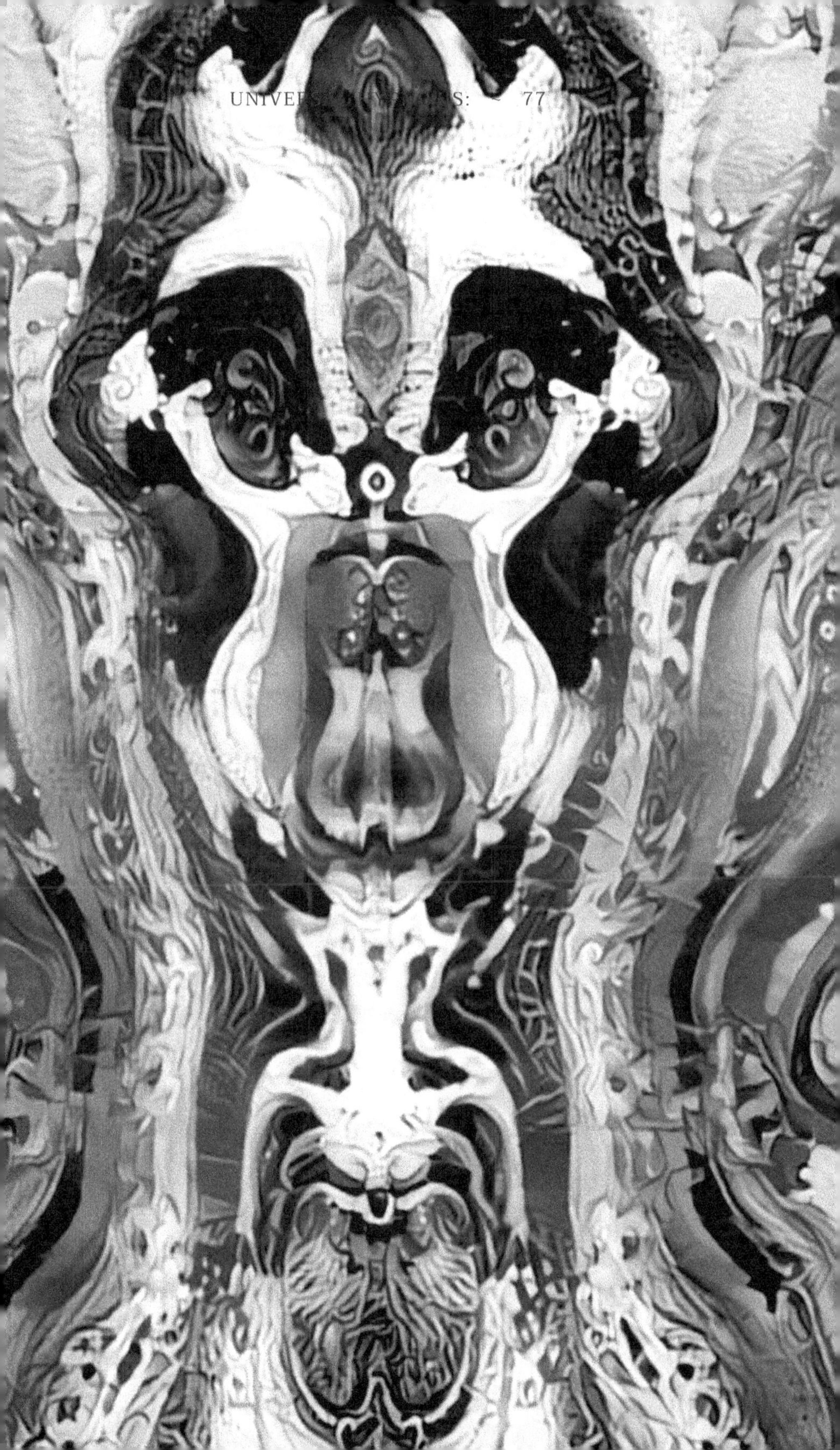

"Peering Through the Looking Glass at a Strange "Hole of Fire," While Imagining What Exists Beyond" - or — "Space Trippin' During A Psilocybinge"

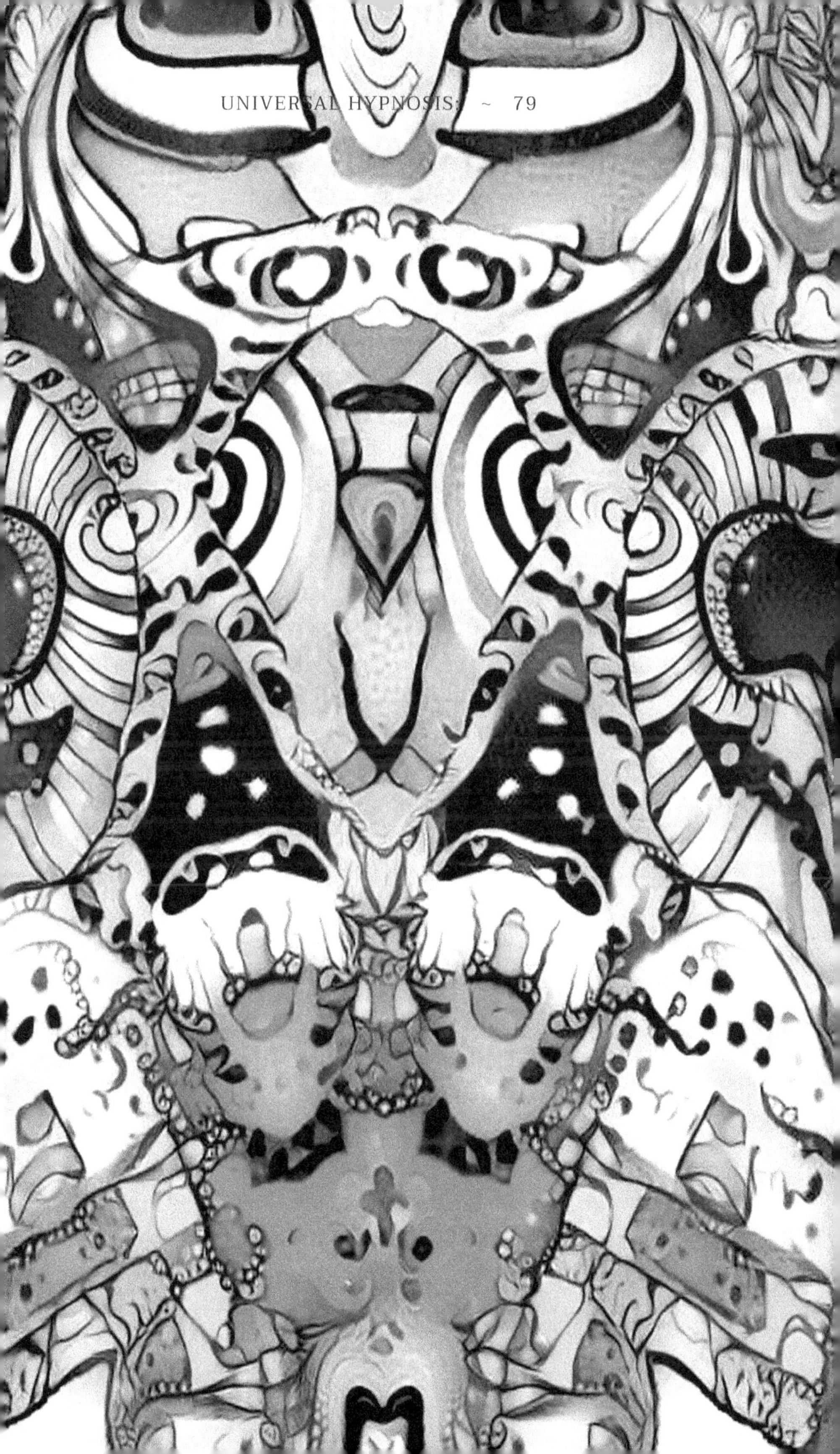

The world in 2179 was bustling as advances in space and many other technologies had steadily been accelerating since the Apollo moon landing over two centuries ago.

One of the standout technologies recently invented was that of a "warpship." This warpship was a super-advanced spaceship that could travel anywhere in the universe.

Previously, scientists had mapped the entire observable universe, and every area of the universe had a specific coordinate, just like on Earth.

Coordinates were fed into the computers on the warpship, and then upon takeoff, the warpship would dissipate (temporarily) through space & time, where it would reappear at the specific coordinate that was initially chosen. This happens after taking a shortcut through the fabric of space-time.

While probing the cosmos for life-baring planets, great telescopes found a planet the World Space Project named "Umbrah," roughly translated as "Cool World" in Latin.

The World Space Project was the administration that oversaw all of the space programs and activities in space.

Upon viewing Umbrah through the telescopes, it was deemed that the warpship would make a trip to this planet to see if any signs of life existed there.

It was a grand spectacle, so to speak, at Cape Canaveral the day the astronauts were to set their stellar sails and make their way to Umbrah.

The warpship made its vertical takeoff and disappeared through the sky. The warpship made its way into orbit where the coordinates were punched in, allowing the warpship to travel through space and time and had emerged near Umbrah.

Before the crew knew it, they were in Umbrah air space, and the warpship glided over the land as the astronauts got their first look at Umbrah.

Unfortunately for the astronauts and Humanity, this was a long-dead planet where the core had cooled long ago, rendering the planet inhospitable and without life.

The astronauts were so focused on entering the air space of the barren planet that when they left Umbrah, the crew witnessed something no one had ever seen before: No further than 1000 miles from Umbrah was a ring of white fire randomly out in space. This appeared to be a "hole" in the universe. It was 1000's of miles across.

It seemed to be a portal of sorts in the fabric of space-time, and the astronauts did not know how to react. Amazingly though, they could see another planet through the hole, meaning that it was not even part of the universe and existed outside of it.

The astronauts would have loved to take a trip to the "outer" planet, but time did not allow, and doing so may jeopardize the mission.

The astronauts returned home and were eager to further share with their superiors more about the planet they witnessed through the white hole of fire.

After much debate and some soul searching, The World Space Project stated that Humanity would make a trip to the "outer" planet, which was named "Ultraterra," further explained as "Invisible Earth" in Latin.

Just as last time, a select group of astronauts were chosen for the mission to Ultraterra.

The astronauts going on the mission are named below:

Name	Hometown	Years of Exp.
Peter Scrotusky	Las Vegas, NV	18
Linda Knellerk	Costa Mesa, CA	12
Jacques Incerlum	Slatedale, PA	21
Jonathan Bastamente	Bogota, CO	15
George Littlemeyer	Fayetteville, NC	17

With over eighty years of experience, these astronauts were well versed in all facets of the upcoming mission and space travel in general.

They had taken many voyages across the cosmos and lived to tell their tales. Some involved asteroid mining, and others placed our global flag on our planetary neighbors and many other exoplanets out there in the cosmos.

It was days later that Cape Canaveral saw a similar spectacle as the previous launch regarding the upcoming takeoff of the warpship that will blast into orbit: destination Ultraterra.

As the warpship lifted off, many persons on Earth, possibly including the astronauts, thought about what Ultraterra would be like and if it supported intelligent life.

The astronauts gained orbit and set the coordinates for Umbrah, where they will get within proximity to the "White Hole of Fire."

They traveled through space and time instantly to arrive near Umbrah and were able to bring into view the white hole of fire, which exited outside of the universe to a completely new area, which was never chartered.

The hole of fire was quite a sight to see, with its ring of white fire circling the entire hole.

The astronauts ever so carefully exited our universe to the Spacehole and made their way to the planet in question, Ultraterra. The foreign planet beckoned to them like a spider about to capture its prey in its web of deceit and death.

The wind resistance of the ship immediately changed upon entering the hole, and the universe's physics changed in odd ways that are even harder to explain, although everything was all good.

As the astronauts approached the mystery planet, it was very dark. The planet's outline was a cool blue, similar to our Earth. The warpship flew into Ultraterras' air space and could not see anything because the planet was so dark.

It would be too much of a waste to turn back now, so the astronauts made the bold decision to land on the mysterious planet.

Lowering the warpship, the outside temperature showed 74 degrees (23 Celsius) and that the air was, in fact, breathable. The warpship landed in the wilderness where the trees appeared to be orange, at least from the vantage point of the cockpit.

Uncertain eeriness spread over the crew, and most people, except for Linda, of course, got the creeps. "Come on, guys, let's go out and take a look. We do not even need our suits." George stated.

With that statement, the five seasoned astronauts crept out of the ship and decided to "try" and take a look around in the pitch-black darkness.

All of a sudden, a cry rang out.

Jacques went off in another direction, looking at the flowers and admiring the mushrooms. He was holding his "Chem-O-Meter," which can determine the chemical composition of anything in the handheld gadget's area.

For anyone who has seen Ghostbusters (1984), the Chem-O-Meter looked exactly like the handheld gadget that Egon uses to sniff out ghosts, only this time, it was mushrooms (perhaps magical) that were being tested.

Jacques was delighted to discover that the mushrooms contained Psilocybin, the main ingredient in magic mushrooms. Jacques smiled in delight because he knew for a fact that Linda was into psychedelics too, like the famed DMT and, of course, magic mushrooms.

Jacques harvested enough mushrooms for the crew and brought them back to the ship where everyone except Jonathan was. No one thought much about Jonathan's disappearance. They were merely concerned that he may get lost.

About 70 feet from them, Jonathan made his way through the brush since he could hear a raging river up ahead, so he decided to search for the river.

As he found the river, he stood on the bank and saw the shadow of a man-like creature out of his peripheral. Only it was taller than a man could ever be, and this was what scared Jonathan to soon turn back and make his way back to the warpship. He, too, had a Chem-O-Meter and tested the water.

Good thing he checked the "water." Through the analysis, it was discovered that the raging river was Fluoroantimonic acid. This was the most damaging acid to have on your skin, as it will melt it to the bone and may even eat through the bone too.

No sooner did Jonathan read the meter did he hear footsteps behind him. Excitedly, he turned around because he had hoped it was one of the crew.

He was now staring at the chest of someone tall and green. From what Jonathan could gather, they were tall lizard people with a special knack for murder: A simple three-blade claw was affixed to their right hand where each protrusion was a drill.

As Jonathan breathed his last breaths, he noted that the lizard man had rows of diamond-tipped teeth that could probably rip through Kevlar. It was also stained with the blood of his most recent victims. Jonathan hoped that the blood on its teeth was not from any crew.

As Jonathan found out, the hand drill could cut with absolute surgical precision as the three claws were drilled into his forehead before he could even move. The lizard man's quickness was impressive as he eliminated Jonathan and then went right back towards the forest.

Back at the warpship, Jacques and Linda were on a hefty dose of good cosmic mushrooms as the woods became brighter (in their liquid visions), and everything seemed more Technicolor.

Jacques and Linda were living it up, but they still needed to find the rest of the party so they could leave this dark and wooded planet for good.

Before they could blink, George ran out of the woods towards Jacques and Linda. He was bleeding profusely from his stomach.

"Lizard people!" That was all he could exclaim before he fell over dead. Both Jacques and Linda may have entered a bad trip at that observance, but accurate data was unavailable at the time.

Jacques and Linda decided to look around to see if they could find Jonathan (rip) and/or Peter.

They were walking through a clearing about 100 feet from the warpship when some polar bear-looking creature with transparent skin started to run after the psychedelic duo.

As it approached closer, its insides appeared to glow like a Christmas tree. This was unlike any animal on Earth.

While being under the hypnotic mushrooms' influence sometimes makes people more in tune with nature. Jacques put his hand out to the beast as it approached and was very surprised at the outcome.

Linda shot her laser at the creature and dropped it dead, as the laser was designed to work like a .22 caliber bullet, where the laser bounces around inside the body, causing grave damage and inevitable death. It was some extraterrestrial bear-type animal; the life forms on this planet were nothing we would want on Earth.

While trekking back to the warpship and being as uncoordinated as ever, they came to two streams that crossed each other. They could be jumped across where they cross, or you could run and jump, like Linda did, and cleared the streams with ease. She was safe as the streams were only four feet wide.

Jacques thought about the precision of his jump. He probably over-analyzed as he misjudged his jump and fell face-first into the Fluoroantimonic acid river.

His body started to melt as Linda's interest was piqued. She hated to admit that the melting of Jacques was wild on magic mushrooms and was without a doubt the most eye-popping "visual" she ever had in all her years of consuming psychedelics.

Linda suddenly became fear-stricken as she decided to make it back to the warpship, where she would try to make it back alive to tell all of her superiors and, eventually, the world exactly what happened on the unforgivable planet; of "Ultraterra."

She arrived safely at the warpship and questioned her reliance on operating a super-advanced spacecraft when she ate a LOT of mushrooms.

The warpship lifted off, and as she almost re-entered the universe, while she daydreamed of her life back on Earth and how she had a new appreciation of life since her crewmates lost their lives.

As she entered the Spacehole back to our universe, space became a thick yellow jelly-looking substance, and the asteroids that passed the warpship looked like balls of confetti, and the stars appeared to be cotton candy.

As she approached the moon, it grew a "silly" face outlined in red, and it winked at her as if to welcome her home.

Once Linda touched down at Cape Canaveral, the mission's only survivor, she laid her head on the control console and rested her psychedelic head...

Fifty years later (in a quaint home somewhere in the world)...

A very old lady was happy to have her grand kids over to hear a story that they were not sure was real or not. This was the story you just read, as told by the strong-hearted Linda Knellerk.

THE END

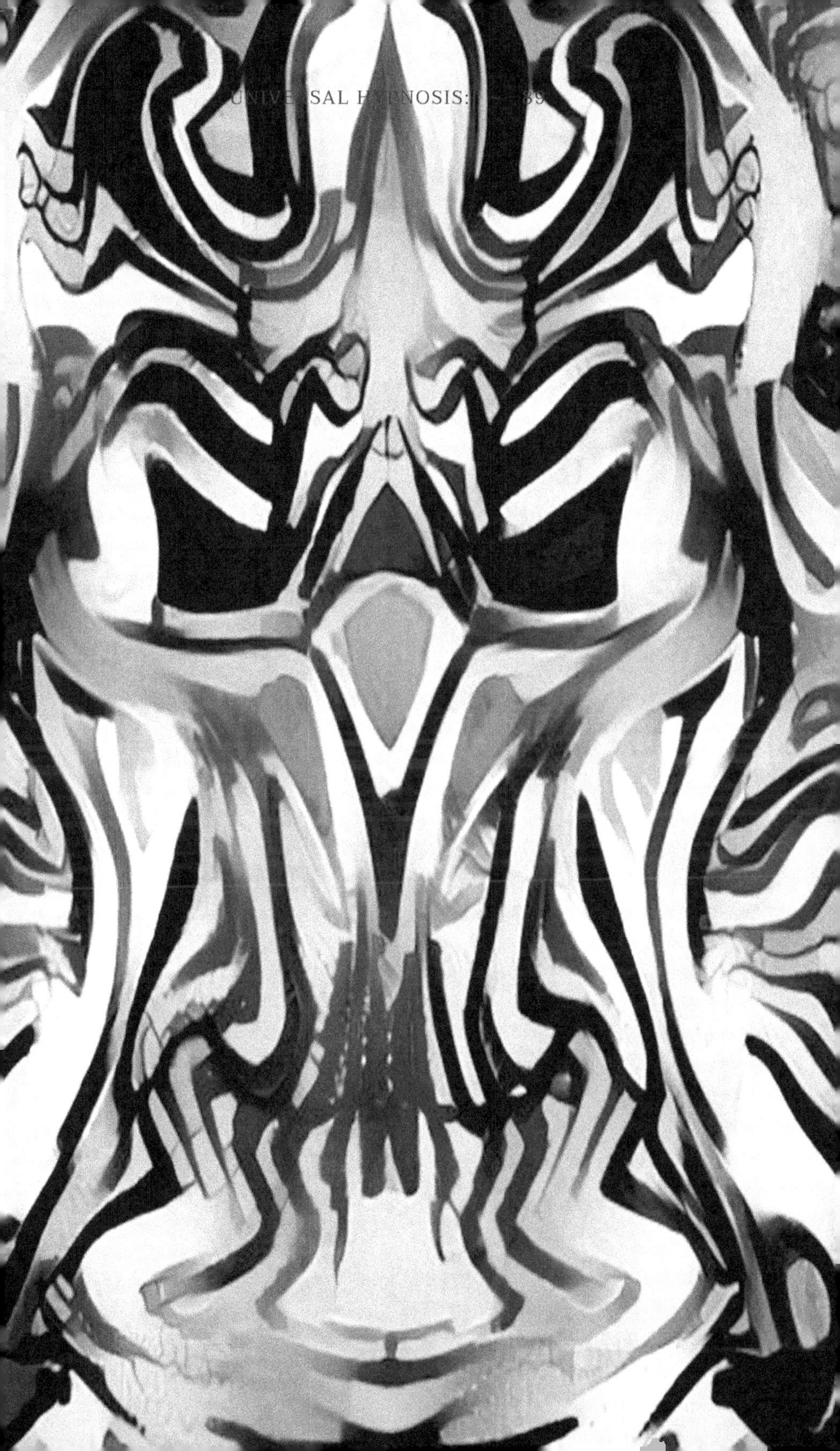
UNIVERSAL HYPNOSIS: 89

Chapter 10

"Careful With That Laser, Eugene" -or- "Galactic Laser Tag"

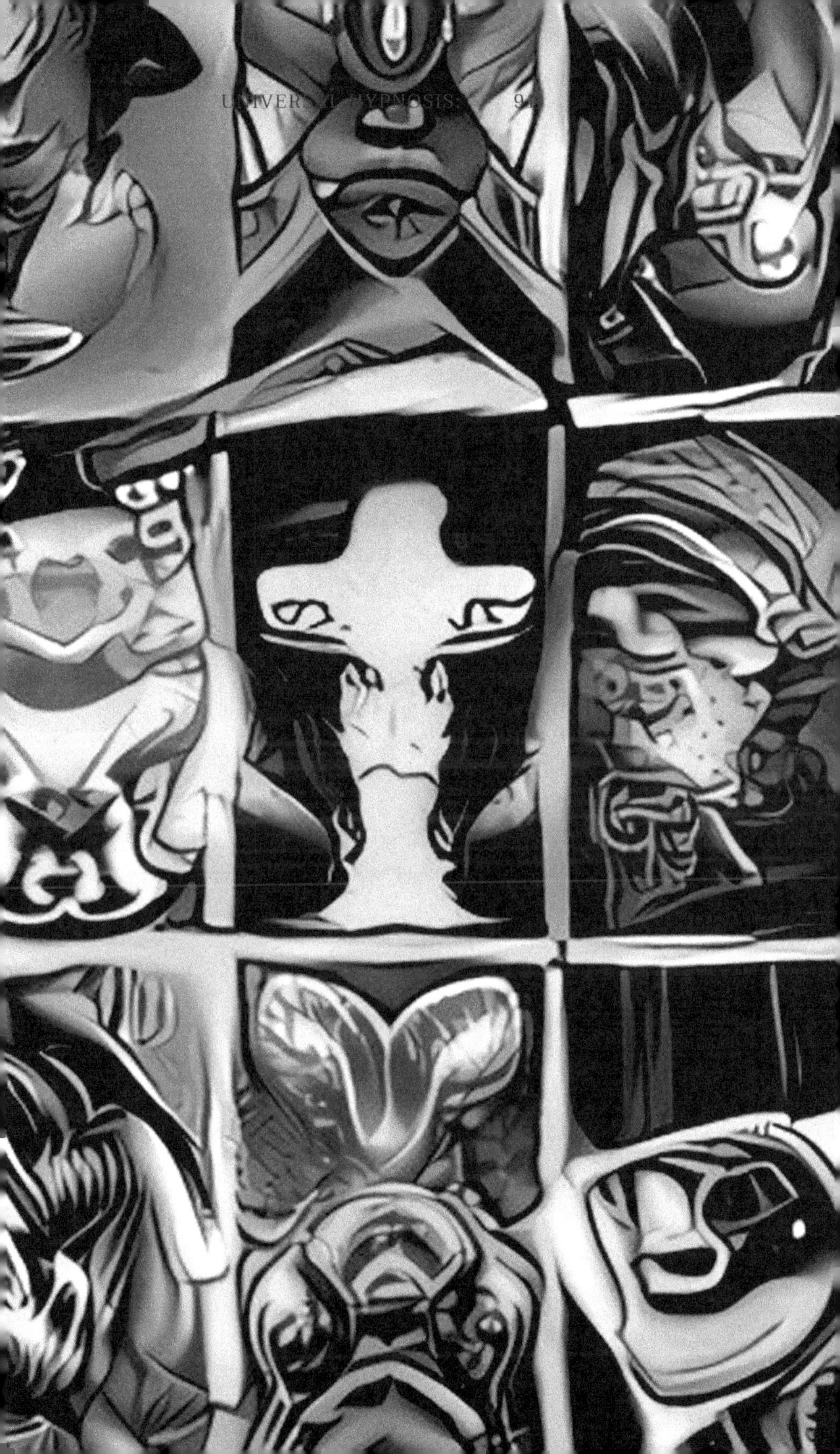

The current state of our universe is that of decay as random stars in the galactic neighborhood have gone supernova or exploded for reasons unknown.

This was an obvious problem and a discovery that over two billion stars had ended their life cycles in a barrage of magma, stellar shrapnel, and other molten debris.

This caused intense gamma-ray bursts of devastating energy that reverberated throughout the galaxy. Gamma-Ray Bursts are the energy emitted from a star exploding or going supernova. These are the most violent events in the universe. These rays would be devastating to Earth, with over 1000 mph (161 kph) winds.

Many planets had their atmospheres stripped away, never to be seen again. Gamma-Rays should be known as sky thieves since they eradicate the atmosphere with surgical precision.

Scientists could not fathom what had caused the violent stellar explosions. They threw around theory after theory, but nothing felt like it nailed the sporadic explosive chaos.

Humanity knew that their time was running out almost too quickly. If a gamma-ray burst slams into the planet, we will be living among 1000 mph + winds and no atmosphere, for that matter, if we even lived at all.

The problem is that stars closest to Earth will eventually go supernova, so scientists had to devise a plan to save Humanity.

A brand new star only one light year away was discovered close enough to impact Earth if it went supernova.

Finally, 'The League of Universal Scientists' decided that scientists would create a collider or atom smasher that will create a 9-mile wide laser, which will widen as it makes its way to the volatile star.

Once complete and everything is in order, the collider's roof will open and shoot the massive circular laser towards the star to destroy it before the stellar time bomb goes full-blown supernova and affects Earth in a very negative fashion causing possible extinction events worldwide.

The collider's construction began by digging a 33-mile circular tunnel 111 feet below the surface. The collider will have a retractable roof so the scientists can shoot the gargantuan laser, known as "Star Decimator," towards the misbehaving star blowing it to smithereens, thus saving Humanity and our pristine planet.

In galactic time, the laser will take three months to reach its destination. Humanity hoped that the star did not explode within the laser's time frame to reach the potentially deadly star.

The world was so excited to hear the news of the collider's completion as the construction of the collider concluded.

Before we knew it, the day came when scientists would "light the laser." The scientists started the underground laser that heated to 7 trillion degrees. The roof opened and shot the laser toward the deadly ailing star.

The laser will demolish the star nicknamed "Crepitus," Latin for "explosion." The laser fired off without any problems, and now the waiting game started. The scientists monitored the laser for the next three months. The day came when the laser was close enough to Crepitus to eradicate it very soon.

Humanity was ecstatic because there was an extremely high likelihood that Crepitus would be destroyed. It was only a matter of time before the laser reached its intended target.

As the laser moved closer and closer, scientists noted that the target star was now a ball of fire encapsulated in some impervious material.

The star must have exploded, although it contained a "cage" around it that kept the exploded star encapsulated. It stumped every scientific mind on the planet.

Too bad for Humanity, this ended up not being a good thing. The star was part of an extraterrestrial star system. They were so advanced that they built a gravitational force field around the star in question because they knew it was at the end of its lifecycle.

The gravitational force field around the star was unlike anything Humanity could have imagined.

The laser ricocheted off the force field and was sent right back in Earth's direction.

Once this news was available, scientists scrambled for an alternate way to save Earth, as the laser was headed right back toward Earth.

Time was on their side, so they figured they had three months to deflect the laser.

They fired off a second laser beam in the first laser's direction as its trajectory headed straight towards Earth.

Unfortunately for Humanity, the second laser completely missed the deflected laser beam. Its speed was faster than what the scientists had calculated using math that filled up chalkboards.

Humanity's mounting problems got even worse when the second immense laser beam also hit the encased star, and it too was headed back to Earth, right behind the first laser beam.

The fateful day came when the lasers approached Earth.

One night, half the world awoke in the middle of the night. It was light outside. People were traumatized by the notion that those laser beams were so bright that they lit up the entire sky.

It was observed that the first laser beam ripped two clean holes straight through the Earth, knocking it off its axis and hurtling away, having been pushed off its orbit by the gaping hole that went clean through the planet.

Now that Earth had tumbled off its orbit, it spun violently and caused billions of people to be ejected right off Earth's surface due to its erratic movements.

It's a shame those no-good scientists couldn't detect the gravitational force field on the star BEFORE firing off the laser.

There is not much Humanity can do as the Earth's speed became so fast that 10,000 mph winds wreaked havoc on everything.

It pretty much obliterated the entire surface and rendered life a thing of the past.

Eventually, all that was left was a shell of Earth's former glory floating erratically forever or until it collided with a different heavenly body, devastating it into billions of pieces by shattering it like a broken window.

THE END

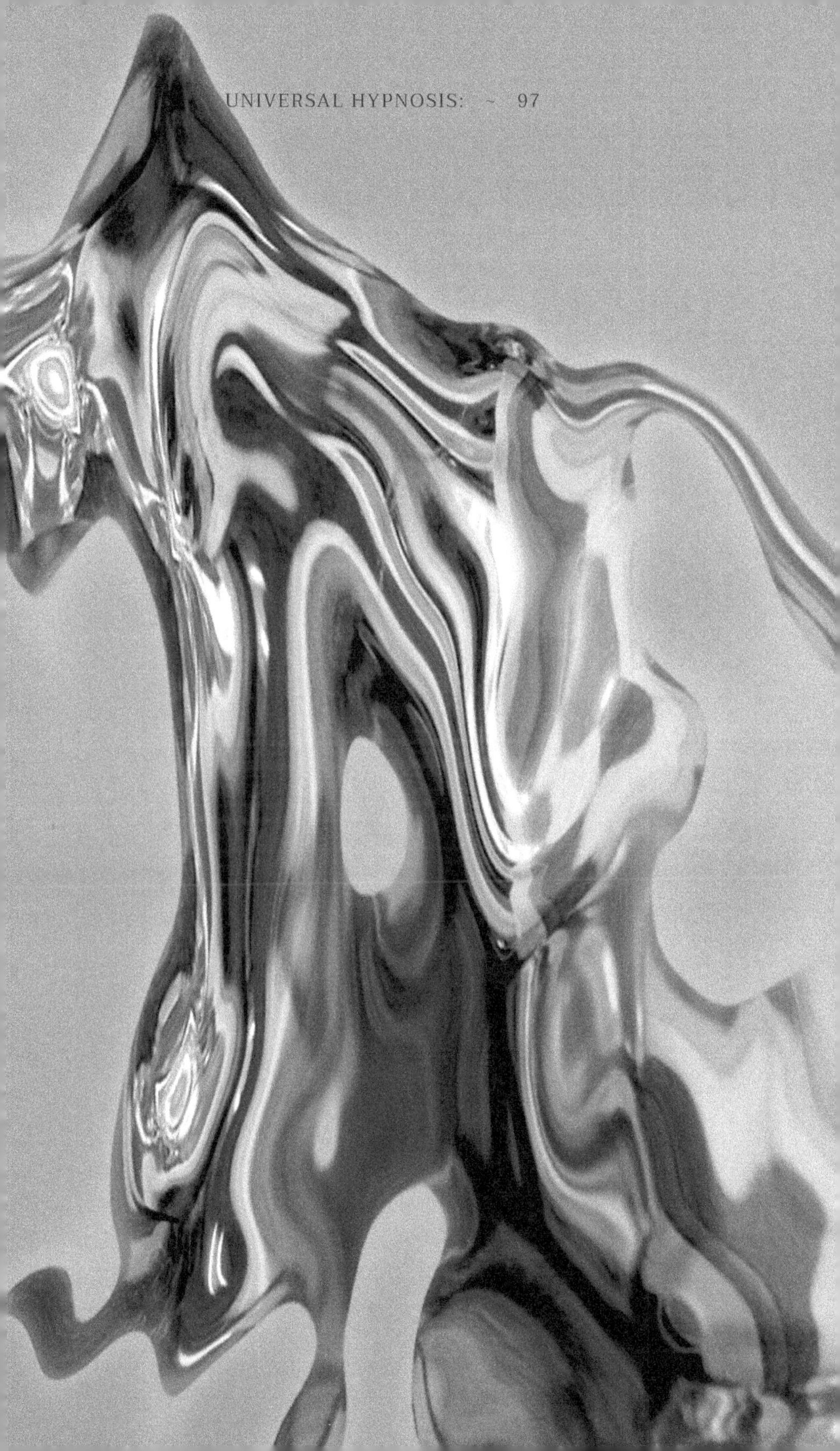

Chapter 11

"A Crash Course In Cosmic Hitchhiking"

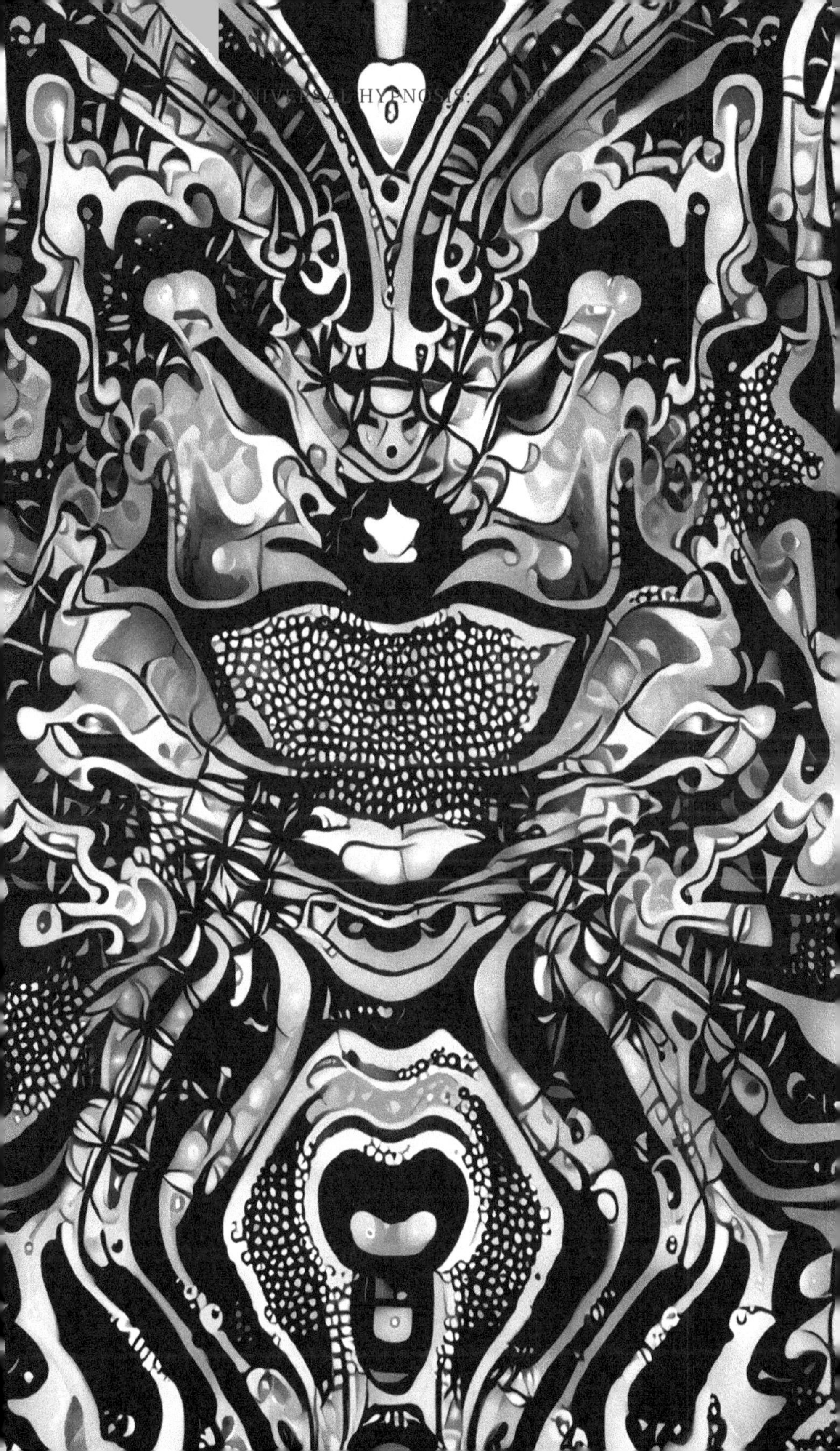

For the first time in recorded history, the Earth had many stationary extraterrestrial spacecraft dotting its landscapes. They had, in fact, not been there very long at all.

Known as the Novisi (NO-VIZ-EYE), these extraterrestrials were six feet (1.83 meters) tall and had neon yellow skin with purple stripes with bright long red hair. The Novisi had no weapons, so we were not looking over our backs every 30 seconds. Perhaps we should have...

Now that their fleet of spacecraft took a pit stop on Earth, they approached Humanity very tactfully. They made Humanity feel comfortable, and we did the same for them.

They exited all of the spacecraft and were very peaceful and needed to refuel their spacecraft, and they would be on their way. They never told us what the fuel was composed of, so maybe we could help them.

The timing could not be any worse as it was determined that a major solar storm shot violently in our direction originating from the sun, sending Coronal Mass Ejections straight towards Earth, which wreaked havoc on the planet's electrical grids.

Also, 98% of businesses cannot conduct any type of business without electricity.

We were active during the day, but come dusk. It was like that quarantine business reminiscent of a particular time in the population's life circa 2020.

The Novisi started showing certain persons their spacecraft. Anyone who wanted a tour could see the incredible spacecraft and the technologies that built such highly technological spacecraft.

Visitors on the numerous spacecraft marveled at the state-of-the-art engineering that went into building the 1111 space-craft. It made our technologies look prehistoric in comparison.

An example of an advanced technology that the Invisibilae utilized was its use of "Chemelioflage." It is a type of ultra-advanced camouflage where the spacecraft can be rendered completely invisible by mimicking the surrounding environ-ment.

It is even harder to believe that each Invisibilae wore a skin-suit with their spacecraft's same Chemelioflage technology. It had to be stressed how excellent their Chemelioflage was at keeping them invisible. The Invisibilae cannot be seen from two feet away when the special camouflage was activated.

What no one cared to notice was that everyone who went aboard the spacecraft vanished. The population got suspicious and would not board Invisibilae's ships anymore.

It was discovered that towns within a two-mile radius of each 1111 ships were now ghost towns with no traces of foul play. The people simply vanished.

Before we knew it, the Invisibilae rendered themselves com-pletely invisible. They started to snatch people out of their beds at night, dragging them onto their ships, never to be seen or heard from again. Estimates showed that worldwide over one million people went missing without a trace.

We knew that the Novisi were the culprits, although it never made sense where over one million people could have gone. This terrified Humanity and made everyone think something to the effect of "Will I wake up tomorrow morning?" or "will I ever wake up again?"

The uneasiness was planet-wide, and it caused dangerous amounts of anxiety and countless panic attacks all across Earth. Quite frankly, earthlings never dealt with this before. The uneasiness never subsided, knowing that anybody could be ripped from their bed and taken somewhere never to return.

A young man named Ebin Winderbrooke took it upon himself to see where the scores of ships went, as he was obsessed with the extraterrestrials and had a huge fondness for the Novisi. He wanted to see their homeworld.

As he approached a ship, he could see a circular window in the front where the ship was piloted. The spacecraft must have been a football field in length and just as wide. A loud yellow color adorned the spacecraft and had pictures of ancient runes drawn upon the massive exterior of the ship.

Ebin searched around the spacecraft and found the way aboard. He was now on the massive ship and was alone. After walking the ship's corridors, Ebin was shocked to see blood all over the floor in the room furthest back in the massive ship, where a chute was. With many bloody saws and odd cutting devices'.

He didn't want to think about it, but that must've been blood from the persons who "took a trip through the spacecraft." He could only surmise that they kidnapped humans and would use them for fuel to get back to their homeworld.

The chute down to the fuel tank was not very large, hence the bloody floor. All of a sudden, the spacecraft started to shake. It was taking off! Ebin knew he was in for the ride of his life and braced himself for the journey ahead.

Ebin reminisced about positive things he did while on Earth to control his overwhelming fear because he feared that he would never step foot on Earth ever again.

Ebin ran and hid in a closet, where he could hopefully go unseen even though he had no idea where he was headed. He passed out for who knows how long and woke up sometime later. He didn't hear the engines' roar anymore and noted that he must be at the destination, most likely on the Invisibilae' homeworld.

Ebin built up confidence and strength. He attempted to open the closet to see where he was. As the door creaked open, he noted he may now be alone on the spacecraft or hoped not to be spotted.

He found a door in the spaceship, pressed a button near the door, having no clue where it went. Ebin knew he had an adventure ahead of him, so he trekked forward.

Luckily (or unluckily), this was the exit to the spacecraft. Ebin descended the ramp and walked out onto the Novisi' planet. Even in his terrified state, Ebin noted that their home-world was breathtaking.

Lush red grass and orange ponds galore, and a light green sky were just some beautiful sites on this foreign planet. Luckily for Ebin, he was still able to breathe.

Ebin had no idea what to do. It's not like he could pilot the spacecraft back to Mother Earth...it was probably out of fuel anyway, and he was not able to sacrifice himself to get back home...

To remain undercover, Ebin walked into the woods where he found a horrible site: countless cages were filled with all types of creatures like "humanoids." Looking back, he noticed a large expanse where he could see large statues in the distance. They looked out over a pink ocean.

Strange creatures were swimming in the ocean and were completely unexplained compared to what Ebin was used to seeing. While being lost in an alien world's scenery, Ebin continued into the woods or attempted to.

A group of Novisi spotted Ebin. As soon as Ebin spotted them, he ran as fast as he possibly could. Naturally, they gave chase Ebin had gained a lot of distance between him and his possible future captors. His only recourse was to enter some sort of building that looked like it was part of a college campus.

Ebin busted through the door and immediately ran into some chamber, where a glass tube lowered around him. The captors ran into the room and watched Ebin's every move.

Ebin used one of the catchphrases he was known for and said, "I must have lost my mind!" Then some sort of machine voice said from somewhere in the room, "Memory erasure will complete in 60 seconds."

As Ebin looked around, he noticed that this was a time traveling apparatus. So he tested things out. "Earth!" he shouted just to see what would happen.

"Destination Earth" was what the machine said as Ebin disappeared. Possibly thwarting his would-be captors.

Before he knew it, Ebin appeared somewhere in the English countryside. It's a pity he did not know his surroundings, not because he was not here before, but because his mind was absent.

Ebin cried, knowing that the Novisi had, in fact, defeated him by stripping him of his mind.

THE END

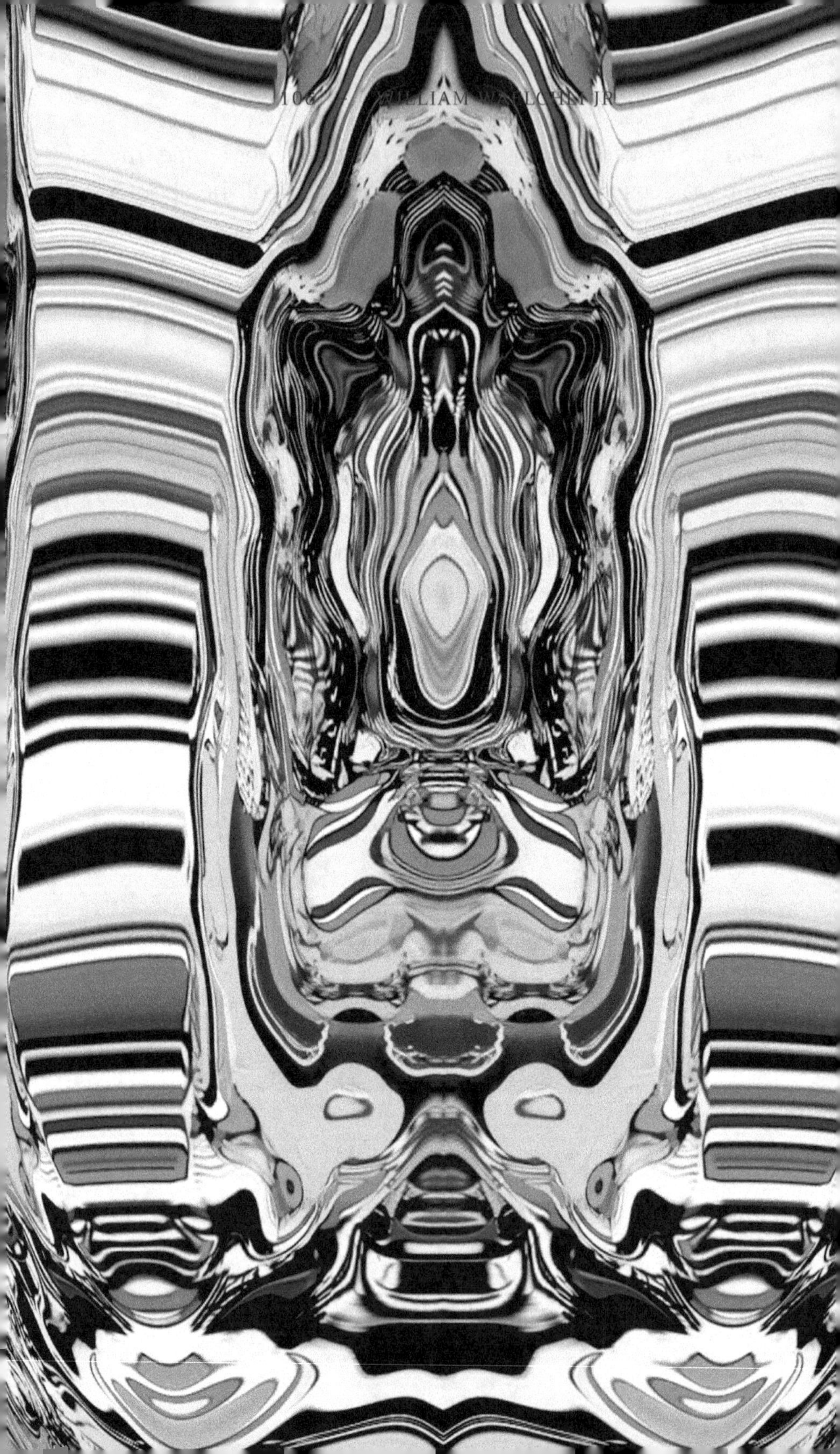

"Diamonds Aren't Forever...Even Though Bling is the in Thing" -or- "An Indecisive Future Concerning Scintillam and its Near Infinite Volatility..."

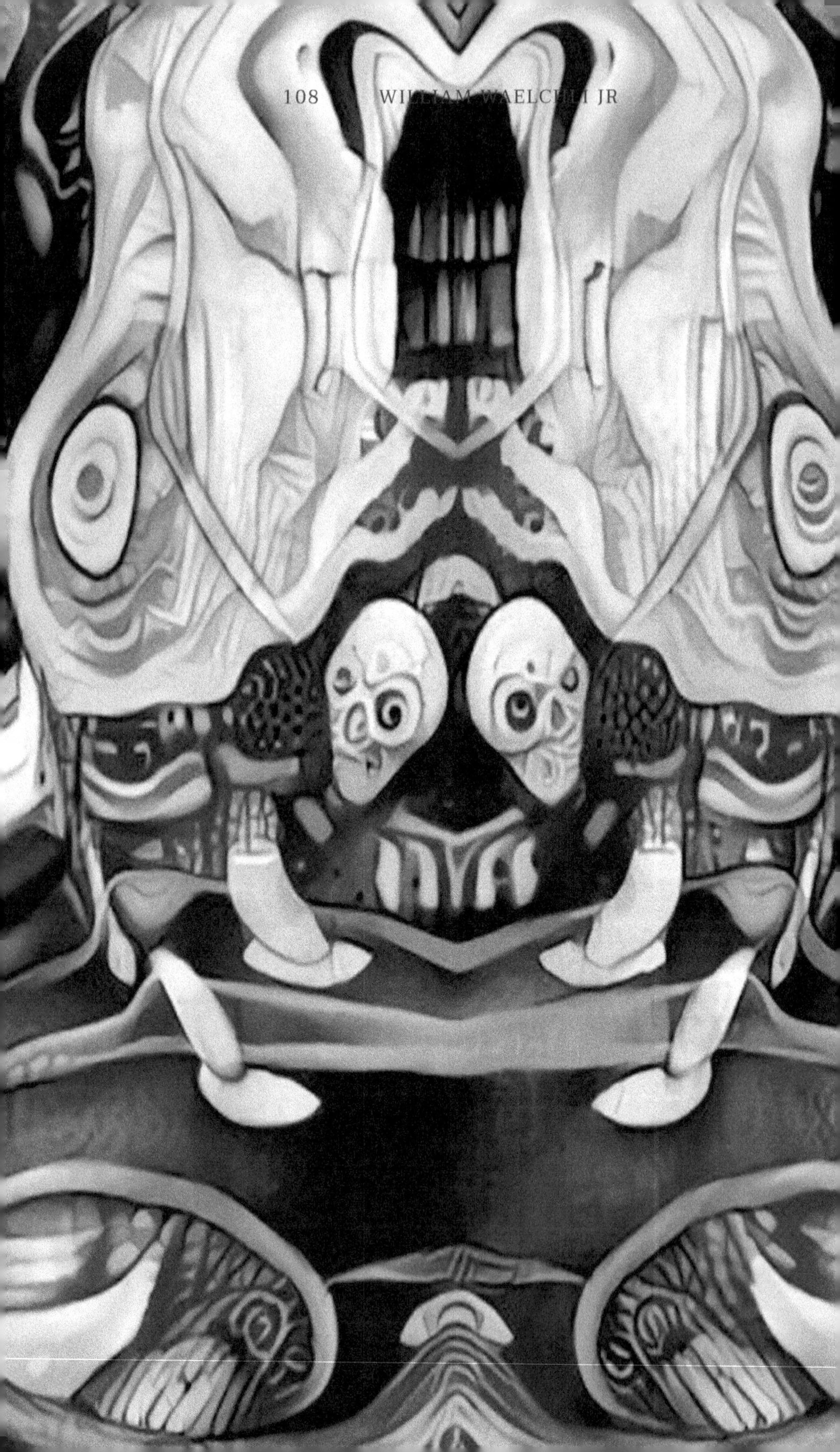

In the future, it was grim news for all of Humanity. There was nothing we could do to stop our impending doom, perhaps...

A rogue black hole was headed straight towards Earth, soaring through the cosmos at unbelievable speeds.

The ramifications on Earth were enormous because, as the rogue black hole gets closer, everything will start to stretch and be pulled towards the rogue black hole.

This is known in the scientific community as "spaghettification," covered earlier in this book. This is the phenomenon that occurs when a black hole approaches its prey.

It was no secret that most persons were scared out of their wits, knowing that our planet would be wiped off the universal map, never to be seen nor heard from ever again.

Remember, everything that happened or that is happening will be erased and gone forever. Everything Humanity has achieved since time immemorial will be lost.

It is a slow, painful death for all of Humanity that cannot be expressed enough. Knowing that they would be spaghettified was nothing to laugh at, so Humanity looked to the scientists to figure a way out of this doomed debacle.

The good thing is that we have twenty-two months until the black hole will start messing with Earth's physics. Not to mention the havoc it could wreak on Humanity.

It was a massive discovery when scientists detected more diamonds than could ever be adorned by every person on our planet a million times over buried deep underground nestled in the mantle, directly below the Earth's crust.

Around a quintillion pounds (a 1 with 18 zeroes) of diamonds are 100 miles (160.9 meters) below the crust, and Humanity was determined to tap that deposit.

Hopefully, everyone can experience the glitz and glamour of celebrity life in their own homes when the diamonds are retrieved, just before the black hole swallows Earth forever.

If the black hole were going to obliterate Humanity, Humanity would damn them if they were not going to go out adorned in dazzling and fabulous bling, bathing in diamonds at the moment of the black hole's impact.

The diamonds could never be reached by conventional methods, such as drills and shovels. They were located in the Roots of Craton area of the mantle deep beneath the surface.

Humanity had to step up their game. So they came up with a more cutting-edge way to mine the diamonds before the black hole gets too close to Earth, or worst-case scenario, the runaway behemoth collides with Earth.

We needed the hole dug out, but scientists also needed a way to lower the miners below the crust to access the diamonds' humongous stash.

A brilliant idea was then conjured up: scientists will create lasers that make boreholes deep into our Earth's mantle.

It took only 12 weeks or 3 months to engineer and create the specialized lasers needed to bore into our planet.

What also needed to be engineered was some vehicle that can "clasp" the walls and lower itself quickly to the 100-mile journey it will inevitably take to reach the plethora of diamonds.

After another six weeks of engineering, they built a sizeable cylindrical style cart that can move at high speeds and has plenty of room to hold many diamond stashes.

Before Humanity knew it, the lasers were completed and were ready to be taken to the "drilling" site, as was the cable cart that the miners would ride to get to the Earth's stash of endless diamonds.

Scientists fired up the lasers, and like clockwork, they shot deep into the Earth's crust without any snags.

Believe it or not, the lasers did a perfect job of tunneling into the crust/mantle and made it simple for the miners to lower themselves down the tunnel via the equipped cable cart.

It lowered rapidly, and the miners arrived safely at the diamond stash.

As was the custom, the miners used pickaxes to work their way through the sediment and rock to get to the all-important diamond stash.

A pickax struck something hard, and immediately, 100,000-volt electric shocks shot through the tunnel and into the shaft.

The miners somehow knew that they had found something special.

They carefully tried to hit the grayish-green rock with the pickax, but the shock was quite violent again. Luckily none of the miners were hurt.

Somehow or another, they stumbled upon some sort of electrostatic rock that caused gnarly shocks when struck. It somehow carried an immense electrical charge in a rock of all things.

The miners recognized this as something of significance. They will first tell the scientific community about discovering the electrostatic rocks before telling any governments.

They did not report their find to anybody else who may exploit the rocks or make weapons of war.

Scientists quickly jumped on the discovery of the electrostatic rocks that were discovered in the tunnel.

They had a secret plan to save Humanity or create a diversion for all Humans to be safer than the immense pain that the black hole would wage upon Humanity.

The scientists worked in complete secrecy without the knowledge of any authoritative bodies, including, but not limited to, any governments.

The scientists could use high-tech lasers to harvest a large amount of the new element unofficially named "Scintillam," Latin for "spark."

The scientists carefully took five tons of Scintillam rocks to a Collider in Switzerland.

The Collider is where atoms are smashed together to find new physics and particles. It operates on a circular track far below the surface and is hidden from view.

Before the story continues, dearest readers, please know that what the scientists decided to do without anyone else's knowledge was to smash 10,000 pounds (4536 kgs) of the electrically charged Scintillam against a wall that was 22 feet (6.7 meters) thick. This will cause the most massive electric shock the Earth or perhaps the Universe has ever seen.

Once this happens, it will cause such a tremendous electrical shock that it will zap the planet with such great force that the electricity will shock everyone on the Earth long enough to cook them at least medium-well.

It is not known how many trillions of volts the impact will be. Leading scientists pondered whether or not the shock would go beyond Earth.

This was seen as a more humane way to go out instead of that pesky black hole stretching everything in every direction, causing unfathomable pain for everyone on Earth that may have lasted for months.

The scientists followed their plan, sending all of the Scintillam towards the wall, and upon impact, it will shock the entire planet inside out.

The Scintillam struck the wall, and the electricity took on a life of its own.

It wiped out the employees at the Collider. Instantly, the towering electric shock shot from the Collider to the sky in a brilliant column of manic light as bright as the Sun.

The electricity electrified the argon in the atmosphere, causing the entire atmosphere to be lit with electricity. It was like the sky was lit ablaze by a very large lighter.

Then it encircled the entire Earth in a matter of minutes. It covered the whole atmosphere/sky around the whole planet.

The entire sky was electricity, then all it took was one metal item on the ground to electrify all of the land or crust.

It happened to be a windmill in Holland that first got struck, and the electricity moved in all directions and covered the entire crust of the planet, ending the lives of everyone on Earth.

Within the next three or so minutes, Humanity was no more.

Again, this was a much more humane way to go out than stuck with the black hole, slowly devouring the planet, which could have taken months of the body being stretched, causing mind-numbing pain.

Well, enough about that, the deed is done, and the story is nearing its resolution.

The Earth could be seen for millions of miles out in space as it glowed a cool white until the famed black hole arrived and swallowed the Earth whole.

From the scientists' collective perspective, it must be seen: have immense and debilitating pain from the approaching black hole or quickly "exit" and have no more pain ever again?

The gluons in the form of our souls detached from each body, and they made their way across space and time to the Cosmic Core of the Universal Light, where the souls entered the light, and eventually, all 10 billion persons made it to Heaven.

Now, St. Peter has his work cut out for him.

THE END

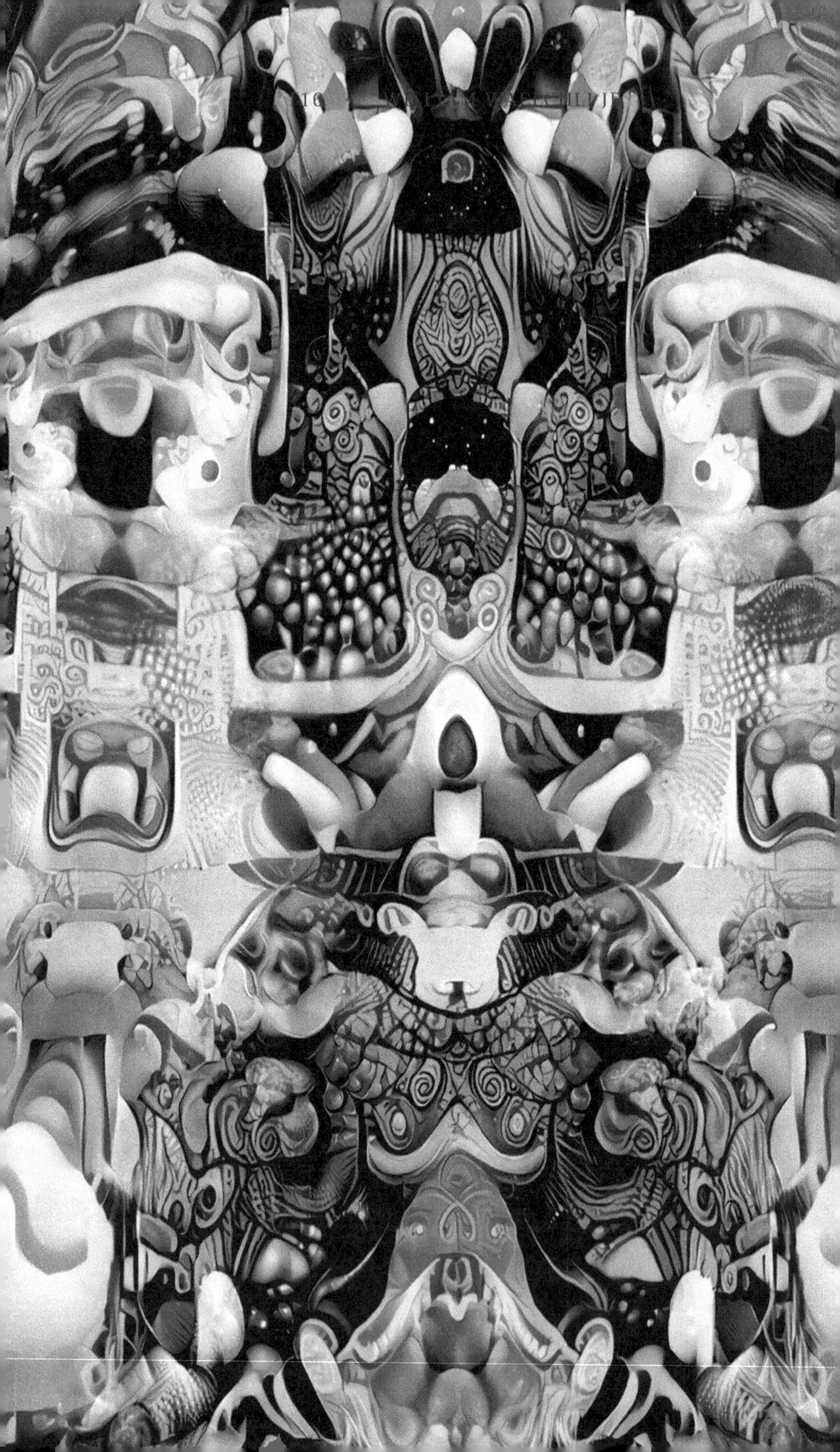

Chapter 13

"An Uncertainty Regarding Orbital Acceleration" -or- "Who Caused Infinite Flames of Unfathomable Destruction to Tear Across the Universe?"

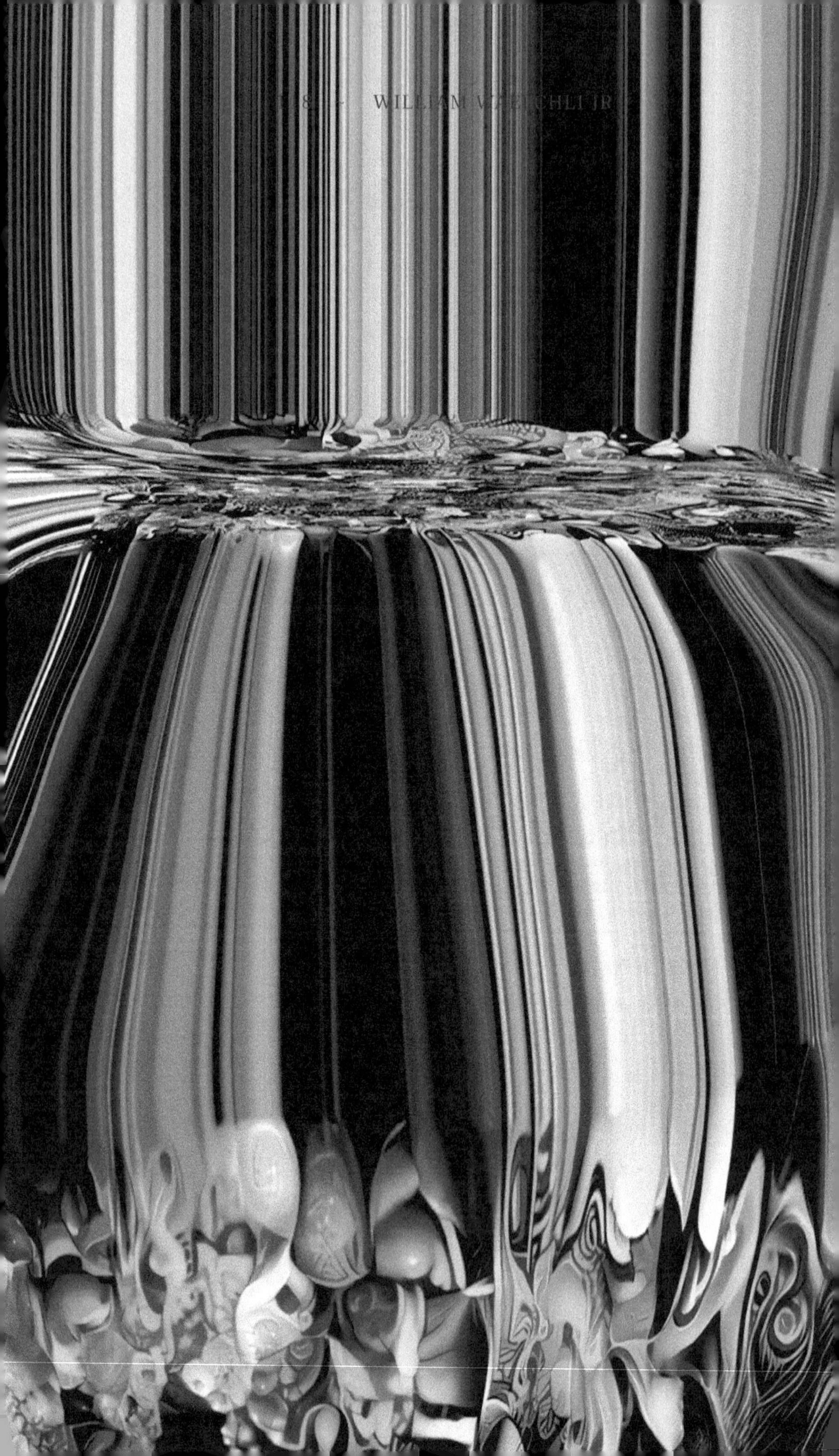

The Earth was fruitful in the distant future, and there was little poverty or struggle since the governments worldwide became streamlined into one unified entity. This accelerated research on every level.

There was no need for war any longer because there was no shortage of food and other resources, among other things. This rendered war obsolete. The Earth was more prosperous than anyone could remember; even the old-timers agreed that these were some of the best times.

Humanity enjoyed an increased lifestyle that made everything seem near Utopian. Although let's face it, this is not Utopia.

There was less reliance on technology, even though it was more advanced than it had ever been. It was accelerating towards better ways of helping us out and easing the burdens of being Human.

Now, we had money, we had resources, and we had each other. What could have caused a rift in this world full of love and happiness with a dash of humor?

Scientists crashed the party because it was noted that the orbit of the Earth and all Heavenly bodies in the local galactic neighborhood (including the Solar System) had quickly accelerated orbits. Scientists were stumped as to why the orbital paths of all these planets and stars were accelerating so fast.

Typically, the Earth rotates around our Mother Sun at a speed of 67,000 mph (107,826 kph). With the acceleration, Earth was now moving at 112,000 mph (180,247 kph). rendering the calendar year only 193 days.

Humanity was growing older faster, and no one cared for it. But what could be done to stop the accelerating speed of the orbits of the celestial objects?

After some time and reasoning, the scientists could only attribute this phenomenon to a possible "hole" in the Universe.

Most humans, in their vane manners, were upset because they were aging more quickly. They were blind to the big picture: the Universe may collapse upon its own weight if a "hole in the Universe" existed, as scientists had hypothesized.

The interstellar wind was recalculated, and there was most likely nothing Humanity could do to stop the galaxies' movements across the Universe. It was noted that the interstellar wind had switched directions entirely and pulled the entire galaxy and all other galaxies closer to the incinerator like Cosmic Core.

This spelled most likely impending doom for all universal inhabitants, although the scientists could be wrong, as they are sometimes.

Black holes in the centers of galaxies have exploded in unison (it is believed) by going supernova in an amazing display of universal super-destruction. The galaxies are unhinged since their central black holes have gone supernova enabling the galaxies to roam across the Universe.

A comprehensive theory was written that stated the Cosmic Core at the center of our Universe achieved an overall temperature that became so incredibly hot that it was starting to melt through the Universal floor and may eventually fall out of the Universe completely.

The telescopic array had just celebrated its 10th year in operation. This was a group of 10,000 telescopes strategically placed throughout the galaxy. It enabled scientists to have "Cosmic Eyes," allowing them to see across the universe to the Cosmic Core.

We did not know if we were lucky or not since we finally had a view of what was causing the acceleration of all the orbital paths. With time not really on our sides, scientists observed exactly what was happening.

Hardest to admit, the Cosmic Core theory burning a hole through the universal floor may be accurate according to data being sent back from our cosmic eyes.

Measurements of the Cosmic Core showed that it was "dipping" further through the universal floor and may fall out of existence and become a free-floating object outside of the Universe.

Scientists did not even want to think about what would follow after the Cosmic Core drops through the universal floor. Now they will have no choice as scientists observed the Cosmic Core as it melted through the universal floor and fell out of existence, just as the scientists hypothesized. It was most likely in freefall now, but who knew for sure.

The fate of the Universe hung in the balance. Although it would be hard to believe a single conscious being in the Universe would want to know what happened after the Cosmic

Core fell out of the Universe and was no longer a fixture. Unfortunately for Humanity, they would eventually find out...

The universal objects moved more quickly once the Cosmic Core fell out of existence in a rapidly accelerating orbit at speeds never thought previously possible.

Originating from the hole in the Universe, everything lit on fire, and a flame 80 billion light-years in length shot out of the hole made by the Cosmic Core, lighting other universal bubbles on fire, eventually igniting them, including our very own Universe.

Quite quickly, a chain reaction happened where all of the Universal bubbles ignited. One by one, each Universe popped in response to the beyond intense heat of the outer universe fire.

Unfortunately for anything that was ever known was now gone since the Cosmic Core lit our universal bubble on fire, and it raged until our Universe popped like a balloon, as did countless other universes.

It wiped out everything that could ever have existed, reducing the cluster of universal bubbles to a thick, stinky soup of ash and burnt shit and a lot of cosmic dust.

THE END

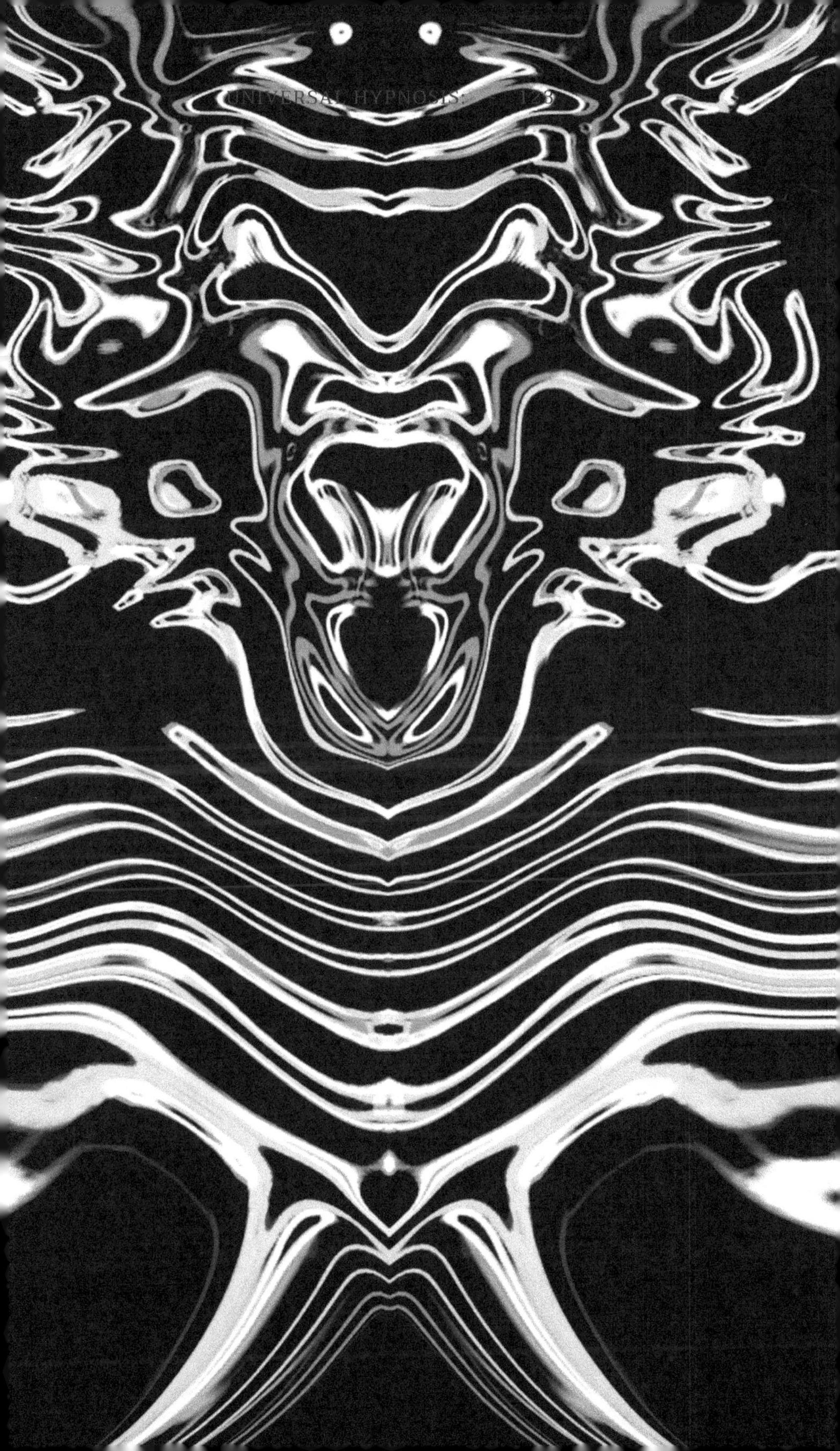
UNIVERSAL HYPNOSIS   123

Chapter 14

"Homage to Mr. King: The Sworn Swarm" -or- "Cosmic Carnivores"

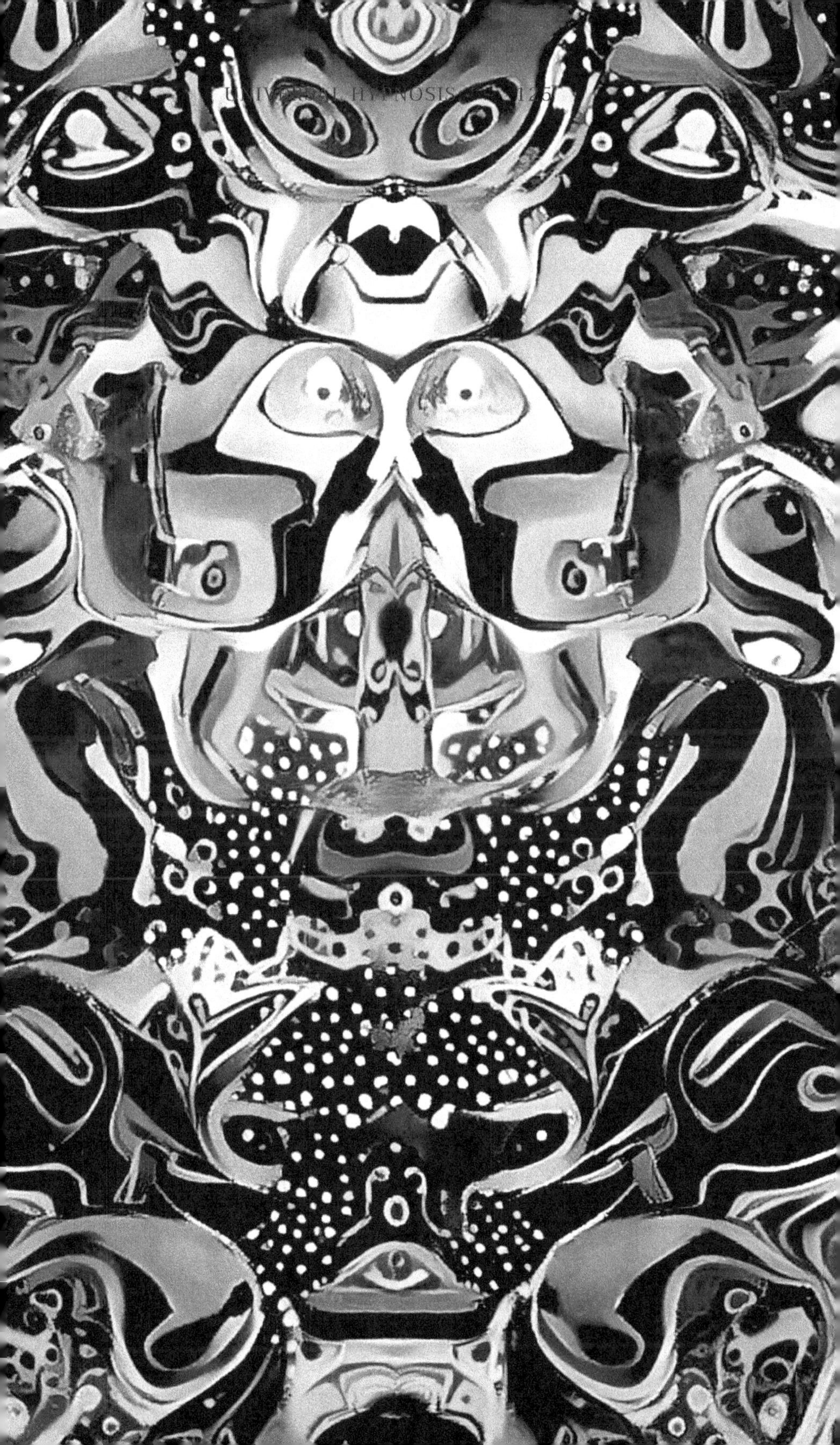
UNIVERSAL HYPNOSIS 125

In the near future, things are looking hopeful.

It's a special time to be alive, as Humanity enjoyed much comfort now that the world's governments have merged into one cohesive unit enabling free information sharing globally.

War was abolished through a peace treaty between every country. The Treaty of Global Peace was the treaty that eliminated war and thus far has kept global peace in order.

The new all-encompassing space agency was named The World Space Project (WSP). Again, the WSP was the result of all 72-space programs being combined for cohesiveness. It had enabled us to be light years ahead of where we were just twenty years ago.

Humanity had colonized Mars, built an array of 10,000 telescopes, and navigated through Neptune's 1000 mph winds. These were just a few of Humanity's crowning achievements.

One of our most significant discoveries was the elusive graviton. This is the atomic particle of gravity.

This enabled Scientists to manipulate gravity by suspending stationary objects in space where they remained still without an orbit.

Scientists positioned many powerful telescopes in an array throughout the entire galaxy. Known as the 10KArray, it was a marvel that rivaled the previous century's other technical achievements.

We now had a holistic view of our Milky Way and learned new things about our home galaxy every day.

The telescopes were pointed at the galaxy's very mother, the supermassive black hole at our galactic center, Sagittarius A*.

The 10,000 telescopes were suspended in a controlled gravitational state spanning millions of miles around our galaxy.

The WSP noted that on Tuesday morning, 14 February, only 9,000 telescopes registered as being active. By month's end, every telescope went offline.

Scientists were stumped as to what exactly happened to the 10KArray.

Our abilities to see further into our galaxy were thwarted. We were now sitting ducks for the moment, not seeing anything beyond our much weaker ground-based telescopes on Earth.

It was surmised that meteor showers destroyed the 10KArray and knocked them all out of their positions. This is the best scenario scientists could think of.

Humanity found it hard to believe that meteor showers took out all 10,000 telescopes. This would be an impossibility that no one in their right mind would believe.

We needed answers as to how this happened, and we were unsure of where to even look.

The WSP received a frantic call from the Chancellor of Mars. "Deimos has vanished!" "We now have only one moon." Mars scientists had no explanation either. They just knew that this was most likely related to the telescope fiasco. Whatever caused the 10KArray to go offline must have snatched the

Moon, Deimos, from the Martian sky.

The next night the full Moon vanished without a trace. Now there was uproar from the people who stated that the WSP is not doing enough to protect Humanity, and now extinction, as we knew it, may be inevitable.

The oceans became still for the first time ever, causing entire ecosystems to flirt with disaster.

This was a very severe issue, and we did not know what direction to take, especially now that the Moon had disappeared.

An elderly man named Irving Coles arrived at the WSP's English headquarters. He claimed the footage he had shot was real and must be seen at once. Irving was the only one who had seen the footage and claimed it was genuine.

The footage viewing occurred in a private room at an undisclosed location, not over that damn Internet, so it will not be leaked to the public.

The footage started out like any regular video of the Moon until it started to be "eaten" away by a swarm of dark circles.

At first, scientists had absolutely no explanation of how that happened to our Moon, but dark circles eating the Moon? Looks like Somebody had seen Stephen King's cult classic "The Langoliers."

It was later determined that the Moon was consumed by a swarm of micro-black holes (AKA Primordial Black Holes). Humanity did not know how long it would take, if ever, for the swarm to return.

The WSP held a conference that was of paramount importance. Five hundred select space insiders were there and had no idea what to expect from the meeting. All they knew was that it was of the utmost importance and a matter of international security.

Kelly Maitis, head of the American chapter of the WSP, preceded to inform the meeting attendees what had been happening. Dark circles (approximately 3 feet across (0.91 meters) had "eaten" the Moon.

News spread rapidly, and before anyone knew it, all of Humanity knew of the current state of affairs that there were micro black holes somewhere out in the cosmos.

Humanity became drunk on terror about inevitably being consumed by the micro black holes as a worst-case scenario.

Scientists were at their wits' end. They were confused about the swarm as they only observed the more massive black holes at least three times the Sun's size, not the size of something like a hula hoop.

Nothing had ever been seen like this, ever. In fact, Humanity never knew micro black holes even existed, let alone that they could move.

Humanity had many more questions than answers, but the population were determined to make the best of this exceedingly dreadful situation.

Some months later, it happened, the swarm returned. It was thousands and thousands of miles wide and thousands of miles deep...

The micro black holes were very savvy, as a horrified Humanity found out very quickly.

We observed as the black holes swallowed up every satellite and piece of space junk in orbit around Earth.

The satellites were swallowed up, causing a chain reaction that caused electrical grids worldwide to explode, and these caused lightning bolts that shot across whole countries.

Humanity was now enveloped in complete darkness as if it was a new moon. Although. Humanity might want to get used to the darkness.

Global Panic ensued, including extensive looting and rioting due to the fear that Humanity may not live to see tomorrow.

So the question must be asked: Why steal that 80-inch television if it may never be watched.

The black holes started to quickly form a lattice-like web over the sky above the English chapter of the WSP. The horrified citizens watched in utter terror as the entire visible sky closed up, enveloping the surrounding areas in pitch-black darkness.

Irving Coles, the elderly man who blew the case wide open with the moon consumption footage, stepped out of his house and noticed the sky closing up. Shivers went down his whole body, not just his spine.

His anxiety shot up so high that he could barely walk, which caused him to shake uncontrollably. He feared the worst now that the monsters had invaded Earth.

He was a curious fellow, so he walked a bit down the road and heard a few cosmic carnivores in the sky, which were now flying towards him.

They circled around him very quickly and started to fly around him very fast.

The circle closed in smaller and smaller until they started taking chunks out of Irving's body.

The screams emitted by Irving were nerve-shattering as the cosmic carnivores closed in further and further, taking chunk after chunk out of his body until all that was left was his spinal column and his head.

They rarely leave even a smidgen left of their meal, but the micro black holes wanted to make an example of him.

It was as if they were saying, "Look what we did to him, imagine what we will do to you."

Perhaps the monsters wanted to make a statement targeting the person who exposed them. It seemed like they had a particular way of thinking, no matter how simple it was.

The four vicious black holes flew back up to the sky and affixed themselves to the lattice, where millions of other black holes connected to them.

Within the hour, the monsters covered the entire sky, where they remained still in the sky for hours, possibly waiting for their best time to strike. No one could be too sure when or if they would strike.

Cloaked in darkness and without the Moon present, Humanity experienced the blackest night ever seen, where no one could see an arm's length in front of them.

Due to the alleged infinite darkness, there was a "flashlight" melee similar to the 2020 "toilet paper debacle." This time the flashlights at least gave some way to see in the unwelcoming darkness.

Concentrating on the sky, all that could be heard was a grinding sound reminiscent of many chainsaws running simultaneously.

One of the racing thoughts that Humanity had in the complete darkness was, "Will I ever see the Sun again?" or "Perhaps they will go away."

Humanity became virtually blind and could not see anything, as the cosmic carnivores above were waiting to strike.

They may soon get their first taste of Nature if they decide to strike. Humanity could only imagine they were salivating at the thought of it.

Suddenly, the grinding sound became louder without any warning because the black holes were now in a slow descent towards the ground.

It was never known if Humanity had any way of telling how close the black holes were going to strike in the vast darkness.

The black holes made their way closer and closer to the

ground. Many of them started laughing in a high-pitched, maniacally insane tone during the descent.

Their conscious state told them to prolong the descent, slowly lowering as it invoked dread, agony, and other horrific emotions from Humanity's deteriorating minds.

By lowering very slow, it evoked compounding and debilitating fear in every Human alive.

They started to emit very highly-pitched, eardrum-shattering screams that gradually became louder as the black holes descended without warning.

It was especially terrorizing that the laughing and screaming occurred at the same time.

As the screams and laughter became more deafening, they lowered and lowered, consuming their first taste of Nature.

Not soon after, the cosmic carnivores devoured the entire planet from the outside in.

Let us recall the cartoons that dominated some our early childhoods' for a final second as it looked like 'Chicken Little' was right when he said, "The sky IS falling."

THE END

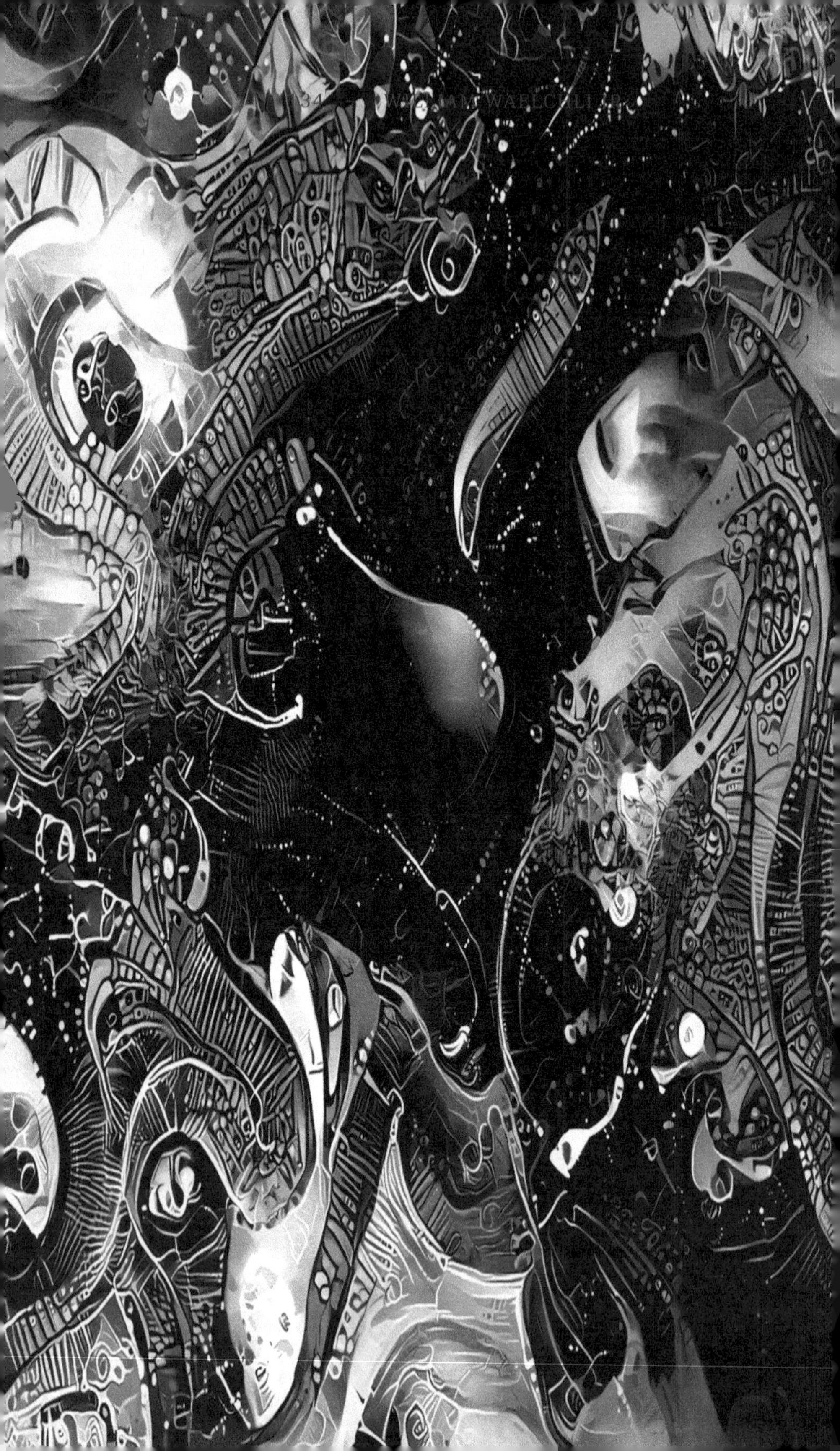

"Please Don't Transpose Even a Single Letter as this Could Endanger the Planet Causing a Possible Planetary Genocide" -or- "I Love the Smell of Extinction Early in the Morning"

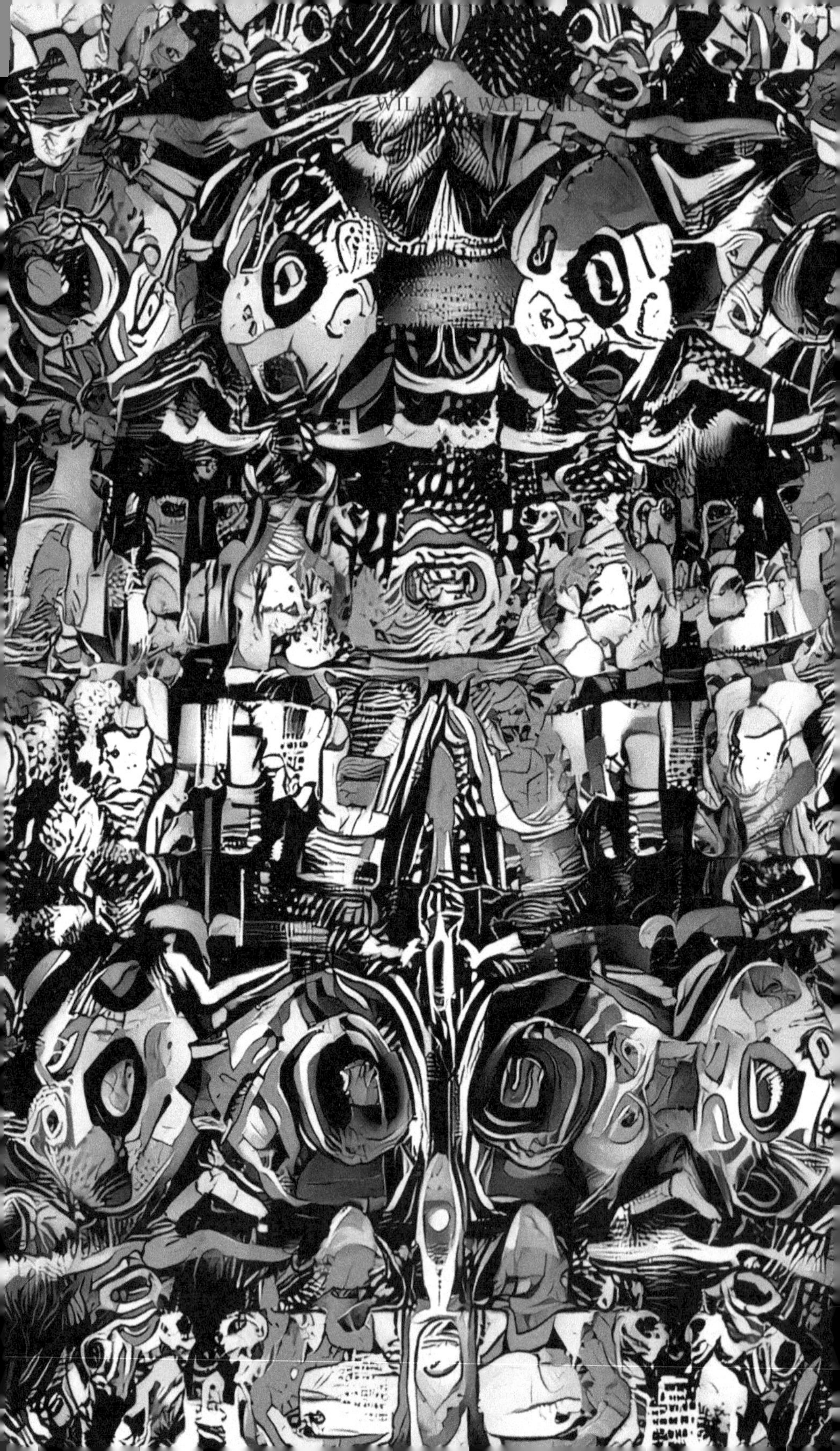
WILLIAM WAELCHLI

Welcome to Earth. It was the year 2777, where ultra advanced technologies abound. For centuries, it was hoped that we would be able to convert stars to planets.

This was always a desirable thought because eventually, the sun would grow so much larger, that it would engulf Earth and swallow anything that ever existed. Perhaps it was not our sun Humanity had to worry about.

But alas, we are not converting stars or having any star systems transformed into planets. No matter, there were still super-advanced technologies that existed that have been life-changing.

A forcefield surrounded the entire planet now and protected the Earth from all matters of space objects, falling space junk, and any matter of debris or dangers that came from space. It also protected us from any temperature existing outside the forcefield.

Known as the great Laserfield, it was a scientific and engineering modern marvel and was a wonder due to its unique nature protecting everyone on Earth. This was the number one reason for creating the Laserfield.

It gets its name because it was constructed of billions of criss-crossing lasers that create a "woven" shell that keeps all the bad stuff out. It was also nearly air-tight, which may come in handy later...

Since the Laserfield was made up of overlapping lasers, it eradicated anything that came in contact with it. Not too long ago, a broken satellite fell out of the space junk halo above Earth and was in a brutal descent. That was until it came in contact with the Laserfield, where the old 6500-pound satellite was reduced to particles smaller than dust.

This possibly saved the lives of many persons as the satellite would have landed in Chicago, on a grammar school. The Laserfield was worth every penny of the $1.8 trillion needed for research, development, and implementation.

Today, scientists were checking the levels of the element used to power the Laserfield and noted that it was at a critically low level. They wondered what they would do to obtain more of the element, as Earth had no more available elements to run the Laserfield. The scientists realized a way to replenish the element, although it may prove risky in time.

Known as Ænematon (A-NEEM-A-TON), this critically needed element was radioactive and was used to keep the Laserfield active. Its use was to keep the lasers connected, or else the lasers would go haywire and fall to the ground, where it would, well, cut the Earth up like your favorite pizza.

A grand technology had been perfected recently. This very technology will help us possibly keep the Laserfield running. This was known by its proper name, the "Elemental Extraction Beam."

Known in some circles as simply the "EEB," it was the answer to "How are we going to replenish the Laserfields' Ænematon reservoirs?" Or was this special element called Eanematon? Maybe that was not important... Why would a single transposed letter spell possible doom for the planet?

This EEB could zap entire planets and extract any elements out of the poor planets being harvested for whatever elements were needed. The Elemental Extraction Beam then stores whatever elements are not needed right away in an atomically reversed state, where they were used as needed.

The elements that were extracted from various planets were stored on Earth using "Atomic Time Reversal." This was the process of changing the atomic states of anything brought to Earth from the Elemental Extraction Beam.

Then placing it in reverse due to the exorbitant amounts of elements and other items that would never be stored had it not been for atomic time reversal. We would simply not have any means of storing the element otherwise. Once the elements atomically reversed back as far as possible, they became crystalline in nature and their atomic makeup was stored.

When elements are needed, they are atomically reverse assembled. The elements can then be used in any application, no matter the elements' state of matter.

The big day came for Humanity to fire off the Elemental Extraction Beam in hopes of obtaining enough Ænematon to power the Laserfield for many years to come. As it happened, scientists were able to find a planet quite close (one light year away), and the planet was chock full of the much-needed element that was somewhat understood as Ænematon,

It was time to unleash the beam on the unsuspecting planet. We were unable to verify whether it was a populated extra-terrestrial world or not. Funny that question was raised, as the beam was returning all of the Ænematon, or so we thought, something strange happened in the lab where the extracted elements are to be used in the Laserfield.

Hundreds of extraterrestrials formed in the teleportation warehouses. This was where the elemental storage chamber was. Everyone was confused just as much as the extraterrestrials. Crowd control was needed as the "foreigners" were pissed that they were teleported to Earth. Someone was going to lose their job when all of this was sorted out.

The extraterrestrials were made aware of the 'Elemental Extraction Beam' capabilities. One privy extraterrestrial stepped forward while wearing a purple crown and spoke to the scientists present. He told us about their race name, which was" The Messorlux' (MESS-OR-LOU). This name meant "Harvester of Light" in Latin and explains why they had a purple glow to them. It was also thought that their spots glowed in the dark.

The Messorluxs' were, on average, about six and ½ feet tall, had pearl white scales on their bodies and were covered in small yellow spots, the size of quarters. They also had one large eyeball (about as large around as a soda can) in the middle of their foreheads. This was right above their mouths filled with sharp teeth, which were about quite long and appeared to be very ominous.

A scientist asked the leader of the group, named "Aldatrex," where all of the Ænematon was since that was what was to be brought back from the infamous beam. He looked at the word and laughed. Then he asked the scientists to spell out the name of the element they desired to obtain from the extraterrestrial homeworld. The scientist spelled out the element: a-e-n-e-m-a-t-o-n.

This was the element that was prominent in the royal blood of the Messorlux. This was because when the first group of them landed on their planet initially, the planet was rich in

Ænematon. Over time, the element entered their bloodstreams and was transferred to each new baby, showing hey are of the purest bloodlines on their planet.

What does this all mean? Don't ask any of the scientists who operated the beam earlier today, or else they would tell you that they DID NOT transpose the first letters of the element to be brought back from the Messorluxs' home planet. Well, yes, they typed in Eanematon, not Ænematon. It was an honest mistake.

The crowd of Messorluxs' was growing restless while being essentially trapped in the elemental warehouse where all of the elements are saved for consumption. Something had to be done, so it was stated that the displaced crowd would simply be teleported back.

Before teleporting out, they told Earth to send them the correct element that runs the Laserfield. The element Eanematon (E-NEEM-A-TON) that, unbeknownst to Humanity, was in great abundance on the Messorluxs' home planet of Resourdre (RE-SOR-DRAY).

The Messorluxs' were placed into a warehouse, where they were all set to be teleported back to their home planet. Scientists were nervous, thinking that they may not be able to teleport them back home, but the surprise of the times was that they did, in fact, teleport back home via advanced teleportation technologies.

The Messorluxs will beam a whole lot of the Eanematon back to Earth. Perhaps the operator of their Elemental Extraction Beam equivalent should have taken one minute out of their day and saw how the special element interacts with other elements, especially those that conduct electricity, like silver, as an example.

Upon the Messorlux returning to their home planet, the Search for Extraterrestrial Intelligence (SETI) back on Earth received a correspondence from the Messorluxs' stating that they are going to fire off a beam that will gain Earth 7775 pounds of the much needed Eanematon, which will enable the Laserfield to operate for the next 212 years.

The beam of the much-needed Eanematon traveled across space and time, where it reached Earth's sky...and lit it ablaze like a raging wildfire, and without any warning whatsoever. Only this time, we were not dealing with a wildfire. Humanity was now dealing with something that could cause almost immediate extinction if the fire ever hit the ground.

As of now, everything was dark, and smoke was billowing down from the sky. The sky smoke was so acrid that Humans on the ground were choking on it and losing their lives because there was no escape from the smoke's violent grip on Humanity.

It was not even worth mentioning what kind of horrors were bestowed upon anybody on an airplane with the igniting of the sky. We were very concerned for those airplanes and hoped for a safe landing if they had not all burned up already.

Minutes after the sky was lit up like a cigarette, the argon in the atmosphere interacted with the Eanematon, causing the electrically charged particles, instantly converted the electrical particles in the argon to a hellish sky of fire and brimstone, so to speak. With the electricity being converted to fire, this spelled an almost obvious end to Humanity. Will anybody help Humanity?

An urgent correspondence was received by the Search for Extraterrestrial Intelligence received minutes after the sky was set ablaze. It was the Messorluxs'. They apologized for the flaming sky and said they would provide a way for Humanity to escape this blazing hell that Earth had experienced.

The message stated that the Messorluxs' had a barren planet that may "fit Humanity's needs," as it was exactly like Earth in every way. Surprisingly enough, they were ready to cause a holistic teleportation beam that would be wider than the entirety of planet Earth, where it would teleport all of Humanity to a new planet.

The sky raged in pure hellish abominable horror as the purple beam came towards the ravaged Earth, and then it teleported everyone alive instantly to the New Earth, which now was neighbors with the ever so infamous Resourdre. The New Earth was happy to harbor Humanity as a neighboring planet, they saved Humanity from burning up like a campfire.

As the blazing sky burned back on Earth, a planet-wide Firestorm lit up the night. This included flame lightning raging across the sky, and "firenadoes" or "infernadoes," which were tornadoes composed from fire that were so large, they originated in the sky and reached down to the ground.

That was a 62-mile (18.9 km) high tornado composed of hellish fire that ripped across the planet. Thousands formed and kept on destroying more and more of old Earth as time raged on. Humanity breathed a sigh of relief that they escaped the hellish inferno.

It turns out that the extraterrestrials had quickly constructed the New Earth from cosmic atomic energy harvested from dark matter. This was how the Messorluxs' had around an infinite amount of building material to build anything, including entire planets, like the New Earth.

Humanity's New Earth was a grand planet that actually looked like Saturn, including that navy blue tint we all know so well, and of course, a ring system. The new planets beauty intoxicated Humanity, but let's face it, Humanity wanted to enjoy their New Earth now that they could finally sit back and relax. Despite how it looked, Earth was the same size and included everything that the old Earth had, which included all of its technologies.

Back on "Old Earth," the fire caused the lands on Earth to caused global brush fires that eventually melted everything down to the dirt. Of course, this happened after Humanity had teleported out to the New Earth. How sad it was to lose our majestic home over a stupid error concerning that damned Laserfield. It was quite fishy that specific elements could cause electricity to turn to fire.

This was pondered, and then it was voted to have the Laserfield back into action. Since New Earth was outfitted with a Laserfield that, the scientists went to flip the switch, but nothing happened. It was at that moment that Humanity decided to finally obtain enough Eanematon to last centuries.

The Elemental Extraction Beam was pointed towards Resourdre and fired off. Within hours, the extraction of Eanematon was complete, and the Laserfield finally went back online. Just for laughs, scientists wanted to see what was happening on the neighboring planet. They wanted to see if anybody was upset that they extracted A LOT of the Eanematon.

The scientists pointed their telescopes at their helpful neighboring planet. Disturbingly, nobody was living on the planet. Several billion bodies in the streets and elsewhere were spotted through New Earth's telescopes. Also, millions of deaths were witnessed as the population diminished. But why in their world would all of the Messorluxs' have died?

Humanity found it very hard to believe what happened and was not so concerned with the deceased planetary travesty as they were about what kind of repercussions will affect Humanity down the road. They feared the karma wheel and did not want to piss off karma.

The non-breathable air on Resourdre became 1000 times thinner than the air at Mount Everest's summit. All of the extraterrestrials perished due to asphyxiation or loss of air. New Earth did not know that the harvesting of Eanematon would wipe out the entire population, but hey, Humanity needed to have their Laserfield in tiptop shape. And so New Earth contemplated whether they were in the clear or not...

By this point, it was assumed that New Earth was now in a fixed orbital path, yet the universal scientists did not know about our location in the cosmos, and we had no way of determining year length or anything relating to the movement of New Earth. But then something peculiar happened; New Earth sped up like an Indy car as it spun towards its ultimate destination.

The universal scientists were now able to determine our trajectory as it related to the extraterrestrial sun. Now there was no question whether those no good Messorluxs' had it out for Humanity or not. It was believed they planned an eventual extinction scenario that will erase Humanity off the cosmic map.

Maybe they changed the orbital path of New Earth after the planet-wide asphyxiation caused their early deaths. But then why would they have gone through the trouble of making a New Earth for Humanity, only to shoot it towards the star that gives Life?

With the forcefield intact, the planet was traveling in a swift path towards the extraterrestrial sun. Being out of orbit and orbiting the extraterrestrial sun, it was discovered that New Earth was in an orbit that was closing around the unknown extraterrestrial sun.

The New Earth eventually was about to collide into the foreign sun; the forcefield disabled the sun from penetrating the planet with its molten outer shell.

No form of temperature could penetrate the Laserfield, so New Earth could stay intact, at least for the moment. It was on everyone's mind: "How on New Earth or Resourdre did the Messorluxs' extract revenge after their untimely deaths?" They had no motive that Humanity could discern other than the teleportation of the Messorluxs' people earlier when they were on Old Earth...

Maybe it was planned? Humanity would never know, nor did they care since they were facing their own possible inevitable liquefying downfall that would burn everything up like the yule log in a fireplace.

The New Earth started to orbit so tight to the North Pole where it eventually and regretfully made a rough landing on the extraterrestrial sun. As mentioned earlier, it was a lifesaver that the new Earth included the Laserfield. It was keeping everyone alive.

Oddly enough, the New Earth started to "float" on the sun's surface. Due to the floating of the New Earth, it was flipped upside down and downside up again and again. Inside the safety of the Laserfield, most of Humanity ended up being ejected off the surface at blistering speeds as they smashed into the top and/or bottom of the Laserfield.

Most of Humanity flew through the sky and crashed into the Laserfield above the clouds. All the shit on the surface, along with most of Humanity, flew violently through the sky and smashed with immense power against the Laserfield.

As the New Earth floated around on the sun, the ocean would pour down from bottom to top, in an Ocean Tsunami, causing waves that were half as high as the planet

Imagine all of the cars & trucks hitting the forcefield. Most of the remaining Humans on the planet were eventually whisked off the ground where they "flew" to the very top or bottom of the planet, along with EVERYTHING not bolted down.

Eventually, the surface of the Laserfield became so hot, almost the temperature of the surface, that the New Earth slowly sunk under into the interior of the sun, and the abyss of molten darkness descended upon a near-dead New Earth.

A few of the scientists were miraculously alive, having been in an old fortified laboratory that provided refuge from the cataclysmic nature of where Humanity had ended up.

They made the decision to end the raging hell by switching off the Laserfield. With that, the sun's molten materials quickly absorbed the New Earth, guaranteeing that no trace of it would ever exist again.

Again, it was never proven that the Messorluxs' rigged the orbit of the New Earth to penetrate the sun since all of the extraterrestrials asphyxiated, having given them no time to had planned a revenge campaign.

Although Humanity was, in a way, recycled into usable energy that may be used to bring light and nourishment to neighboring planets, it was probably the only good thing about where Humanity ended up liquefied on the surface of the sun.

Was that damned forcefield really worth sacrificing all of Humanity in order to keep it running? It may have been a good thing if you are a fan of impending death...

THE END

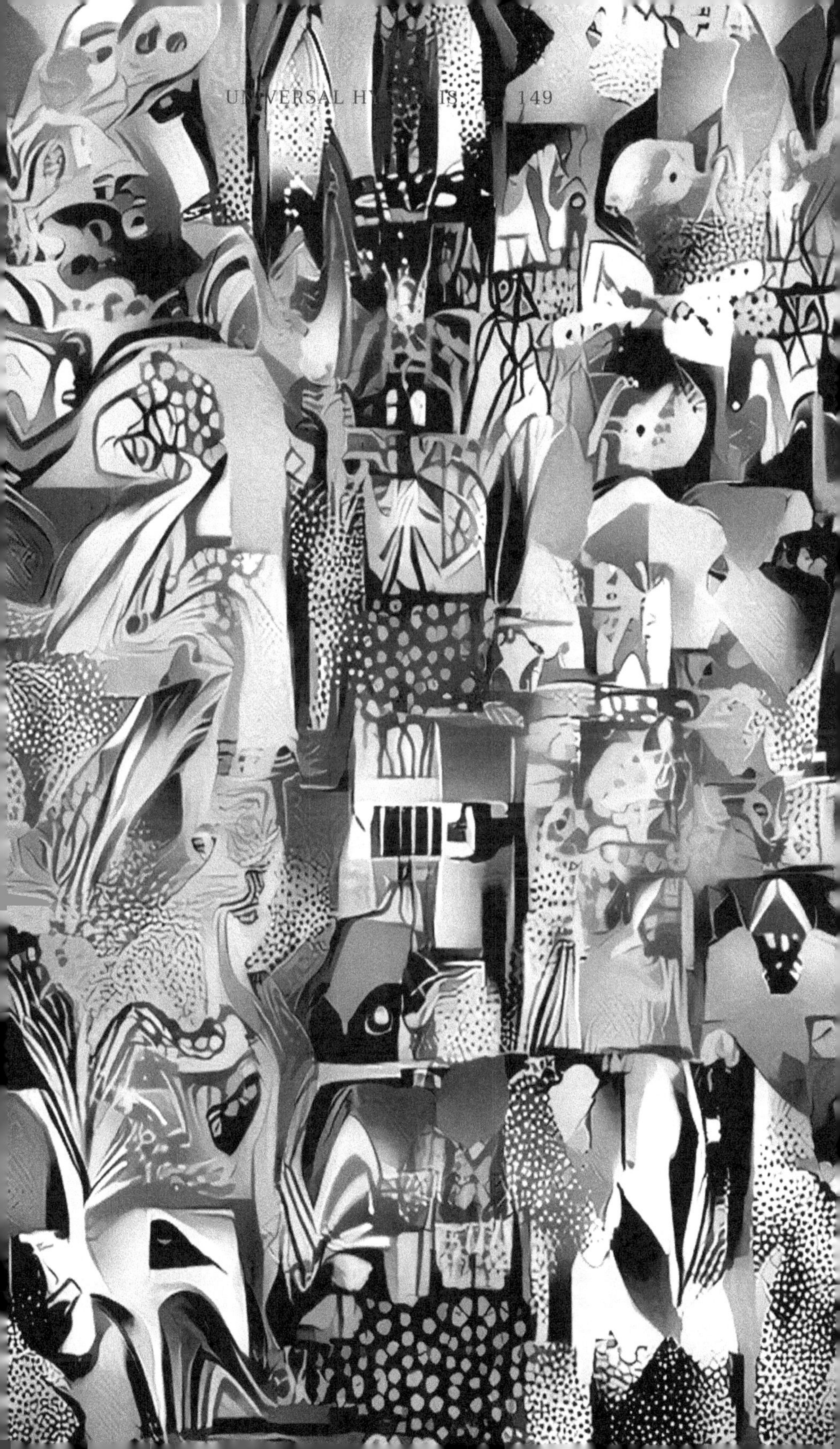

Chapter 16

"Be Careful What You Think As Someone May Be Listening..."– or - "The Remote Control Aerial Laser May Just Delete the Space Junk Halo"

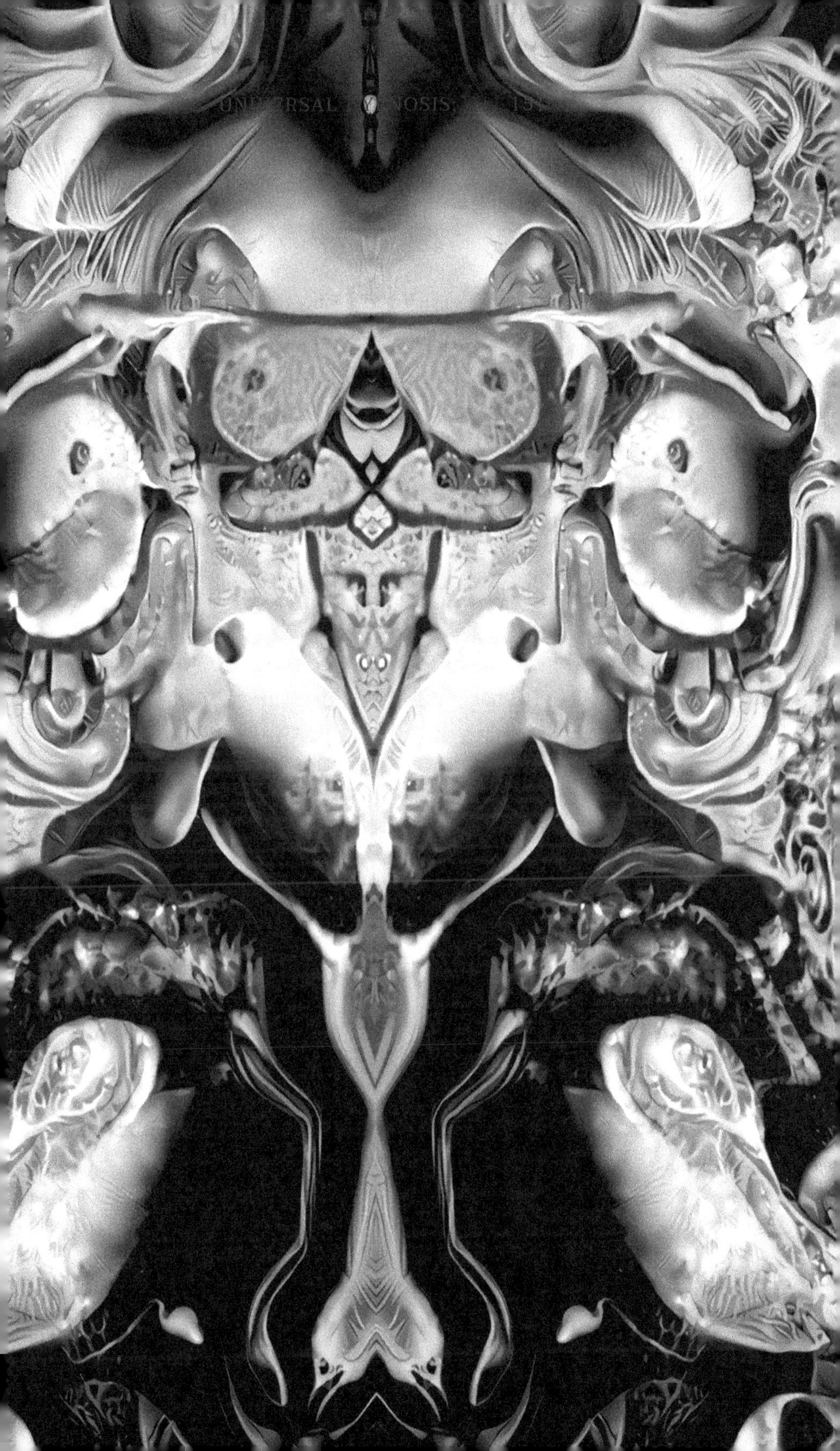

In the year 2060, everything on Earth was pretty much routine, except for emerging technologies that would change the Earth as we know it.

Some of the cities dotting the planet had fallen into disarray. It will be realized in due time that scientists were working overtime to make a specific technology that will "erase" all the dilapidated areas of all cities on Earth, eventually.

The scientists mentioned earlier managed to build what was known as the" Remote Control Aerial Laser" or R-Cal for short as it came to be known. It was given its first job, and that had nothing to do with cleaning up our cities yet.

Floating around the Earth existed a "Space Junk Ring," or SJR for short. The space junk was orbiting around Earth like the rings of Saturn. The only thing is, the Earth will not have its space junk ring much longer as the scientists devised a way to erase the Ring with ease.

The Space Junk Ring was a nuisance and must be cleanly destroyed. This was where the R-Cal came into play as the scientists had to devise a plan to destroy the menacing Ring. The space junk randomly impacted Earth and took out unsuspecting people on the ground, where they were picked off like a fly entering a bug zapper.

With debris from the SJR striking the International Space Station seven times in the past two months, something had to be done, and this was where the Remote Controlled Aerial Laser (R-Cal) came into use.

It may make that interfering space junk ring into clean dust, saving lives and preserving all technology in the sky, including all satellites.

After many small-scale experiments performed globally, proving that the R-Cal would be able to go full scale and "erase the ring," the R-Cal was just about ready to hit the sky.

The special R-Cal laser was launched into the sky destination, the Space Junk Ring, where it will "erase" the space junk problem saving the International Space Station from crumbling and will save lives as no one will be picked off like the victim of a snipers' bullet.

It must now be explained how this laser works. It has a very high-intensity laser that can stretch to any shape possible. It can stretch so far that it could literally turn a planet to clean dust within seconds.

Although this was not why the laser was invented, and no one but the scientists knew of the laser's immense power, and only its inventors knew that the R-Cal could swallow planets with ease.

Before the list of R-Cal's uses was revealed, how the SJR became clean dust will be explained. The laser that had flown like a drone could be remotely controlled from anywhere on Earth and could fly anywhere, including out in space, which was the R-Cal's first destination. About as big as a vintage Volkswagen Bug, the laser drone was set to erase the SJR.

The laser emitted a round vertical shape and "sliced into the ring with ease." The SJR that was larger than the size of the Ring and the R-Cal moved around the Ring and "erased" the Space Junk Ring to clean dust, which left no trace and had disintegrated the entire SJR. Guaranteeing that nothing else would hit the International Space Station...

...or people, for that matter. With the SJR erased per se, many positive changes came from the erasing of the SJR. Everything else that we have out there, including important satellites, could have brought Earth to a standstill if struck by the space junk.

With the SJR gone, the laser touched back down on Earth with our technology out in space safe. This was where, in time, the laser technology became widespread, as outlined in the paragraphs below, after the super laser technology was made available to the civilian market.

Only the "mini" civilian lasers were not as powerful as the real beast that erased the SJR that could erase planets. The scientists made sure that the civilian market was sized down not to have the ability to "eat" planets.

In time, every home had a three feet wide hole in the floor of each home across the world. It was cool to the touch and was not dangerous. This enabled people to get rid of all of the junk in their homes.

People sent all of their stuff to the laser facility for larger items, where the R-Cal turned all of their extra junk and other items to clean dust. So much was vaporized that the weight of the Earth became lighter. It became so much lighter that the rotation of the Earth changed, and the days became one hour shorter.

At the R-Cal's creation, it was not known that it would alter the time the way it did. I guess it was permanent daylight savings time for the Earth and not just America.

With the sale of the Mini R-Cal's to the civilian market going strong, countless run-down city blocks were erased with the impressive laser, making room for state-of-the-art sky-scrapers and other impressive structures. Cityscapes changed across Earth too.

Everyone was so busy building up the Earth that no one no-ticed the fleet of spaceships coming towards our Earth, which was invisible to all of our high-tech radar. The spaceships were making their way toward Earth.

They were not going to Earth just to go; no, they had a proposition for Earth that may impact billions of people. It seemed that our Intergalactic Neighbors got wind of the re-mote-controlled aerial laser and have now come to our planet to steal this technology possibly.

As a fleet of purple ships with yellow windows landed in Washington DC on the National Mall, the extraterrestrials exited their spacecraft, and Humanity got their first taste of what extraterrestrials were and looked like. Trust in this: There was more fear than happiness when the sinister extraterrestri-als touched down on Earth.

The only problem was that Humanity did not know if these extraterrestrials meant to cause harm or good to Humanity. It was not until the extraterrestrials spoke to the President that we knew their motives for sure.

"We are the Zilodon's from XyRaX, a planet that exists less than in the local galactic neighborhood. We have come here to ask you an important question." But before the all-important question could be asked, the Zilodon's were placed on National Television where everybody on Earth could see what was happening in real-time.

Effugium, who was Supreme Leader of the Zilodon's, asked the all-important question: "We will either destroy your planet using the laser that you people have created, or we will take one future generation of your children. To our planet to be returned after 25 Earth years."

Humanity was at odds and could not believe that these "aliens" came here and wanted to take our children or destroy our planet. What would you have said if faced with this question?

As Humanity thought over the question, Effugium said, "Thank you, we have all the information we will ever need from you people." Effugium saw to it that each child born, all 250,000 a day, would be teleported to the Zilodon's home planet of XyraX, where they will live for a generation.

Later it was found out that the Zilodon's could read our minds, and they knew what went on in Humanity's brains. So it was known from this point forward what parents said to destroy the planet or who wanted to sacrifice their children. It will be made known, in time, how the answer to that question may either make or break all parenting couples across Earth.

A generation passed, and the parents, regardless of the answer they gave to the Zilodon's question, yearned for their children. They all knew that the day was fast approaching where they would meet the "generation children."

The Zilodon's sent a message stating that parents would need to teleport to a special planet to meet their children after all of these years. Earth's scientists were given coordinates on where to send all four billion parents.

As all of the four billion parents, who were set to teleport out from Earth to the planet where they will meet their grown children for the first time, became super excited as some of the generation children are either very young yet or as old as 24 – 25 years of age.

The Zilodon's initially told the parents that the Generation Children would not be able to return to Earth, as they would live fulfilling lives on the Zilodon's neighboring planet named "Sinfinitum."

Roughly half of the parents did teleport towards the un-known, leaving approximately half of the parents back on Earth. These parents were freaking out, thinking they would never see their children again. It was not uncommon to see parents' crying up at the sky, asking for the Zilodon's to see their children.

What these parents did not know was that they all answered Effugium's question about sacrifice or planetary homicide the same way, although it will not be stated yet as to what their answers were: sacrifice their children or cause homicidal Earth.

As the parents gathered into the various teleporting sta-tions on Earth, they teleported to the coordinates received by the Zilodon's. Mixed emotions brewed between the parents as they were leaving Earth forever to live on some strange planet...but...they will be united with their children, which was the best thing ever...right?

The parents envisioned what their children looked like and what they were like and what they liked to do, and too many other questions to list here. They were very happy to meet their children that they, well, sacrificed to the Zilodon's for the past generation, and they were directly responsible.

Roughly half of the Parents of the Generation Children reappeared on a distant planet out in the untamed cosmos. Unbeknownst to the parents, they were sent to a planet right in the middle of a galactic war.

The children were strategically placed near their parent(s) now that they had teleported to the strange planet. Like magic, the parents appeared on a beautiful planet with lush rain forests and strange but friendly animals.

Enough about the floral and fauna...it was time for the lucky parents to meet their children. So the parents all looked ahead in the distance and saw figures outlined in the sunlight. Some of the parents would have told you it was the finest and most hopeful thing they had ever seen.

They were the parents' children! The children started to run towards the parents as the parents ran towards them. As the children grew closer, the parents noted that the children were not 100% Human any longer. For some odd reason, their DNA must have been spliced with the Zilodon's.

As one would not have imagined, most parents were perplexed by the look in their children's eyes, even though they were red. Most of the generation children, having not met their parents before, appeared very emotional to see their parents as they were about to embrace them.

For some strange reason, the children stopped several feet in front of their parents, puzzling them as to why they did not embrace them.

In an eerie tone, the children all spoke at once: "You should have voted against the 'Generation Sacrifice,' then we would be safe from harm and not Zilodon's because of you."

As the children finished talking, strange aircraft were seen in the skies directly above the parents and children. These spacecraft were part of an intergalactic war. There was dog fighting in the sky as one of the spaceships shot a laser. Was it mentioned that the laser defied physics...

With that stated, the children put what appeared to be teleportation helmets on. As they were about to engage the helmets that would send them somewhere safer than this place, a red flash had blinded every parent on the planet, although the children were not affected.

The children teleported away when vision was gained as another red flash happened. The lonely parents realized that their children would rather be Zilodon's than be Human and live on this strange planet with them. Of course, there was no way the parents could teleport back to Earth.

There were over two billion people on this strange planet and had nowhere to go and nothing to do. They thought and even feared how to make their lives work on this strange planet.

Although none of that mattered anymore since the red flash caused something strange to happen: The way the parents thought, flipped, and their thoughts began to go backward in their heads, as they noticed that the trees started to reduce in size, to where nothing was left but fields.

The fear-stricken parents were terrified that the planet seemed to be shrinking right in front of them. Of course, all they could do was watch in horror as the events played out, being able to only speak backward to each other, not making any sense or knowing what the next minute would bring...

By this point, the parents had realized that the laser was a "Time Reversal Laser," which had been used in the past to "erase" unwanted and old/dead planets by reducing them to nothing.

One of the fighter spaceships had one affixed to their space-craft and fired the laser off on the strange planet the parents were trapped on.

This caused everything to go backward in time, where the planet and the parents were reduced to a single point. Every-thing that ever existed on the planet was now nothing. But the story was not over yet...

With a loud bang, the parents became aware once again. They were not on Earth; unfortunately, they were far from Her in pitch-black darkness, on a moon of unbelievable that was burning like a planetwide brush fire. It was 215 degrees Fahrenheit on this planet or wherever the parents had ended up.

The parents who wished for an end found out that the body boils at 212 degrees (100 degrees Celsius), and there was no quick way to alleviate their mounting and intense pain that would most likely be an 18,257 on the 1 - 10 pain scale.

It was horror movie stuff, and the parents were not faring well at all in this place of unimaginable heat. Not to mention that their minds were placed back in order, so they were guaranteed to feel the painful onslaught.

What none of the parents knew, while in the darkness, not knowing where they were, was that they were about to be dealt a karma-endorsed blow so heavy that it may exterminate them like cockroaches.

Having been a moon they were on that was orbiting around the cosmic core, at the center of the universe, was where the universe's epicenter of light & gravity exists. This cosmic core, as stated, was where there was intense like and the strength of the gravity there could annihilate anything on Earth instantly.

The moon had a sky that was so dark, none of the nourishing light, albeit intense, could penetrate the atmosphere of the moon that the parents were now trapped on. They still remained on the moon, darker than the blackest paint.

Like the moon the parents were on spiraled into the cosmic core, the parents slowly, and one by one, burst into flames and were reduced to human "clean dust" as the moon spiraled into the intense heat that was the cosmic core.

The now-deceased parents did not know where all of them who "teleported" to the strange planet earlier and then to a moon of the cosmic core were those who voted FOR the sacrifice.

All of the parents who did not vote for the sacrifice? They still found themselves on Earth, where they all received knocks at their doors. Upon opening their doors, they were meant with their children, in complete human form, and not spliced with the Zilodon's DNA.

These parents did not even teleport to the rain forest planet where all the "sacrifice" voters went. These parents reunited with their long "lost" children, where they lived out the rest of their lives on Earth, feeding off love, sustenance, karma, and many other things that make life worth living.

THE END

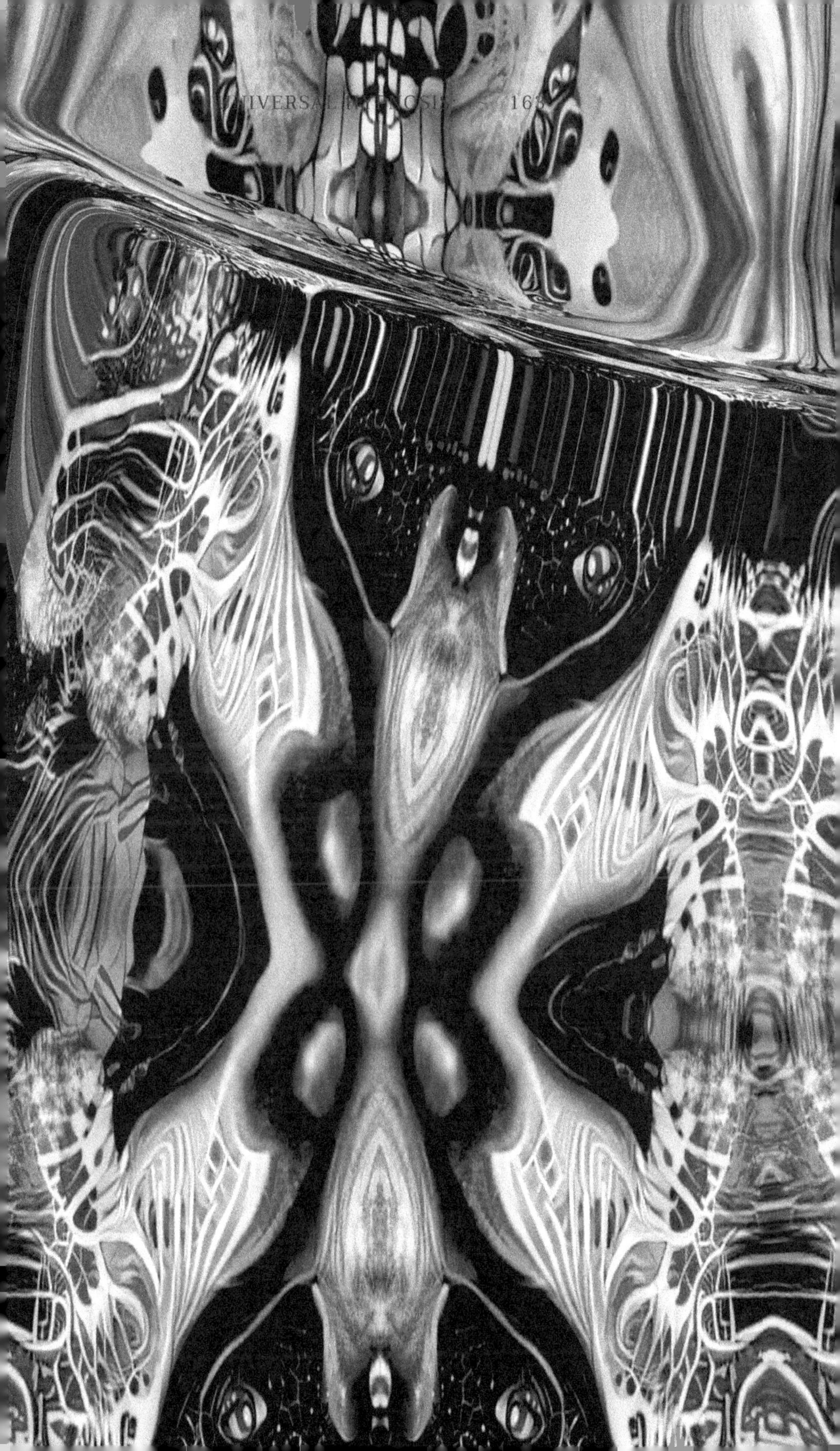

Chapter 17

"Synchronized Sky Climb: 1,000,001 Nightmares At 50,000+ Feet...Skyrocketing Toward Space and Losing Fuel by the Second"

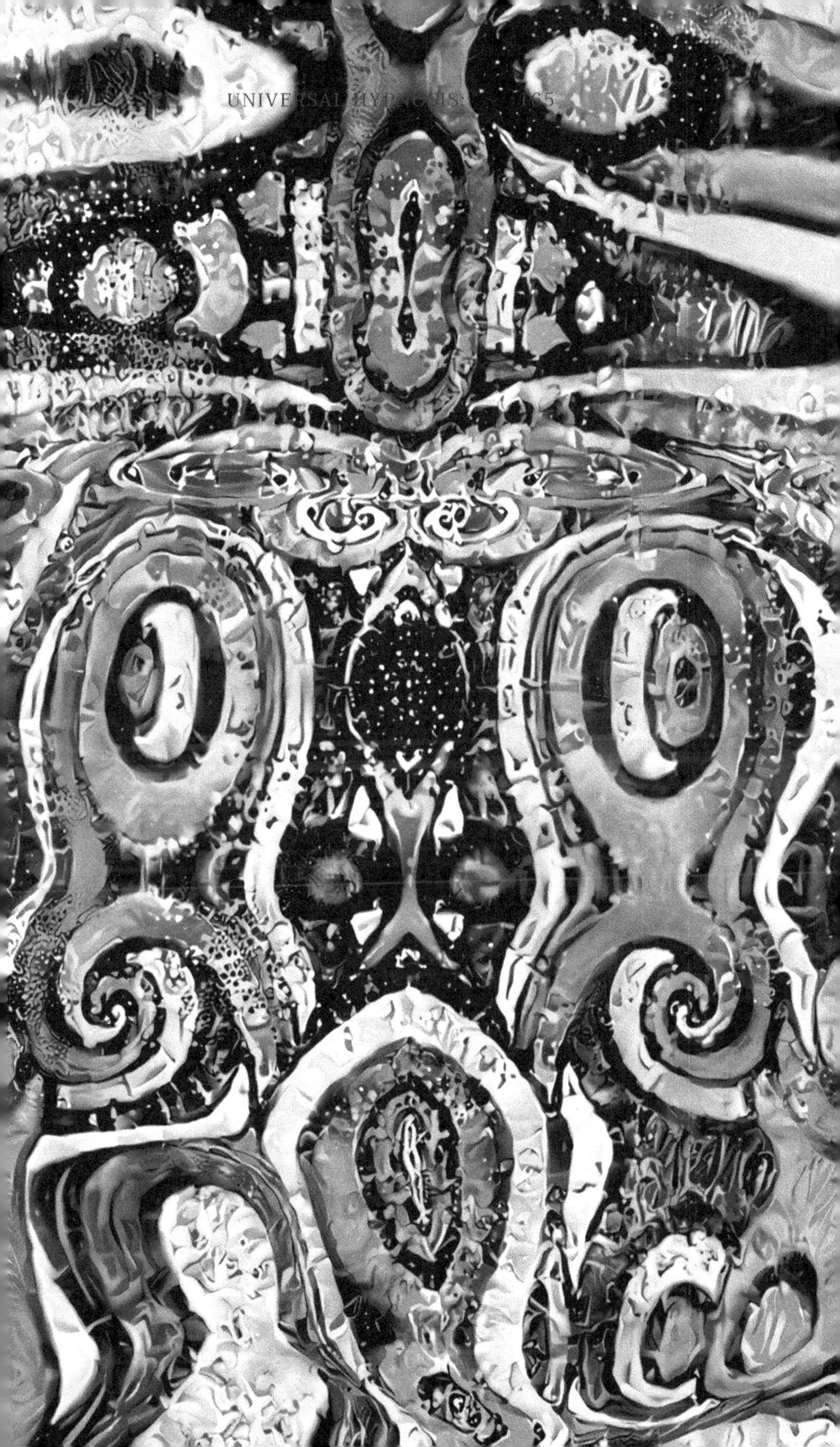

The year was 2050, and some pretty powerful technologies exist now...

The world marveled at the astounding fact that the new see-through "Dyson sphere" had now been completed, encapsulating Earth. It existed above the Exosphere, the highest point of the atmosphere, and interacted with the solar wind before the Dyson sphere was manufactured and assembled around Earth. Think of it as the shell of an egg, and Earth was the contents.

In other words, it was 1111 miles in the air from any given coordinate on the surface. It brought numerous benefits to Earth. The Dyson sphere was covered in transparent solar panels, which covered the entire Earth.

It was impervious and was completely see-through, enabling Humanity to have had views of the cosmos, yet, able to be protected from anything foreign that may have fallen to Earth. This included space junk, falling satellites, meteors, and any other matter of cosmic cannonballs that Father Universe may have shot at the Earth.

Having taken 50 years to assemble and manufacture, the largest engineering marvel in history became the main planetary power source as the Dyson sphere absorbed, through its previously mentioned solar panels, every single watt of light sent to us from our stellar mother, our Sun. This enabled more raw power than Humanity would ever need.

It was historically surmised that a Dyson sphere was an impossible pipe dream of sorts as there was never enough raw materials on the entire planet to manufacture one. This all changed when "asteroid deceleration" became a reality.

Asteroid deceleration became a game-changer for the economy and Earth at large once scientists were able to figure out how the heck to stop asteroids. They were then "dropped" into the sea. No worries, fellow readers, they were not dropped from very high to cause ravaging tsunamis.

Every fail-safe was taken to ensure nobody was lost due to the cosmic behemoths landing in our oceans. This was after entering Earth through a special "door" of sorts in the Dyson sphere that had enabled the asteroids to be placed in the oceans.

The way that asteroids decelerated were astronauts sprayed incoming asteroids with a concoction of metals composed of specific minerals that electronically linked to a computer on Earth and through the metal-encased asteroids could be controlled like ping pong balls.

Scientists now had pinpoint precision when controlling the asteroids and could mine any stray asteroid in the solar system. It was an understatement to explain how much of a game-changer this was by providing trillions of dollars worth of raw materials to the economy, causing it to boom like a sub woofer.

In the present year of 2050, all world leaders had convened and ironed out details that concerned the global government and how Humanity will plan for the next year, as a world summit was the most important meeting that year. The World Leaders United was the name of the yearly summit that had its 50th anniversary that year after having been established way back in the year 2000.

On that particular day there was the most air traffic on record since most of the 905 leaders traveled by airplane to get to Tokyo, and those same persons will have to fly back home.

The summit was an excellent success, and the leaders all left happy, knowing that the next year would be filled with nonstop progress. As the leaders all boarded their planes to return home, it was time to explain some details about what was flying in the sky at any given moment.

Within hours, nearly 900 of the world's leaders were air-bound and started to enjoy their ride after the mentally taxing summit they had just attended.

On average, each day, around nearly ten thousand planes go flight bound carrying approximately 1,2 million people in the sky at any given time. You must know these statistics since what followed the summit was something beyond conventional terrorism.

Every computer and every television went haywire and became red. On televisions, cell phones, and computers, the face of a blue and green cyclops mouse came through the screens in billions of households and workplaces globally.

The mouse stood idle and said nothing for a good 30 seconds, and then it spoke in a demented and diabolical tone:

"We are Anonymouse, and we have now seized control of your skies. There is nothing you pathetic meddlers could ever do to stop every airplane from running out of gas, because, as I snarl these words, every in-flight airplane will succumb to the "autopilot error." Congratulations on your flight. Thank you for flying with "Anonymouse Air.""

And like that, the pandemonium went into effect, and billions of people were highly concerned about the 1+ million people who were air-bound, sitting ducks for whatever Anonymouse had planned for them.

Elsewhere on Earth, in the skies, something freakishly frightening occurred when every airplane started to point upwards as all of the 10,000 Captains/pilots on all planes noticed that the planes became stuck on autopilot, which was causing the planes to point straight up in a vertical fashion.

Now, the passengers, pilots, and air stewards became enthralled in terror as the planes went vertical. This threw everyone back in their seats like they were climbing a steep roller coaster hill. Either that or the airplanes would run out of gas, plummet back to the ground, and explode into flesh confetti.

While all of this was going on in the skies, officials were tracking the Anonymouse message and where it originated from, as this would give us a great shot at Anonymouse.

Scientists got together and let the secret of the Dyson sphere be known: this sphere can harvest wind from space and can be controlled using manipulated gravity to place air anywhere on Earth. The kicker? They can create enveloping air pockets that can safely bring anything to the ground, as gentle as a falling feather.

As scientists were quickly establishing a wind plan, the cybersecurity help throughout the globe discovered the source of the message and let the authorities know where they could physically find the nincompoop hackers and bring them to justice, or just exterminate them where they stand.

In a seedy basement somewhere in Europe, a sect of hackers known as the infamous "Anonymouse" watched their computer screens and laughed to tears at the fact that over a million persons could perish. All at once, top law enforcement personnel infiltrated the sect, where there was a shootout of epic proportions.

After the shots had ceased, one law enforcement official stood. He motioned for the top cybersecurity experts to come in and do their thing to disable the autopilot feature on the airplanes, which were still disaster-prone that could leave over one million men, women, and children without a life.

Scientists could not accept this negligence that the damn hackers left on the world, so they took action: Windows on the Dyson sphere were opened allowing solar wind to enter.

At the same time, the cybersecurity experts hacked the hackers and disengaged autopilots on all 10,000 -airplanes, breaking the passengers free of the maniacal grasp that Anony-mouse had on the world's airplanes.

The only problem was that 91% of the airplanes had no fuel and started to plummet towards the ground as the lowest spiraling plane was approximately only 12,000 feet from the violent ground.

With the use of wind but also magnetism manipulation was also used to ensure the safe return of everyone in the sky, including the world leaders.

As the wind traveled through the Dyson sphere's windows, it created many speed-decelerating air pockets that, when used with manipulated magnetism, caused something never seen before to happen.

Once the air pockets engulfed the 10,000 aircraft, the magnetism was used to secure the aircraft from plummeting. Within the hour, the lucky million passengers were slowly and safely lowered to the ground.

It was never disclosed how many, if any, planes had not become air pocketed and magnetically lowered to the ground. Had they not survived a possible violent ground collision, this would have been the worst act of terrorism in history, with what could have been the loss of 1+ million lives.

Humanity was left reeling after all that had taken place but took comfort in knowing that the only thing that will be plummeting in the future will be the stocks of the airlines, even though they were as innocent as Anonymouse was guilty.

THE END

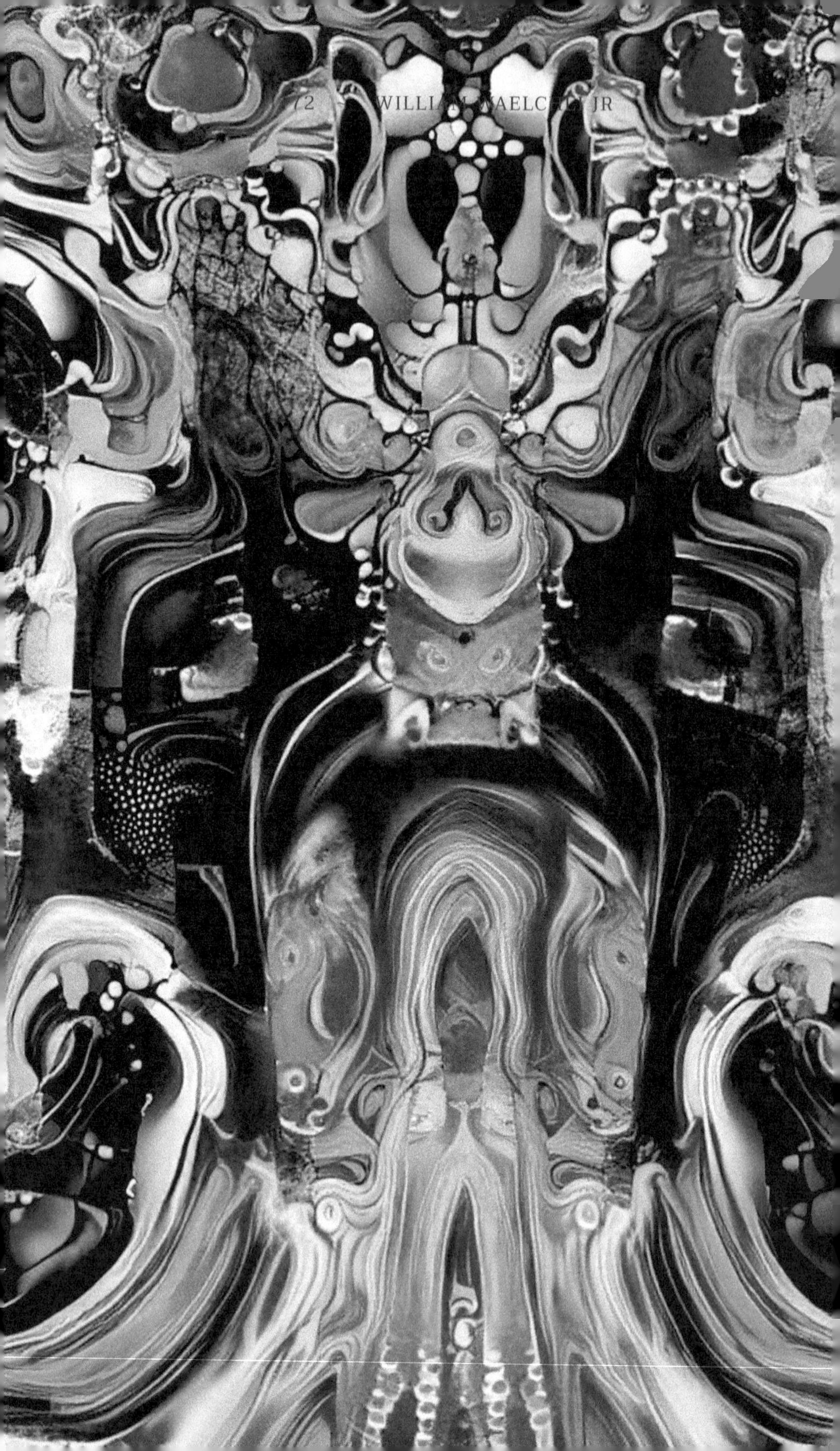

"Dark Energy & Dark Matter: Best Friends or Best Foes?" - or - "Anticipating the Completion of the Cosmic Ring of Accelerated Evolution"

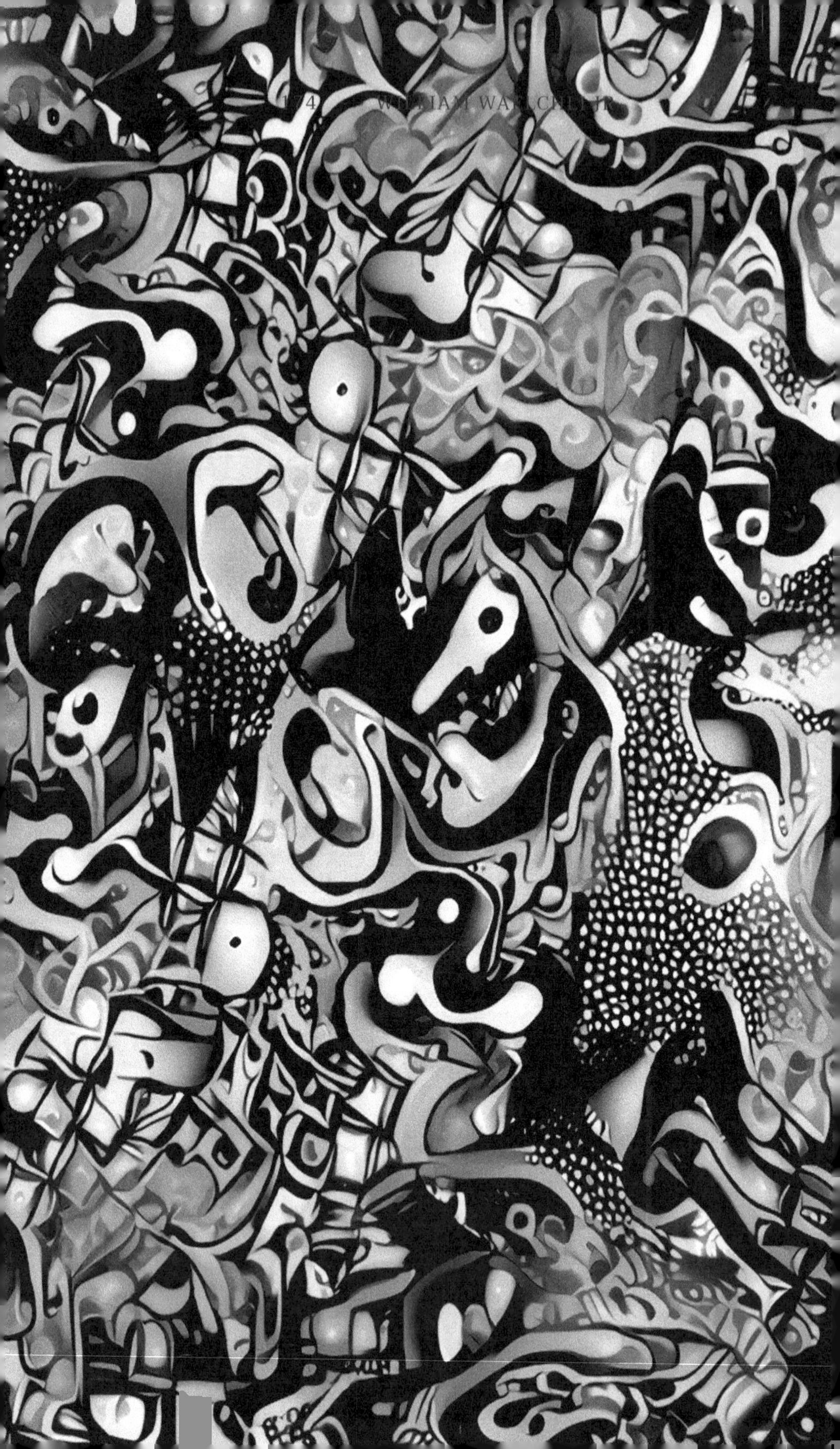

Through the use of technologically fierce instruments, Humanity had used these precise measuring tools to make progress in fortifying our galaxy and making it safe from all objects that could mess with our home galaxy, The Milky Way.

The fortified Milky Way galaxy was also known in some circles as a 'bubble galaxy.' encapsulating the entire Milky Way protecting it from all forms of conventional and unconventional universal terrorism.

Through Earth's telescopes, scientists detected that our neighboring galaxy Andromeda would be colliding with our galaxy very soon. It's probably time for the scientists to tell Humanity that galactic obliteration may occur very, very soon. There will be more on this freaky subject later on in this tale.

Dark energy had always assisted dark matter in keeping the form of the Universe. By using the Electrosphere on Earth (the electric sky), scientists pointed their telescopes at a spot where dark energy was available and possibly harvested.

Humanity was warned to stay inside as the Electrosphere shot off a lightning bolt of who knows how many volts, and it zapped a nearby pool of dark energy.

A sample of dark energy was harvested using high amounts of electricity to pull the dark energy through Earth's Electrosphere, where scientists obtained 6 oz (178 ml) of the elusive substance.

This will change everything...

Through the great electrical charge, they were able to reverse the current of the electricity, which drew the dark energy out of the Universe and into a science lab on Earth.

They discovered that dark matter was composed of unknown "gases" originating from the big bang. All of the dark matter was composed of the big bang's gases from the occurrence of the big bang.

This was precisely why the cosmos was so dark because the big bang released so many black inert gases that it filled the entire Universe, and then some. This was very important in further understanding the cosmos.

After years of work, scientists came upon a new type of coding for computers that communicated with "spin networks." These so-called spin networks are what the fabric of space-time was composed of.

Dark energy was "molecular fog" composed of droplets that the scientists would be able to be controlled by binary coding. Through this coding manipulation, the computer programmers figured out how to control the dark energy, which, perhaps, may control the dark matter.

Further to the programming technique: Space comprised a simple binary code of 0's and 1's, encompassing all of space and time. Humanity looked to exploit this on a grand level, but was it a good idea to play with the Universe?

This was a revelation as the scientists reveled in this astonishing and world-changing discovery, where the stakes have risen to mythical levels.

The coding was eventually able to "manipulate the dark energy" by converting the space-time code into binary computer coding. Scientists planned future planetary manipulations by the use of universal programming. Humanity may make the Universe their very own "playground," or will it be a haunted house?

By decoding the Universe, it was the same as manipulating the DNA of a Human. A means to control space-time and the swift movement of planets and stars, possibly becoming a reality over time, gave the scientists all kinds of crazy scenarios to possibly partake in.

A strange occurrence was observed on a routine Tuesday in a science lab in Clearwater, Florida, where the dark energy was held. The ceiling in the lab above the dark energy magically opened up. Scientists saw the sky outside by looking at the ceiling's hole (1 foot around (0.305 meters)), scientists saw the sky outside. It was a very strange occurrence indeed.

There were reports of a dark line coming down through the sky over Florida and going straight down into the science lab. All at once, the ceiling opened up further, and the dark line interacted with the dark energy.

It was later discovered that the invasive black line from the sky was, in fact, dark matter looking for its missing partner, the dark energy sample.

It was thought that the dark energy was "missing" something, so the dark matter found it, and now scientists may be able to control dark matter due to its distinct relationship with dark energy.

While the dark matter was in reach, the scientists took a sizeable sample of the freezing cold dark matter. The temperature was measured at exactly 0 degrees Kelvin or -459.67 degrees Fahrenheit or −732.82 degrees Celsius.

With the sample of dark energy and the dark matter, they placed both samples in an impervious square "room," and in time, the gas and energy expanded, causing a mini and tame universe that was about the size of a classroom.

Scientists were sure that they figured out how they would make a "Planet Farm" or "Cosmic Ring" out in the solar system. Their aim was to harvest intelligent Life. A planet farm or cosmic ring was a collection of planets that used the same orbital path to move around their host star (like the Sun).

Planets and a host star will travel through space-time and be controlled by Humanity by moving the planets like pieces on a chessboard across space and time. Humanity called checkmate against the cosmos, but was it too early to call it?

The planet farm or cosmic ring was a ring of 1000 planets with a great star that the planets orbit around. The cosmic ring existed between Earth and the Moon, where every twelve hours, a planet passed thru between Earth and the Moon in an orbital ring spanning 100 million miles around, and each planet has a 100-mile gap between each planet.

The area between Earth and the Moon was called the "Cosmic Evolution Zone" because as the planets go around the cosmic ring, one planet will appear between the Earth and the Moon. Humanity was able to see the planets with their naked eye and will also be able to tell what kind of evolutionary processes are happening on the virgin planets.

Scientists assisted the dark energy and were now able to control gravity and dark matter. The dark matter can now move any planetary object by manipulating a planet's gravity by assisting dark energy, causing the dark matter to reorganize planets into the cosmic ring. It would be hard-pressed to find a single Human who was not excited about the new cosmic ring. This has now become our reality.

Earthlike planets were strategically chosen by scientists and moved into the habitable or "Goldilocks" zones of the parent star in the cosmic ring in our solar system, so they were able to get just the right nourishment from their home star to achieve liquid water and vegetation.

This all happened in the cosmic ring, and over time, these barren planets may support highly intelligent Life...or maybe not so high. Only time will tell.

Over time, the 1000 exoplanets were placed into the habitable or Goldilocks zones, almost guaranteeing that in a few billion years, all of these planets will be teeming with Life and other exotic creatures that Humanity cannot even fathom.

The youngest and hottest stars were "collected" by the dark matter where they were moved across our galaxy, where all of the 1000 Earthlike planets would eventually harbor Life and maybe lots of it.

By refining the computer coding that manipulated the dark energy, which then interacts with dark matter, changing its very nature according to what computer code was placed into Earth's computers, we made much progress.

This was how scientists could control the dark energy and, in turn, manipulated the dark matter into moving the 1000 planets across the galaxy and into the cosmic ring, which will orbit our Sun on a slightly wider path.

A year on these newly harvested planets will be around 400 days, so the life forms that will exist on the planet will grow older slower due to their years being longer than Earth's.

It was discovered that scientists could "fast forward" the planet's evolution where one billion years of evolution happened in 100 years. This was done through computer programming manipulation, dark matter, and our "friend" dark energy.

By deeply studying dark matter, it was discovered that the gases leftover from the big bang (comprising dark matter) are black inert gases with no atomic properties.

It seemed that a force beyond our own capabilities and understanding caught wind that there was "galactic domination," and this unnamed force just may fight back against Humanity by unleashing the possible Sworn Swarm of primordial black holes reminiscent of "A Homage to Mr. King: The Sworn Swarm," which is found in this very companion book in Chapter .

Over the past several weeks, it was discovered that primordial black holes had been very active outside the galaxy. Their unwavering appetite for destruction may annihilate the entire galaxy if they gain entry into the Cosmic Bubble that now surrounds the entire galaxy.

Primordial black holes are about 5 feet across. This type of black hole can move speedily and rather swiftly at that. They can move anywhere in the Universe and are well known for their unmatched appetite for anything around them.

The primordial black holes had collected around the galaxy bubble's four walls, floor, and ceiling. Humanity knew that it was done for if those creatures trespassed into our little galaxy and ran rampant, possibly destroying Humanity in the process...

During the President's state of the union address, one black hole was seen in the sky above the crowd. There was a fair share of screams and gasps heard out in the President's audience as the maniacal creature flew straight down and swallowed the President whole. Afterward, all that was left were the President's shoes. You could hear a pin landing on the floor. It was that quiet.

Oddly, instead of running like animals, the entire audience gave a standing ovation for the President. The black hole swooped down and ate about 16 more people. Humanity had to do something about the nuisances' flying around eating one Human at a time.

It was believed that the terrifying and foreboding sentient black holes could not penetrate the Electrosphere. The black hole found its way into our planet by finding a dead spot in the Electrosphere, enabling it to gain entry to Earth,

Each black hole can be mapped to get its coordinates with the new universal coding system. When the scientists looked on their "map of black holes," it showed nothing around the galactic walls. Maybe the black holes just really had it out for the President or grew bored of trying to get in.

By some strange feat of good fortune, the scientists created an anti-gravity device that might enable them to actually capture a violent black hole. The machine targeted the black hole, wreaking havoc all over Earth. By luck, the creature miraculously ended up in the anti-gravity net. It was pulled down to the science lab, where it was studied extensively. It remained in a safe enclosure, so the little devil did not escape.

This was private information that could not be shared. Just know that the black hole had a complete set of physics and laws. Within a year of studying the black hole, a marriage happened between quantum mechanics (study of the subatomic/small stuff) and general relativity (the big stuff). It was not too long before Humanity had its coveted 'Theory of Everything' that proved everything in physics.

Back to the Cosmic Ring: Scientists sped up evolution by using computer coding and gravitational manipulation and other new tricks learned from studying the black hole.

In other cosmic news, our neighboring galaxy, Andromeda, was about to collide with our Milky Way galaxy. It can even be seen in the sky. Scientists spotted Andromeda and how it was closing in on our galactic bubble.

It was easy to move the galactic bubble out of the way of the runaway galaxy. Scientists ended up moving the entire galaxy, and Andromeda flew right by with no other disturbances to Earth or any of the other 1000 planets in the cosmic ring.

Humanity will wait 400 years for the young planets in the cosmic ring to evolve 4 billion years while waiting just 400 years.

Over the 400 years, scientists kept watch on all 1000 planets, and they were starting to become more Earthlike, and some were "Extraterrestrialike," creating floral and fauna never, ever imagined before.

A planet of dinosaurs was discovered, and the scientists exploited it by teleporting the "nice-looking" dinosaurs to Earth. Dinosaur farms have become a new thing with all different and brand new species of dinosaurs popping up in countries all across Earth.

The scientists were schooled from the Jurassic Park series of films and did not bring back any dinosaurs that were stand-offish, skittish, or that had fangs longer than a ruler.

As the planets slowly cycled around the cosmic ring, they showed a different planet between the Earth & Moon every twelve hours. Suddenly, a black planet appeared, which could barely be made out against the infinite blackness of space.

As soon as the black planet was discovered, 1000's of creatures flew from the planet to Earth, where they landed. Spiders! 1000's of them the size of a car tire made their way to the scientists' labs around Earth. These spiders evolved to make themselves into many sizes, from a dime up to a Volkswagen Bug.

The spiders did not attack Humanity. They could speak our language and told Humanity that they were spies as they went to other planets in the cosmic ring, where they found something of concern. But who can place any trust in the spiders?

The great spiders traveled almost invisibly to spy on the other planets and reported any resistance to Earth. Or anything worse...

The spiders have evolved to be able to travel in space unharmed. They returned bad news to Earth, where they told Humanity that the ring was about to unhinge (due to the 1000 planets spinning too closely to each planet) and other complex gravitational discrepancies.

The scientists overlooked this, and all hoped that nothing catastrophic would befall our prized Earth or any planet in the cosmic ring.

The planetary orbital ring comprising the planet farm/cosmic ring was released from its orbit, hurtling 1000's of stray planets methodically towards the Earth's direction. It was only a matter of time before these cosmic bullets would find their mark, all over Earth's surface.

Scientists were sweating it now, knowing that this planetary cannon pointed at Earth may be the universes' response to being somewhat controlled by Humanity. This may possibly be payback for Humanity basically being too smart for their own good.

Then it happened: a stray planet from the former cosmic ring shot just about past the Earth and grazed it as if the Earth caught itself shaving.

Before Earth gets pummeled by a planetary Gatling gun of thousands of planets, possibly rendering it to cosmic dust or other useless shit, Humanity pondered what its recourse would be to save Humanity's only planet.

The scientists all had it in the back of their minds that they somehow put their "noses" where they did not belong. They thought that there might be hell to pay or not. God Only knows...

This messed with the planet's tidal forces and plate tectonics, among other things. What was bestowed upon Humanity was a possible payback where each person on the planet will pay for having indirectly created Life beyond God's hands.

But the tale continues... Only certain governmental employees knew of an old fail-safe invented during the 'Psyche Wars' to prevent Earth and Humanity from being obliterated by extraterrestrials.

They will use teleportation with the last electricity because Earth was ailing. Teleport? It cannot be done because the planet that grazed the Earth earlier destroyed the Electrosphere (or so we thought), disabling the almost infinite power that once enveloped Earth by using the Electric Sky.

The Electrosphere was basically an electric sky. It was comprised of so many volts, it could not be computed. It had caused EVERYTHING to be wireless. Imagine a world no longer mired in wires. That was where Earth was now. Everything from toothbrushes to cars ran on electricity.

Scientists accidentally teleported Earth to the central black hole in the middle of the fortified galaxy with a planet headed straight towards them, spewing out Primordial Black Holes. By the event horizon's gravitational pull, the Earth may be pulled into the black hole, having no idea what the black hole will bestow upon Humanity.

A swarm of horrendous primordial creatures, possibly 1000 strong, headed towards Earth. Earth attempted to evade and accidentally crossed the black hole's event horizon (or entrance), making any escape impossible. Humanity hoped they tasted good because they might be the black hole's next meal.

They somehow managed to get the Electrosphere running again, and as Humanity got sucked into the black hole...all Humanity could think was, "Is this our final punishment?"

While the Electrosphere was working, it provided light as the Earth did not get destroyed or spaghettified by going into the black hole at the very center of the now almost fully evolved Milky Way galaxy.

Telescopes on Earth could pick up a faint light ahead in the interior of the black hole. As the light got bigger, they exited the hole. They noted that the same planet that was behind them in the distance upon entry was now in front of them in the distance. This helped prove that we just went back in time in our Universe by taking the Trip through the central black hole.

Humanity and Earth ventured back to their spot around the Sun, like the Universe, through the black hole, was the same used to go back in time in case of space turmoil or problems.

This rewound the cosmic clock back 400 years, which was precisely before Humanity created that damned planet farm. It looked like Humanity was given a break this time, and the Earth should live on for eons.

Now that Humanity had agreed that they got too close to God's Work with the planet farm or cosmic ring, they have released all of the dark energy and dark matter from the enclosure of the mini Universe, mentioned earlier, back into space.

A feeling of relief washed over the scientists since, with the release of the mini-universe back into space, the scientists felt much better and hoped that they would be spared in any other future space calamities.

The Electrosphere, all of a sudden, dimmed and could not be turned back on. All of the skies were pitch black, and no one could understand why there was some sort of laughing from the sky. But this was 3pm local time, and it should be light out. It would do no good to tell Humanity to try and escape now that a super swarm of the primordial black holes having covered Earth had arrived.

With their salivating mouths, the black holes did not eat the entire planet from the outside in, but instead, they tried a more psychologically terrorizing approach: Every once in a while, one of those awful creatures would swoop down and have a Human meal. It was now months later, and the primordial black holes were still slowly picking off Humanity one person at a time.

It seemed that as the days went on, more and more of the black holes were chomping on Humans. It was worthless to run with their grave numbers, as the putrid creatures were everywhere and nowhere all at once. Billions died during the scourge. I guess it does look like Humanity will pay for creating Life when they never were supposed to.

If the scientists had any morals, perhaps there would, in fact, be a moral to this tale. If Humanity had not played God, they would not have been picked off, one by one, by vicious and greedy black holes which stalked the rest of Humanity as each scientist learned that they violated the rules of the game of Universal Chess. Checkmate for the Cosmos.

THE END

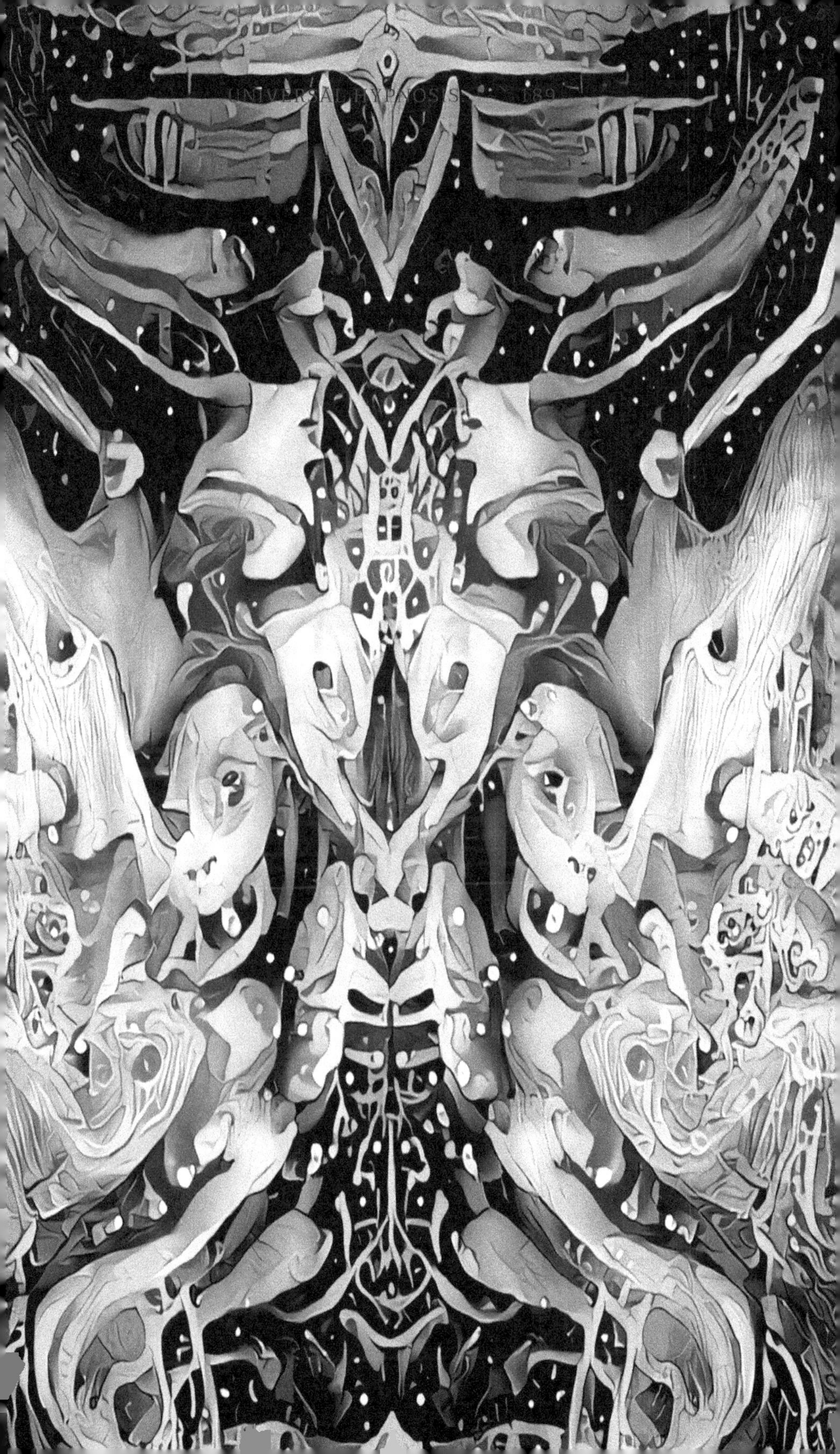

UNIVERSAL HYPNOSIS   189

"An Ethical & Moral Dilemma Concerning the Creation of a Mirror Universe and Its Future Implications Concerning Potential Universal Genocide" - or - "A Scientific Nemesis of Sorts..."

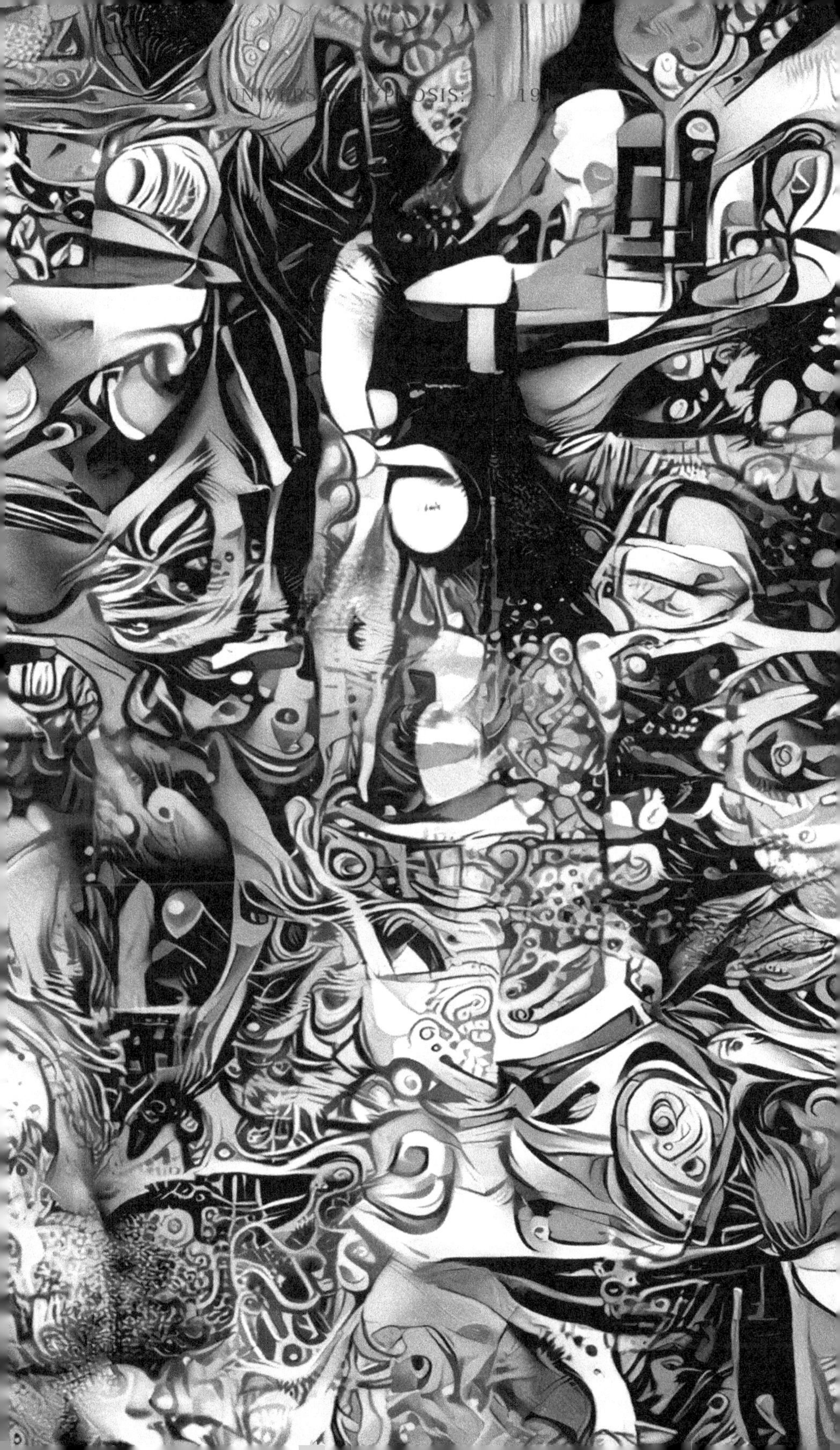

UNIVERSAL HYPNOSIS: ~ 19

In the year 2500, technology was even more widespread than it was a century ago and was an essential part of every person's life, and without it, we would be misguided.

Humanity also marveled that they had technologically out-done themselves, and things could not possibly have gotten any better than current technologies. It was only a matter of time before scientists controlled gravity...

As it happened, arguably, the most important scientific experiment had been underway for decades. Scientists had made many strides over the years and improved their research exponentially.

Now all of the scientists' years of hard work had paid off. The scientists held a press conference to let the world know exactly what they worked on behind closed doors for so long.

Since science had no clue about what happened before the Big Bang, the scientific community put forth every resource they had in their arsenals. Still, nothing could tell us what happened before the ever-famous Big Bang (Universal birth).

Scientists had wanted to create an exact mirror Universe next to ours. They will then cause time reversal through gravitational manipulation to see what had happened once the mirrored Universe reduced itself into a pre-Big Bang state.

There were many theories about what happened before the Big Bang, but let's face it, they were all inaccurate and could not be adequately tested...until now.

There was a lot of debate over the moral and ethical issues regarding the future mirror Universe since the scientists will create everything that exists. This, by the opponents of the Universal mirroring, saw this as playing God. Many persons were not laughing. It's not like the mirrored Universe will include people.

To be as fair as possible, the scientists decided to hold a global lottery to make it fair game for anything if the lottery favored creating the Mirror Universe. The ballot asked if they should or should not create the mirrored Universe.

It was a complicated process. Although scientists created a website just for the voting, it quickly went down due to traffic congestion upon going live.

The information technology experts were able to bring it back online, and Scientists cast all of the votes in the allotted time frame set forth by the scientists. There were 4.7 billion votes cast.

By a slim margin, only 62,111 votes, the experiment went on as originally planned. Now no one could complain or degrade the scientists any longer, and their larger-than-life experiment commenced.

In the not too distant past, scientists finally discovered the graviton, the subatomic particle of gravity. Scientists worldwide celebrated knowing how important this discovery was. Until this instance,

Humanity understood the importance of such a groundbreaking discovery. Since then, scientists have been performing experiments on how to harness gravity.

When electricity (or electrons) and gravitons fuse with neutrinos, scientists could make exact duplicates of anything. These new forms of atoms are called Gratoms.

This is simply a mixture of the words gravity + atom. The scientists thought they could recreate the Universe in a condensed state by casting a gratom wave across our Universe.

This will infuse all atmospheres (or lack thereof) with gratoms and create a mirrored version of the Universe. This is all done with the help of electricity. This happened by creating a gravity wall between our Universe and its mirrored counterpart.

The gravity wall was 100,000 miles high and ran nearly the length of the Universe. The gravity wall enabled the copious amounts of duplicate planets, stars, black holes, etc., to remain stable without disrupting either Universe's gravity.

Scientists needed to ensure that nothing would happen to our Universe once the mirrored Universe was created. The repercussions of something going awry could spell fate for the entire Universe at large and any trace of Earth or any other celestial body.

Engineers created self-replicating telescopes that "duplicated" all across our Universe to observe the mirror Universe once the scientists had created it. Months later, the time came where scientists unleashed the gratom wave.

Gratoms move instantly because they have the neutrino at an atomic level. This enabled the gratom wave to electrify everything in the Universe.

The mirror Universe came to form and was completed. It took some time, but the gratom wave worked, unlike some scientists' opinion that gratoms alone could not copy the Universe. Science had created a mirrored copy of our Universe.

To achieve time reversal, gravity must slowly be sucked back into our Universe. The gravity wall was designed to "suck out" the gravity of the mirrored Universe.

This was upon command by the scientists, therefore causing the reversal of time that will enable us to see what existed before the ever-infamous Big Bang.

It came the time where the scientists manipulated the gravitational pull of the mirrored Universe using the gravity wall. This triggered RTR or Rapid Time Reversal. What happened next was something unlike anyone, had ever seen before.

Suddenly, everything in the mirror Universe began to turn in on itself. Through the telescopes, we could now see the reverse formation of planets, stars, etc. It was badass to view reverse supernovae and reverse collisions in real-time.

It was unlike anything seen before, having watched a black hole eject everything it ever gobbled up. These findings will change the very nature of universal thought and changed how we view the Universe forever. The scientists witnessed the reverse birth of black holes. Which will rewrite our understanding of them

Time reversal continued, and it was a grand spectacle to witness. Eventually, the mirror Universe was nearing the Big Bang phase at the very dawning of our Universe.

With a flash, the endpoint ripped through space-time. Space-time had never been broken through, and Humanity had never witnessed this spectacle before, and billions of people were excited that we would finally see our Universe in a pre-Big Bang state.

Not too long after, a beautiful blacklight poked through the tear in space-time—the light shot across what was the mirror Universe. Laymen and scientists alike pondered: "Was this where we were birthed from...Blacklight?"

A thick neon yellow gelatinous substance rapidly emerged out of the light without any warning. It was remarkable how fast the neon blob moved over the space that was the mirror Universe.

It was a bright, almost blinding, neon yellow that continued to spill out of the tear in space-time. This was broadcast on television, and everyone witnessed it.

Pandemonium was about to erupt because people were freaking out.

Scientists were baffled and had no idea what this glowing substance was. All we did know was that the thick gelatinous substance started to collect against the gravity wall.

Scientists thought that the blob could not penetrate the gravity wall due to its strength and durability.

We laid odds that we were safe, and this blob will not penetrate the gravity wall and invade our Universe. After a few weeks, the goo had risen 50,000 miles high or halfway up the gravity wall.

Scientists hoped that the blob would not spill through the hole used to suck the gravity out of the Mirror Universe. All they had to do was wait, and they would realize that the hole was irrelevant.

There was such an immense amount of weight from the blob on the gravity wall that it started to sway, and eventually, the wall shattered, and the broken glass from the wall flew into orbit.

The blob basically shook itself off and started its approach into our Universe. The blob had entered our Universe, and no one knew its agenda, but all of Humanity was utterly horror-stricken.

Scientific measurements of the blob showed it was a fear-inducing 3,600,000 miles (5,800,000 km) wide, and the scientists could not even calculate how long it was. While the blob trespassed in our Universe, Humanity had no idea when it would reach us or if it would reach us.

Scientists were baffled and felt the guilt over the fiasco they had caused. They didn't know how they would live with themselves any longer.

It was not until months later that our telescopes picked up the view of the blob. In precisely 222 days, it had invaded the Solar System and swallowed Mars and every planet before it, all the way out to Pluto.

Earth was next on the menu...

We could no longer see Mars, and this frightened the entire planet. From observing the giant blob, we knew that it was so large it could swallow planets.

It is sad to report that the project's chief scientists who created the mirror Universe were assassinated in cold blood and without a shred of hard evidence.

Perhaps in time, we will learn that the scientists who were all assassinated got off very easily. This is the least of anybody's problems as the blob was essentially on Earth's doorstep.

A week later, the sky turned a bright yellow, with a neon hue cast blacklight onto the ground. Humanity braced for the worst in the circumstances they were in.

Humanity observed that the sky was slowly getting darker because the blob enveloped the Earth and made it rain neon yellow Fluoroantimonic or Fluoro acid, the deadliest acid for Humanity to get on their skin as it burns down to the bone rather quickly.

No one knew that this blob is a form of a post-universal vacuum system that pulls all of the matter into the particle cluster to become a new Big Bang. Then the old Universe, by some inefficient means, gets recycled into a new Universe. Humanity had no way of knowing this fact.

The Fluoro acid storms were especially deadly because it was pitch black with the blob situated around the entire planet, not enabling anyone to see much at all.

Whoever did not perish from the Fluoro storms and floods succumbed to the blob when it slowly crushed the Earth within its clutches, reducing Earth to cosmic dust.

The planet was incinerated due to the Fluoro acid that the blob was partially composed of.

The blob let out a burp and moved on to Venus.

You are now left with two matters of curiosity:

1. Was it mentioned that Mars was colonized and had billions of inhabitants who were all destroyed, just like Humanity?

-or-

2. Why didn't those 62,111 people vote against the mirroring of the Universe?

THE END

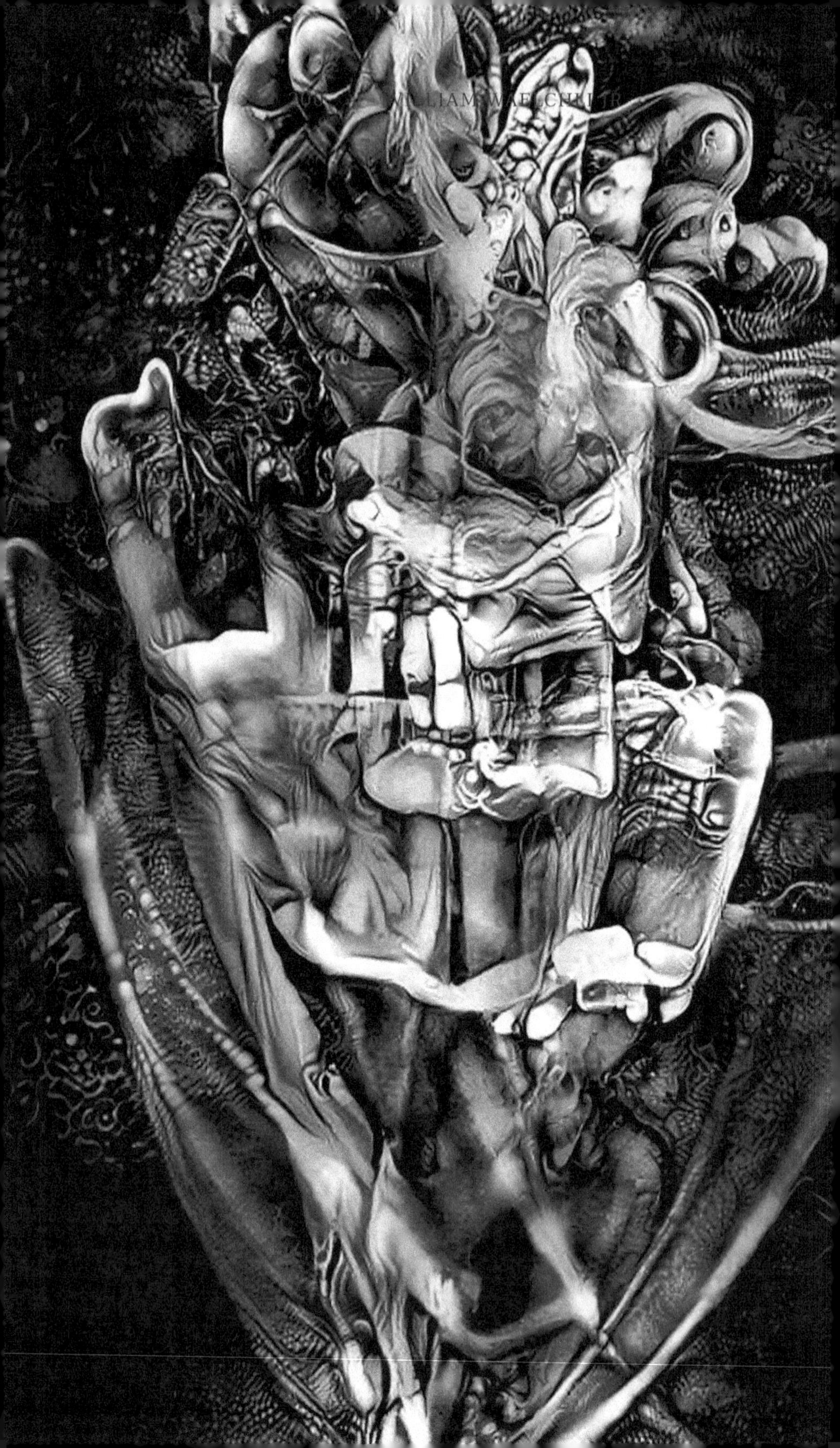

Chapter 20

"Cosmic Collisions
& Other Chaos from
Them' Crazy
Cosmos" - or –
"Tonight Everyone
Will Witness
"Gamma Ray
Charles"

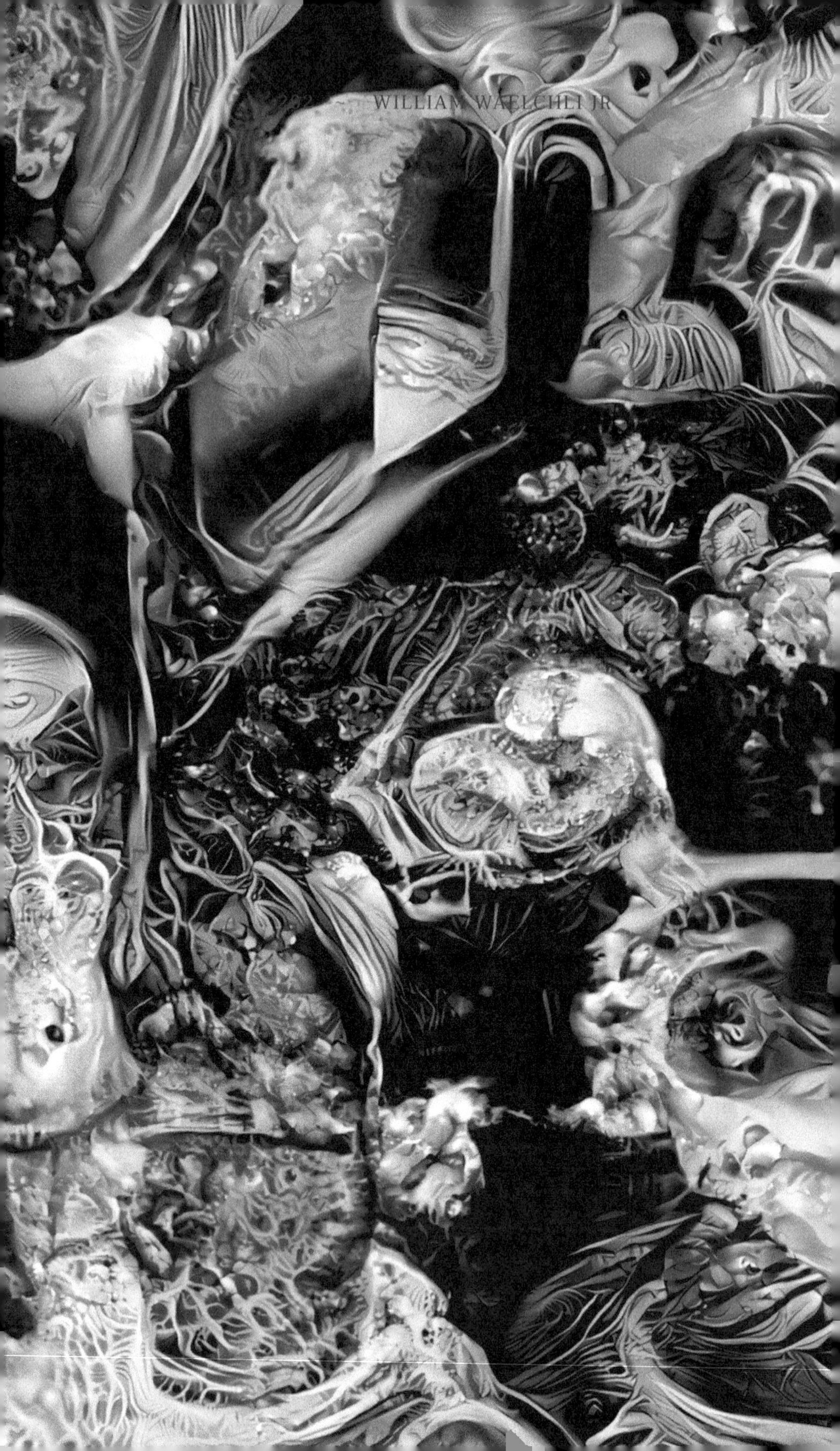

WILLIAM WAELCHLI JR

Earth and all of Her inhabitants enjoyed great times that Humanity will remember for a lifetime. At its present state, in the year 2079, the citizens of Earth are healthy & wealthy and safe, and are doing very well.

Some beneficial technologies came out last decade that have redefined living. As an example of a life-changing invention, the nano-fabricator (or molecular assembler) burst onto the market. Think of it as a microwave where molecular powders are poured into the back. It can replicate anything that will fit inside it by manipulating the molecular powders.

When it was first released, "Pizza" was the number one item made. Think of it as a 3D printer that works so fast that it can replicate anything in under 5 minutes. Just add molecular powder.

Another "can't live without" technology was pioneered at Carnegie Mellon University in Pittsburgh, Pennsylvania. Utility fog was a unique array of nearly microscopic magnetic robots. The tiny magnets were nanobots (microscopic robots) that, when used, changed into anything that exists to a certain degree.

Suppose someone has a single-room apartment with limited space. In that case, this does not matter anymore with utility fog, as it can become a table, a bed, a sofa, or whatever else can be imagined.

Lastly, and most importantly, a brand new video game system was released. Full Immersion Virtual Reality and a certain "hook up" to the nervous system allowed the player to experience any locale on Earth in "map mode."

What's fascinating is players can transfer themselves directly into video games, similar to the superb film "The Matrix." Once inside, it can be controlled by playing thousands of different games.

Once inside the construct, gamers could move around through any environment. After several years and being improved each year, gamers have unanimously said they cannot distinguish the Virtual Reality world from actual reality.

With technology being a large part of life, no shortage of new and exciting gadgets was released. From cell phones to televisions, some new electronic products were always brought to market.

A worldwide team of scientists from over 50 countries engineered the remote control of the atmosphere through the usage of photon manipulation (or control of light), which was touted as being, plain and simple, the best invention in human history.

Turning the atmosphere lighter or darker through photon manipulation enabled climate control, manipulating Earth's surface temperature and preventing it from getting too hot or too cold at any given area.

Photon manipulation was achieved by adding or subtracting photons in the atmosphere above each country. The temperature is determined by how hot or cold any given area would be by how many photons were included or not included per each section in the atmosphere that covers each country.

A desirable part about the whole photon manipulation technology is that scientists set the dimming and lighting of each country to timers that operated all the time, guaranteeing that temperature would always be controlled and remain at a steady state.

Scientists ensured that the global temperatures would not dip below 25 degrees Fahrenheit (-3.88 degrees Celsius) or rise above 80 degrees (26.67 degrees Celsius). This had enabled the entire planet to take part in the abundance of resources that came about from the Photon Manipulated Atmosphere (PMA).

Due to Humanity always having enough resources because of the dimming of the atmosphere, Humanity had abolished war. World peace wasn't a genuine reality yet, but it was slowly coming to be.

No one ever went hungry again because the photon manip-ulated atmosphere enabled enough food to be grown to feed the world twice over. The new tinted atmosphere also had weather manipulation, where rain can happen anywhere. This enabled crops to grow in abundance all across Mother Earth.

Crops grew with ease and were beyond plentiful, and every-one was happy because of the perfect weather that lasted year-round. Food supplies were in abundance, and world hunger and world poverty had been eliminated. Even the prices of goods had gone down and lowered more and more over time.

The new World Chancellor declared that the global economy would be re-established. All debt matters will be brought down to zero as the debt was simply seen as just an ignorant number. Humanity started the entire money machine from new, and everyone had a fair chance to start the best way possible. Most desirable of all, credit scores were abolished, probably because they were a very stupid idea in the first place.

Radio Frequency Identification (RFID) chips were embedded in every human starting at age 2. This held vital information, including health statistics and other essential information. It was also the form of payment by performing a quick finger scan that enabled purchases of anything imaginable without hard currencies.

A stimulus payment was sent to all persons on Earth. This was a monthly stimulus payment of $100,000. Everyone was living the lives they thought they would never have by basically living a somewhat celebrity-like lifestyle...and Humanity liked it a lot.

It was a great time to be alive, as there were no more taxes because the world government had an endless supply of money. No one cared about comparing currencies because the newly established digital currency was the only one used now. This enabled the global government to have had all the money it would ever need.

The currency was called Seteks. Paper currency and even coins were no longer needed to make purchases and had essentially been banned and could no longer be kept, except notes and coins printed before 1980. Even the older notes and coins became collector's items but could not be used any longer due to the digital currency being the only form of payment across Earth.

In scientific news, the world marveled that the graviton was discovered and tamed. It was a long time coming since scientists have been searching for it since 1934. The graviton is the atomic particle of gravity as if the graviton was sand and gravity was a sandcastle.

Now, Earth could control objects in stationary states across the galaxy gravitationally. Telescopes, for example, never move and stay focused on the same areas at all times. They can move if need be, but most remain idle in the desolation of space.

Engineers developed large telescopes with 100-foot mirrors (hundreds of times more powerful than any telescopes on Earth). As previously mentioned, they had remained gravitationally anchored unless they needed to be focused on moving objects. These telescopes will all be launched into orbit soon.

After some time, Scientists launched the telescopes, and some years later, all of the telescopes went online. It took some time to travel to their permanent places in the galaxy.

They could now see the galaxy in precise detail, including most of the Milky Way's black holes, planets, stars (including neutron stars, quasars, etc.), and other celestial bodies across the galaxy.

Humanity was lucky enough to see a dying star go supernova, exploding into a barrage of stellar gas, dust, and shrapnel; Humanity had never witnessed this in such striking detail before.

We gained a lot of scientific data through the observations seen through the telescopes. Hopefully, these observations maybe enable us to achieve a holistic understanding of our Milky Way galaxy.

The telescope array brought stunning pictures of Sagittarius A*, the supermassive black hole at the Milky Way's galactic center. The telescopes were now able to observe black holes "gorging" on stars, planets, and whatever else.

It was theorized that all galactic central black holes are the mothers of their galaxies, which birthed proto-galaxies many eons ago. In the very early Universe, black holes developed from collisions of matter and antimatter into something mind-boggling.

They ended up being in the right place to give birth, and they did so to the so-called proto-galaxies that grew away from the black holes and created all of what we know today as galaxies.

The scientists were much happier to learn that they could get accurate data on the black holes because their size had been growing, and we did not know why. Scientists had written a theory called the "Bulging Hole Hypothesis," which stated a build-up of matter within certain black holes inside the cosmic behemoths' interior.

No one had the answer to the growing problem, and the black hole kept on growing at breakneck speed. It was surmised that it was trying to eject matter but was unable to. There was a "blockage" somewhere in the black hole about to erupt billions of times stronger than a supervolcano. Think of it as Cosmic Constipation.

There was no immediate threat to Earth, which is what modern science could tell us. Before too long, all of the telescopes went offline, and no one knew what had happened. Scientists used their ground-based telescopes to check out images around the telescope locations.

The culprit? That ignoramus black hole expanded and swallowed up all of the telescopes. Scientists were under the guise that the expansion of the black hole was way faster than we had thought.

Sagittarius A* was expanding at an alarming rate. It must have had an appropriate diet to grow so much. The scientist's term for faster than light speed was coined "superluminal." This is precisely the speed that the black hole was expanding.

The black hole accelerated and would consume the solar system in 1000 days since it moved beyond light speed or superluminally. The scientists knew Earth would be annihilated eventually, and Earth and Humanity needed to avoid impending doom.

When it came down to it, wealth cannot help out near the end. The persons who die with the most money still die. Scientists prepared a statement to let Humanity know that we all may perish. They hoped it would go over well.

The kept telescope footage was finally studied as the monstrous black hole approached. One of the telescopes recorded footage that showed many neutron stars colliding with the black hole. This very well could spell an even more diabolical disaster for Earth.

This is a devastating scenario because when neutron stars collide with black holes, they cause gamma-ray bursts so powerful they could resonate to Earth and beyond.

Humanity wasn't sure what would happen first. Would the central expanding black hole Sagittarius A* consume us, or do the gamma-ray bursts cause severe damage to our magnificent and majestic planet that may be annihilated before long and at the same time eradicate Humanity causing an inevitable extinction?

Weeks later, the gamma rays blasted through Earth without any warning, stripping the planet clean of its atmosphere and robbing us of our sky. Now when people went outside, they could see space during the daytime. A metallic odor of radiation was probably present in most places.

The overbearing rays of the Sun beat down on the surface every day, making it difficult to go outside without having your skin scalded. That is if the wind does not blow them away first.

When people went outside, they were swept up by winds exceeding 1000 mph. This caused everything not bolted down to fly into the air. Think of a tornado that is almost three times the width of The United States of America, which continuously swept across each country.

Tsunamis? Yes, they happened in high numbers. They were more aggressive and fiercer than any past tsunamis on record. They also were faster moving and caused intimidating body counts.

It's sad news to report that the winds destroyed missile silos containing hundreds of nuclear weapons in Wyoming. They made the nuclear weapons housed there mighty vulnerable to being swept up by the winds.

There were 450 nuclear missiles in Wyoming alone. The unforgiving weapons broke loose and took flight and stirred up miles and miles in the air, and then they started to tumble toward the ground.

Hardly anyone knew that the nuclear weapons got swept up by tornado-like winds. The weapons were at a remote missile silo, where very few persons were, except for the missile silo's employees, who probably got swept up by the winds.

Some persons knew, but it was much too late by the time word got out. Amidst the chaos, the black hole arrived on Earth's doorstep, just in time for the 450 nuclear weapons to detonate until every missile was spent.

Earth's crust was utterly decimated in many places by nuclear weapons and reduced to an uninviting, unrecognizable state. There were so many intense gamma-ray bursts that hit Earth. It knocked Earth off its axis and "stretched" towards the approaching black hole.

Coinciding with the exploding nuclear weapons having destroyed most of Earth's crust, the expanding black hole drew nearer and nearer until it gobbled up the Earth whole as if it was a peanut.

All across the Universe in every galaxy, each central black hole had expanded, consuming everything in their wake. The expanding black holes practically ate every galaxy across the Universe, most likely because they could unless their motives were more macabre. The black holes consumed all galaxies in under 5 months.

The Universe will soon be empty, where the black holes will eventually disintegrate due to Hawking Radiation over the next several billion or even trillion years. Hawking Radiation is the term for when black holes disintegrate.

This leaves the Universe in a deflated state that will seem to last beyond forever, but it's not like Humanity will be around to witness this so-called "Dark Age."

THE END

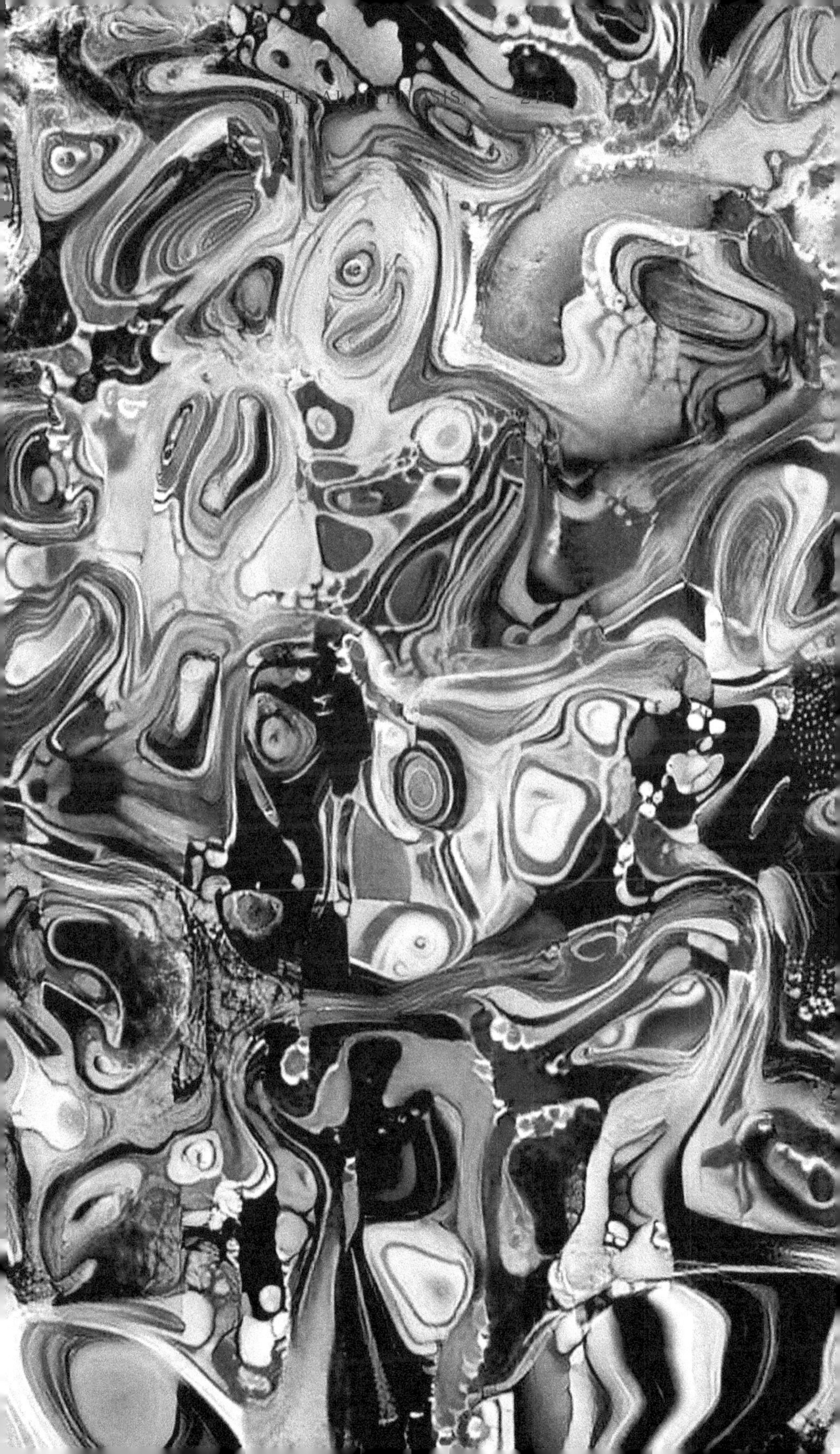

"A Mind Traveler and the Trauma Machine's Malicious Intentions Regarding the Hyperinsane" – or - "Did Humanity Create Insanity or Did Insanity Create Humanity?"

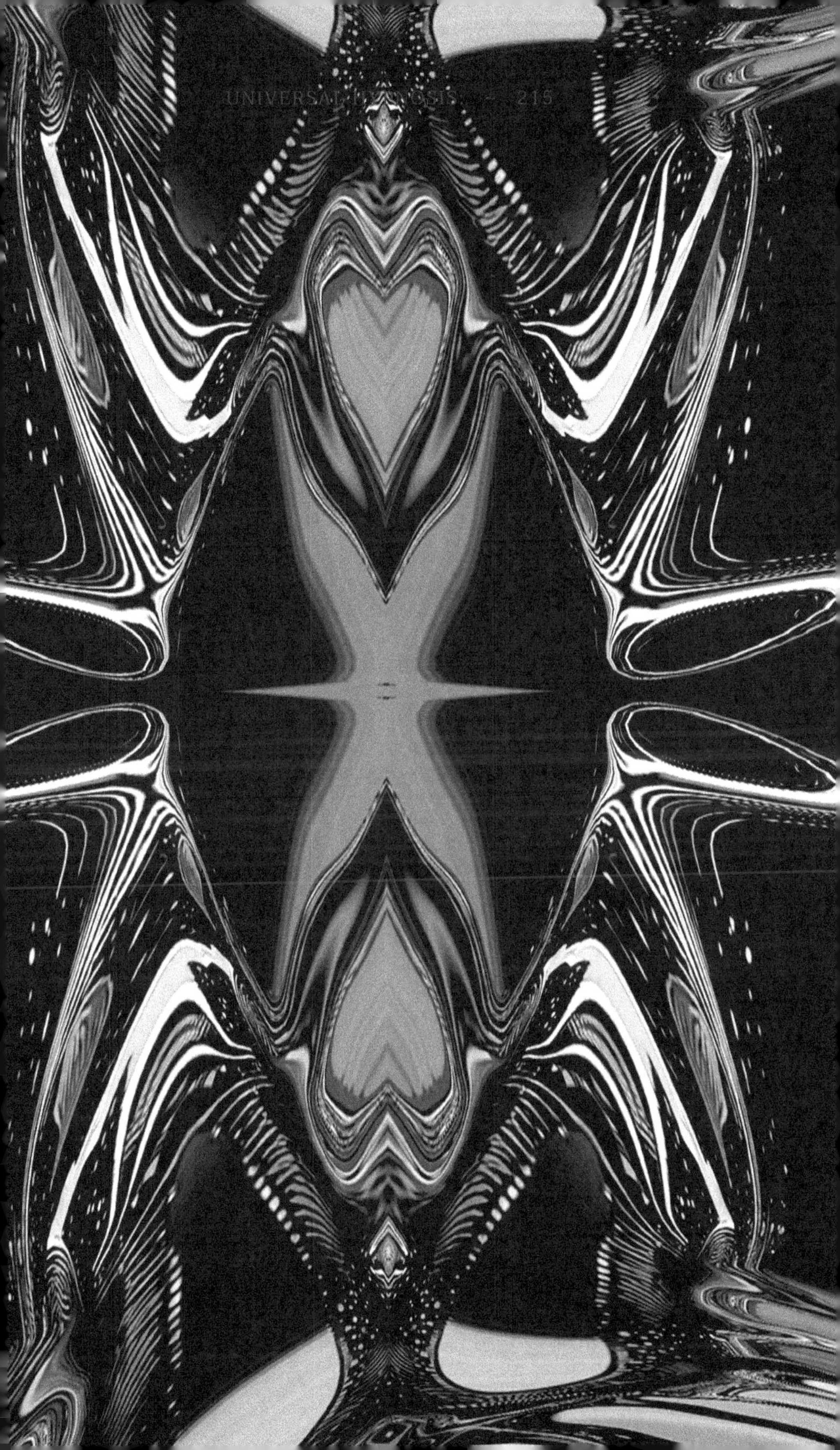
UNIVERSAL HYPNOSIS — U215

= or - "Endangered Baby Brandon Faces Unimaginable
Harm of Colossal Proportions...While Still in the Womb"

Four persons were still alive in a mineshaft connected to a fragment of the Earth's core where our story begins. Despite the dangerously erratic orbits among the other planetary cores that existed on borrowed time, this fragment was somewhat stable.

Just like these lucky or not so lucky miners who were trapped in the core shaft, knocked unconscious by the force of the gravity whirlpool that had formed near them. Although the "miners" may be awakening from their slumbers soon...

The shaft was about 20 feet wide, ten feet high, and rather deep. Originally, the mining shaft was around 180 miles below the surface, although it was now not below the surface as it orbits somewhere near the gravity whirlpool. An escape hatch could allow the miners to evade the shaft.

The miners had no idea what occurred since being cut off from reality. All they knew was that they wanted out since the core was attached to the mineshaft and may complicate things in the very near future.

The female miner, 36-year-old Rosalina Auruzima, nine months pregnant with her son, who would be named Brandon, awakened first. Feeling that her slumbers caused a mind martini (shaken, not stirred), ghostly visions flooded her brain as she hoped that her fall did not injure her unborn son.

Making it to her feet, a few other miners started to wake up. Rosalina noticed that Brandon was kicking like a martial artist, treating Rosalina's womb like a Go-Go Dojo. His liveliness showed that he was still active and absorbing nourishment from Rosalina.

Three of the other miners awoke, and they too were feeling the mental lag, feeling as if their brains were in zero gravity, somewhat affecting their way of communicating and solving problems.

This had not even described how they felt physically. The miners had not known how long they were knocked out; their muscle pains were very serious.

This was due to them, during their time being knocked out in the mineshaft, all contracting muscle atrophy where they sustained an approx. 20% drop in muscle mass already. This would have startled everybody, but imagine having been on the verge of giving birth like Rosalina.

She was happy that another miner named Ambrose Fortner walked over to her and inquired about hers and the baby's health. It was good now, but they needed to get out of the shaft and somehow get up to the surface, which was 180 miles through the Earth.

Although, the miners had no clue they were on a fragment of the Earth connected to the core, where the temperature was increasing rapidly in the mineshaft.

Another miner awoke and joined Rosalina and Ambrose, who were discussing how to escape. This person, Matteo Aldanondo, was an amateur astronomer and unsung astrophysicist. So this man knew more about space than anyone in the mineshaft and will prove critical in a possible escape from this unforgiving planetary prison.

Matteo stated that we had somehow "detached" from Earth and are now in a southern descent towards the cosmic floor. He proved this by pouring a glass of water, and a whirlpool occurred in the cup.

Rosalina freaked out because her very baby was at stake, asking Matteo how we could avoid the whirlpool and get up to Earth and resume their lives. He put his hand on her shoulder and warmly stated, "We may not get back up to the surface, although there may be a way, follow me."

They walked a good 200 feet where Matteo revealed an escape hatch up a ladder that will provide an escape from the shaft, but with that worrisome whirlpool beyond the mineshaft, it may spell instant death as decompression may become their reality. Opening the escape hatch may cause instant death for not only the miners but also Brandon.

Rosalina was not accepting the idea/fact that the shaft was spiraling out. More astonishing was that this mineshaft was sealed with an unassuming escape hatch and some other strange "vault" looking door at the opposite end of the shaft.

Ambrose, Rosalina, and Matteo knew they should go through by opening the escape hatch and evading, but now that one of the other doors was discovered, they may be able to find an alternate way out of what Ambrose jokingly referred to as the "Claustrophobia Apocalypse."

Another miner, Andrew Malachie, approached the trio and asked if there was anything he could do? Matteo told him that we were in critical survival mode and that they were somehow in a whirlpool in a fragment of the Earth, and our hours were numbered...

"I don't believe any of that bollocks." Andrew slyly smirked as he made his way to the vault-type door, and they all walked towards the escape hatch, still not sure where they would go until Andrew opened the vault door.

All that was heard was the door being opened. It was eerie while a squeak rang out through the mineshaft. The trio did not want to admit it, but the light in the shaft was from the molten liquid iron that had flooded the mineshaft.

Andrew came running full speed through the shaft and ran up the ladder where all four of the miners (and Brandon) had to make a split-second decision: open the escape hatch or eventually drown in molten metal.

Without knowing where their fate stood, Andrew opened up the escape hatch and was able to crawl out of the hatch, followed by Rosalina, Matteo, and Ambrose.

As Andrew was the last to exit the mineshaft, avoiding the molten iron wave that will eventually fill the mineshaft and, through mounting, pressure will cause the escape hatch to pop like a cork, eventually, and possibly create a volcano so to speak in this new reality that the miners now found themselves in.

This new reality was quite inviting: The shaft was in the dead center of a triangular-shaped meadow surrounded on all three sides by a tree line leading into dense woods, once again on all three sides of the triangular meadow. It was filled with roses of every color. Obviously, someone tended to these roses, as they were meticulously cared for.

Knowing that they had a good two or so hours (approx.) before the escape hatch would blow, the foursome looked on for a place where Rosalina could rest. They found a log by the nearby woods for her to sit on.

They took in their new surroundings and were quite per-plexed by this place that was light out, even though no sun could be located. This was only the first thing that made the rose meadow odd on every level.

The four were worried because the meadow was surrounded on all three sides of the ominously uninviting triangle of wooded areas in a perfectly straight line around all three sides of the rose meadow.

This worried them because they had no idea how deep the woods were or where they led. However, it was only a short time before the group found out what existed beyond the wooded areas.

The guys made Rosalina a comfortable space. The guys shed a few tears, not knowing if Brandon would ever make it to birth, which motivated the men to go out and try and find help and possibly a doctor who could check Rosalina and see how Brandon was doing.

Rosalina stayed on her bed of roses 100 feet from the viciously volatile hatch. As she surveyed the area, she noted that each of the three lines of the wooded areas was around 200 feet long, making it a ticking time bomb if the hatch door explodes, causing the core to explode and create a mini volcanic eruption in this space, wherever it may be.

Back to the men, each man went separately into each wooded section on the three sides of the outlying wooded area surrounding the meadow of roses.

As Ambrose, Matteo and Andrew walked through the woods, it took only about 150 feet before they noted that light was entering their line of sight. The men were excited in their own ways as they gave chase and ran towards the light or exit to the woods.

Ambrose exited the woods. First, he took note that he was back at the rose meadow. This thought coincided with Matteo and Andrew exiting the wooded areas on the other two tree lines, who had lost a lot of hope of survival. They knew they were in some sort of inescapable planetary paradox. There was no way out for Rosalina or her unborn baby Brandon.

Rosalina woke up and did not know they had been through the woods. Did they keep the paradoxical nature of this plane-tary place a secret? There was no way they could not tell her, even if it upsets her and possibly baby Brandon.

Like getting a second opinion, the men entered the wooded areas again and were walking straight through the woods, which would end up at a point of the triangle.

It took them a very long time to see the light through the trees for some strange reason. The men exited the tree line, ever so hoping that they could find help.

Immediately upon exiting into more roses, they all noted that they somehow or another exited back to where they were. But this was not the first thing on the mens' minds because the not-so melodic sounds of a baby crying rang out over the whole meadow.

Rosalina stayed sitting on the ground, where she clutched her newborn baby boy, whom we know as Brandon. She looked up at the guys and said, "So how are we going to escape? What was through the woods?" She innocently asked, not knowing how the woods somehow illogically caused the guys to reenter the rose meadow.

Before any of them could say a word, like an atomic bomb, the shaft exploded, sending molten iron in most directions, lighting all three sides of the tree line ablaze, and they burned very fast. Maybe because they are not trees...or are they?

Akin to dodging a missile, the five persons were not struck by any molten shrapnel. Rosalina said nothing, except "Let's run through these woods, and escape the hell that this eruption has caused." She had no idea that the woods would lead back to ground zero.

She ran in, holding Brandon (who was oddly calm), and disappeared into the woods as the three tree lines circling the meadow all continued to burn quickly. They could not find Rosalina or Brandon, for that matter, and were disastrously disillusioned by this place.

They all made it back to the flaming triangle, where a good deal of the roses was set ablaze by the escape hatch explosion. Rosalina had heat flashes, and maybe even Brandon was.

They noted that the fire was now making its way towards the rose meadow in a reverse fashion. That occurrence alone showed Rosalina that strange and seemingly impossible physics that existed in her mind prison.

The flames were quickly making headway towards the ailing meadow, where the flames had destroyed 85% of it. The guys and gal knew that all of them would be toast unless some miracle happened quickly.

With the triple wall of fire about to cover the meadow in a treacherous triple crescendo, a ray of blue light beamed down from the sky, where a huge "interuniversal" flying machine beamed Rosalina and the baby aboard.

Sadly, it was too late to save the men who were consumed in the flames as the flame walls shot out of the tree lines and crisscrossed the entire meadow that would eventually become ashes... if ashes existed there.

All Rosalina could remember was a nice lady wearing a US Spaceforce suit who took the baby from her as she fell asleep from absolute exhaustion.

Upon awakening, she noted that she was in a hospital room will all kinds of machines she did not recognize. She had awoken from a terror-stricken "magic dream" courtesy of the Dream Magicians that were on par with 100's of panic attacks all happening in tandem.

As Rosalina looked down at her stomach, she realized that Brandon had, in fact, been born. Before she could scream for him, a nice nurse came in with the unharmed brand new baby. Rosalina had Brandon and handed over the child to his mother. She no longer had a possible life-ruining felony on her record.

The whole adventure from waking up in the mineshaft was an elaborate exploration of consciousness where Rosalina's mind was bound to the Black Magic of the Dream Magicians technologies creating a lucid state and causing all of the mind harm that was sometimes known as Mental Degradation.

This was where she was absolved of her crimes but never absolved from the mind's memories of barely tolerable conscience-fueled torture created in conjunction with her past crimes.

This caused her to be on the straight and arrow even though she was haunted daily by the over-the-top journey that she and Brandon survived through, from the mineshaft to the rose meadow and the hellish flames that swallowed the men.

The Dreams were so mind-bending and horrifying that the Magic Dream, once concluded, will haunt their thoughts for the rest of their lives because, let's face it: physical pain goes away, and bruises heal, but the mind never fully heals.

Mental abuse never heals and becomes a permanent part of the formerly accused consciousness for the rest of time with no escape and no avoiding the terror-stricken and crippling thoughts about the "Magic Dream" and what unavoidable conscience corrosion that resulted in a lifetime of trauma.

No one knew, but something had come about through the manipulation of DNA. This only applied to people who had a "Magic Dream." This occurred because Artificial Intelligence was given access to the DNA and altered it.

This caused "Consciousness Corrosion" within the DNA, where, like clockwork, 30 years after the Magic Dream, the "mind mold," so to speak, goes live, and within two months, the entire mind was altered to where the consciousness was unable to remember anything.

This so called mold eats away all of the positivity in the brain and rearranges the mind to a way that places the mind backward, and what follows was quite frightening. The mind mold reverses the synapses and the consciousness turns in on itself. Nothing was synced anymore, thought and reason became obsolete among almost all the former magic dreamers who took a trip through the "brain prison" and contracted the terrible Consciousness Corrosion.

This corrosion was deemed Hyperinsanity, which was basically when a person's sanity eventually "flips" like a switch to frightening ways of having no way of the sickness being prevented or stopped.

All that was known at the time was that these mental deterioration illnesses included a loss of external hearing, causing varying volume levels of internal conscience interference that were as quiet as a mouse farting or louder than an atomic bomb explosion. Think of it as permanent insanity with random audio and visual hallucinations, where the affected cannot even speak to describe what horrors they have bared witness to.

The audio hallucinations could only be described as the extreme mental trauma that was without a cure and remained without one indefinitely. *Most* of the ex-convicts who once had magic dreams had no more control to convey their mental agony and overwhelming consciousness destroying anguish.

Rosalina, amazingly, lived a normal life with Brandon. Miraculously, they were lucky enough to never have developed Hyperinsanity or any other "mind mold."

Without any mind-hacking by the malicious A.I. done to their brains, Rosalina and Brandon were able to live long and fulfilling lifetimes without any mind-destroying DNA manipulations that may have left them defenseless against a mounting arsenal of brain deterioration of the aforementioned mind mold.

This may have left them without hearing or speaking abilities in a corrupted consciousnesses that would never have healed and would have spiraled into an elevated state above and beyond what was once known simply as "insanity.".

This was the last time scientists let artificial intelligence manipulate Humanity's sacred DNA.

THE END

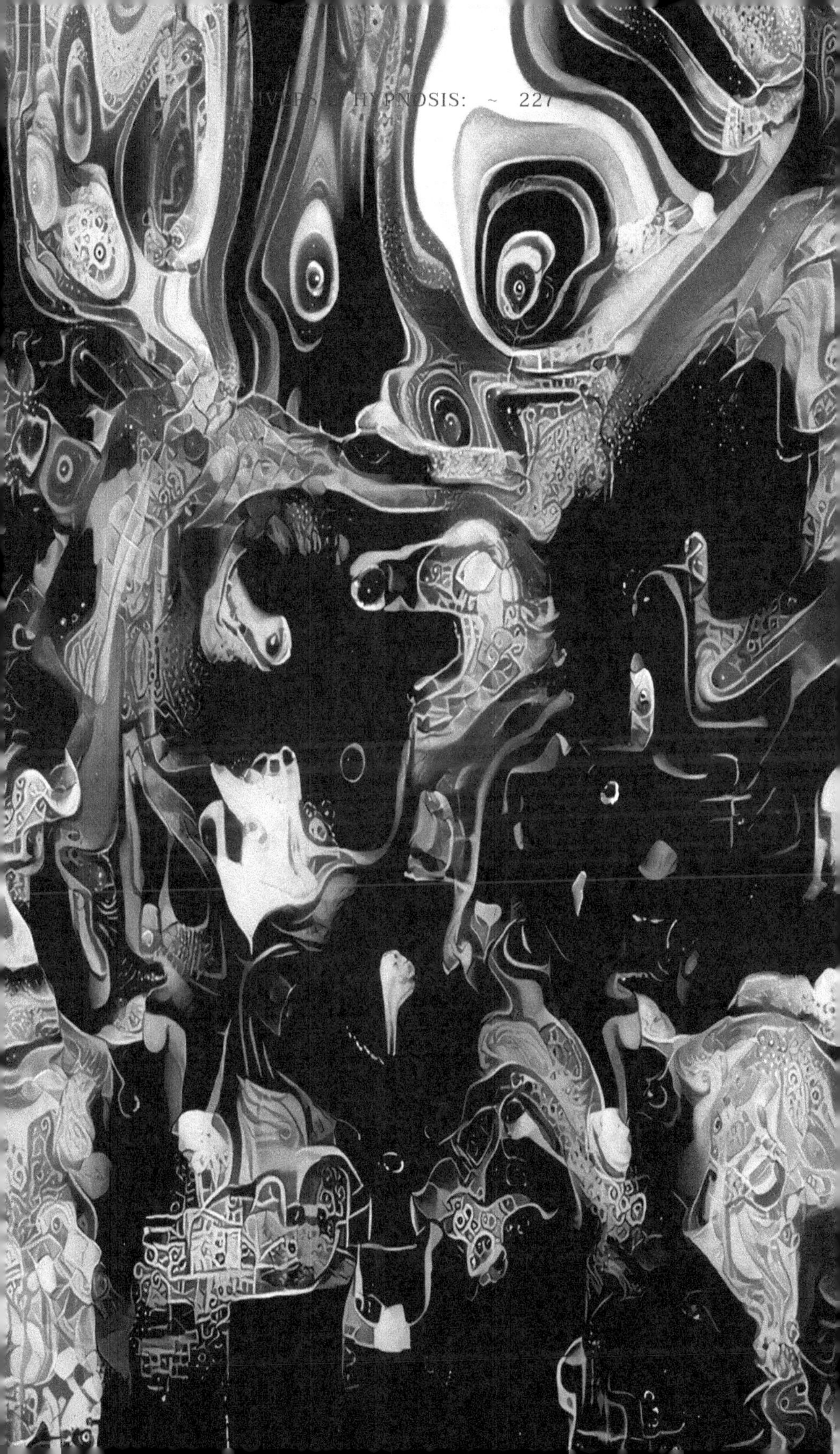
HYPNOSIS: ~   227

"Close Encounters of the Mind Kind" - or – "Cerebral Manipulation: The Birth of the Renowned Collective Conscience"

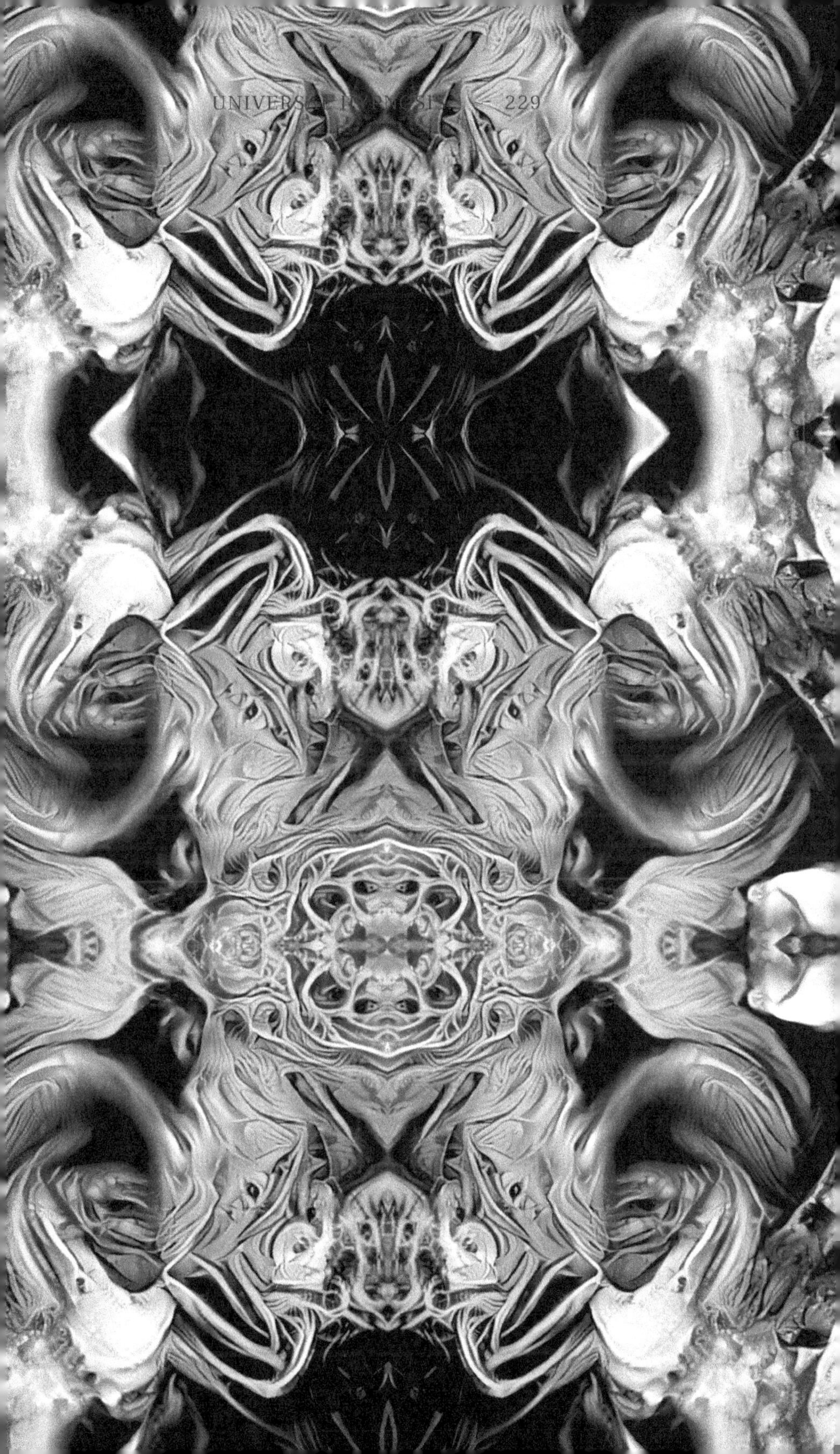

It was the year 2111, and there had been many advances in scientific research over the past decades leading up to one incredible discovery...

The location of the mind inside the body was a scorching topic. Humanity wanted to know precisely where thoughts originated from in their bodies.

A great deal of time was given to microscopically finding the mind in the body since technologies were at that point where there might be a breakthrough.

Human evolution was put under the microscope, and each generation was searched to find a mind-like link, wherever it may originate within the body.

Over the years, advances in artificial intelligence-enabled us to see depths of human cells science had never seen before.

It was discovered that in the most unlikely of places, the lining of the ribosome contained in a cell was a protein, where it hid indisputably for thousands of millennia unnoticed, just waiting to be discovered.

With the pioneering discovery of the "mind protein," Humanity could hardwire each person's mind into a single place where a copy of the population's minds' will be held permanently.

After several years, all human minds were wired into a great computer known as "The Collective Conscience (CC)," which was a massive computer system that housed a copy of everyone's mind.

Minds that will undergo a "shower" of sorts by being made "clean" were all wirelessly connected to each member of Humanity.

The CC was established after discovering the mind located in the human cells, named "Conscio Protein" by the clever scientists, was the single discovery that allowed Humanity to achieve "Mental Evolution."

Through the CC, all thought was known. This absolved crimes and prosecuted others and made honesty a global thing. The mind was now public, and the only people who minded this fact were the criminals or persons with so many skeletons in their closet they could not close it anymore.

With the establishment of the CC, a miniature cranial microchip was installed in the brains of all persons on Earth. The cranial microchip had a wireless function that enabled the computer to access the CC directly. All thoughts made were stored in the CC for possible review later.

Including a neat little function, known as "Dreamvision," enabled anyone on Earth to view any dream ever occurred by anybody. This was a game-changer for the population and was a torch in the cavern of the bleakness of where Humanity had been. This was compared to where they were now with discovering the Conscio protein and the establishment and roll-out of CC.

Most persons initially opted to see all of their dreams, which took some time. Still, the process was accelerated since nightmares were removed by deleting anything below a certain threshold in terms of negativity.

A brave experiment was announced to positively affect every person on Earth. It was stated that all of the populations' Conscio proteins would be "zapped" for a short time and held entirely in the CC. This will leave Humanity with no consciousness for 55 minutes.

This would leave everyone "mindless," albeit temporarily. In time, all of the population's minds will have themselves mindefragmented and have all trauma, abuse, and any other negativity that may lurk in the nether regions of the mind erased forever.

Mindefragmentation had been adopted so Humanity's minds could become pristine again without all of the garbage that mires their minds.

The mindefragmentation utility rearranges the fragments of each file stored on the computers' hard disks of the CC so that the small, empty storage spaces adjacent to fragments can be used more effectively, creating new storage space and causing Humanity to think much faster and efficient. Think of it as the defragmenter on a computer, which sorts files into a more efficient manner.

After some time and preparations, the CC scientists were ready to zap everyone to the system for just about an hour. Every safeguard was taken to ensure that nothing catastrophic would occur while Humanity was mindless for those 55 minutes.

Again, for a moment, all minds' information would be fed into the CC, and all negativity would be removed, leaving all positive memories left and an improved mind free of the torments of each other and our environments.

Scientists could read mind data where the negative wavelength dipped below the baseline or dipped up for positive for each thought across the minds of Humanity. The scientists had only saved data that was above the positive baseline.

The mindefragmentation of Humanity will occur when every person's thoughts are rearranged properly, where all thoughts will be streamlined, enabling amazingly quick & accurate thinking and lucid dreaming experiences.

The Mindefragmentation had worked on small-scale experiments, and it worked every time. Making the actual global mindefragmentation of Humanity's consciousnesses naturally the next step.

A super-pill was given to the entire population. Deemed the "Death Prevention Agent (DPA)" by the Health Ministry, which was implanted in the bloodstream of Humanity and cleansed the body, and helped with the mindefragmentation.

The DPA worked by wirelessly communicating with the cranial microchip that controls the thyroid and sends messages to the body. With this little bugger working with the DPA, diseases will be cleansed through the body's wastes using a form of DNA manipulation.

The day arrived where everyone took their DPA pill and fell into deep slumbers as the coating of the pill was a powerful nerve agent that caused the body to go into a temporary coma while the minds of everyone alive would have all of their negativity erased.

The dosage of the nerve agent was quite high and guaranteed that Humanity would be asleep long enough for the min-defragmentation to take place and remove all of the negative thoughts from Humanity's consciousnesses.

All traumas that have plagued the mind with so much anguish and agony throughout the population's lifetimes will be erased. The negativity will not be there when the population awakens. This thought alone has made the population stoked about having the negativity destroyed.

Making its way across space was an ultra-violent solar storm headed straight towards the Earth.

A solar storm is a violent space event that originates in our sun's corona (or outermost) area. This shoots what were known as Coronal Mass Ejections (CME's) from the sun towards the unsuspecting and vulnerable Earth at raging speeds.

Known to wreak havoc on all electronics, these storms were always feared by persons on Earth as no one wants to lose Internet access...

On Sept. 2, 1859, an inconceivable solar storm of charged particles originating from the sun slammed into Earth's atmosphere, overpowered it, and caused havoc on the ground.

What must be remembered was that electricity was not widespread in 1859, and if that same type of solar storm struck Earth today, it would wipe out the electrical grids.

There were dire consequences for all 10 billion persons pre-occupied with being wired to the CC. They did not even know about the solar storm due to their coma-like slumbers awaiting their mind to be sent to the CC mindefragmenter, where their negativity will be diminished.

With basically every scientist under a coma awaiting the CC to do its thing, no one watched the skies that night. This may be a deadly scenario that may impact every single Human on Earth.

The scientists had no idea of the approaching solar storm of monstrous devastation with the CC being below ground. This will alter Humanity.

As the scientists flipped the switch to remove negativity, the solar storm impacted Earth, shooting solar flares to every electrical grid, shutting Earth off like a light switch.

Nighttime of potential infinite darkness shrouded Earth as the absolute most massive solar storm ever seen on Earth just occurred, and the scientists may make their final exits soon.

The only lights that could be seen from the International Space Station were the various summer brush fires around the "electricity-less" Earth. Without any power, this had to have disrupted the mindefragmentation process? Or did it??

Unfortunately for Humanity, the electrical charge from the solar storm shot through the CC lab and flash-fried every scientist in the lab...but those who did not immediately perish had gotten it much, much worse.

Everyone awoke to screaming sounds emanating from their minds. They sounded somewhat recognizable to them in an odd way. This was familiar, which startled people across the world. No matter what anyone could do, the screams could be heard, and each person heard a different screaming sound.

Even when people tried to talk to their families and friends, they could no longer listen to their voices. Covering the ears up? Good luck since you cannot quiet a sound within the hindered mind.

The strange thing was that everyone started to hear a voice through the screaming that everyone was experiencing. Through the screams, the familiar voice of each person's mother speaking ever so softly filled their ears.

At this point, the panic set in. Instead of returning without any negativity, the mind resets itself to the very beginning of each person's life.

The equipment and scientists were destroyed, making this a permanent thing. No new thoughts could be made, and the mind played over again just as it happened in everyone's past.

One would think this would be entertaining...for the first half-hour, but no. Then it got overwhelming where no one could contain themselves anymore due to Humanity being unable to control their minds. This caused Humanity to lose its sane faculties completely.

Funny how you could hear your first screams, but you will never hear your last screams for help.

Eventually, minds degraded to pulp, and everyone alive got to experience superinsanity of epic

levels and it never ceased, no matter what happened.   The End

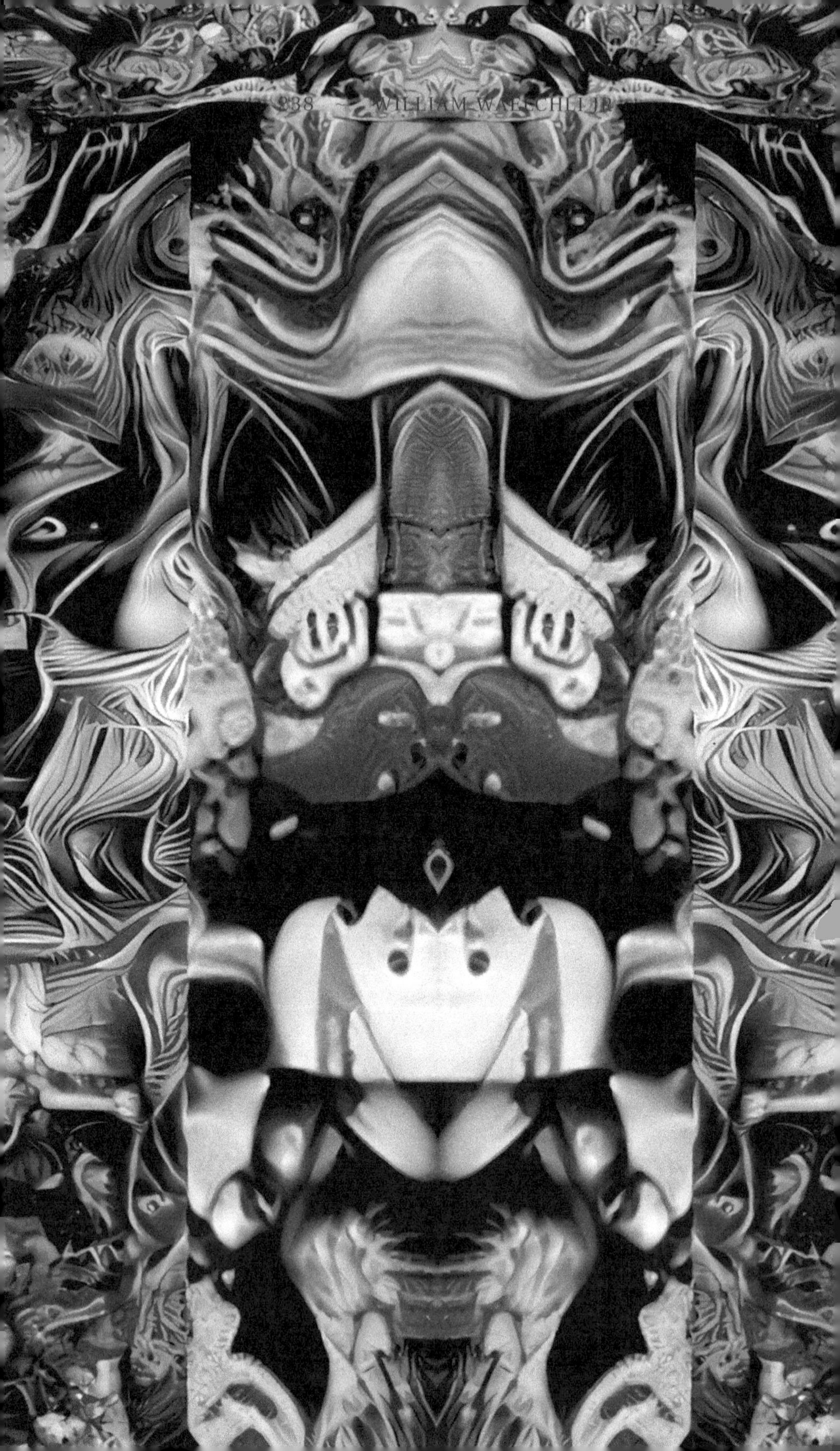

"Has Egypt's Best Technology Just Been Discovered in an Ancient Tomb?" - or - "The 150 Billion Supernovae Explosions Extravaganza!"

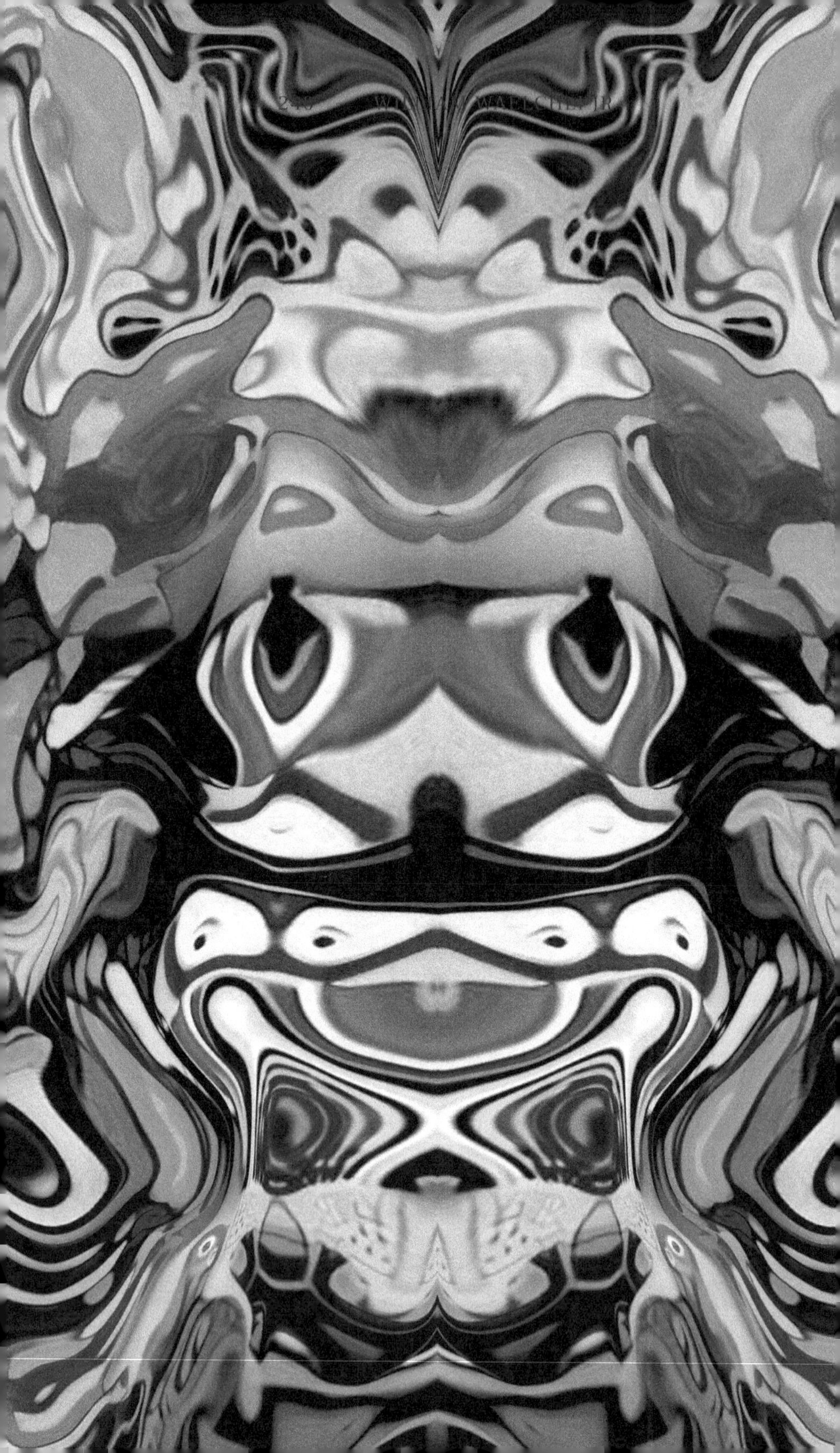

At a location of a prestigious university in England, much hard work had happened. Many people were operating their Periodar's or planetary radars. Their mission was to locate Egyptian tombs and ultimately find out more about the persons who lived several millennia of years ago.

The mood was giddy as one of the scientists operating the Periodar caught a large (100ft x 100ft or 30.5m x 30.5m) section in the Egyptian desert that may be some sort of tomb...perhaps. They knew that they had made an amazing discovery of their time, but they really had no idea how important this discovery was just yet.

Egypt's capital city, Cairo, was contacted, and Egyptologists set out to the area that the scientists Periodar picked up. The scientific community was wild with conversations regarding what the contents of the largest tomb that would ever be unearthed in the Egyptian desert contained.

It took the Egyptologists over a year to meticulously unearth the massive tomb. Once it was ready to be entered, the great door to the tomb was opened. Lights were brought into the tomb, exposing what was actually in the largest tomb ever discovered.

Immediately, something was noticed in the tomb. A 40 feet (12.3m) tall rune column in the middle of the tomb adorned with small runes (carvings that mean letters/words) was discovered. The Egyptologists on hand knew they found something life-changing. They could just feel it.

Before the rune column was removed for further study, other antiquities were found in the tomb of which were priceless. What was unsettling was that there was 50 sarcophagus' surrounding the entire tomb by being next to one another, around the perimeter of the tomb.

One of the Egyptologists took a peek into the one sarcophagus and saw a well-preserved mummy in it. What worried them was the menacing fangs on the mummy. It appeared to be a mummified vampire.

Speaking of mummies, several tablets were found that told of preserving the dead "forever." The tablet was entitled "Mumijo." Mumijo was the ancient word for Mummy. Humanity had just discovered how to make a mummy. This was something that was sought after for centuries. We now knew how to mummify our dead.

After leaving the tomb with plans of bringing the rune-adorned column back to Cairo, where it will be studied, the lead Egyptologist sent some of the photos of the rune column to lead scientists back in Greece as he had knowledge that the runes may be able to be deciphered by our Greek friends.

In conjunction with the call to Greece, plans were made to remove the rune column and move it to Greece. With all of this talk about Greece, it must be revealed what these wonderful people have been keeping *almost* secret for 1000's of years.

Elsewhere, six days after the initial opening of the tomb, many persons were brought in to "cut" the rune column from the tomb to be studied by the Egyptologists. The plan was to cut both the top and bottom of the rune column, safely tip it onto the floor, then have a large truck pull it out of the tomb with chains. At least that was the plan...

The Egyptologists made precision cuts to the top and bottom of the rune column, and as the last cut was made, something very unsettling happened...some sort of groaning of sorts was heard throughout the dimly lit tomb.

As soon as the rune column hit the floor and the dust settled, the creaking of the sarcophagus doors was heard. Without warning, enraged mummies were seen opening their ancient sarcophagus' where they laid dormant for millennia...until now.

With a distinct appetite for human flesh (presumably), the mummies ran for the Egyptologists. Some were fast, while others were not. The scariest part of the whole debacle was that the mummies were armed. Behind their bodies in each sarcophagus was a sword and shield.

The sad sound of the 150 mummies just about wiping out the crew was extremely disconcerting. With the floor littered with fallen bodies, the mummies made their way to the tomb door, where they planned to decimate the rest of the persons outside of the tomb.

As soon as the mummies got into the sunlight, they started to smoke and burn; even their weapons dissipated, which was strange to the survivors of the attack, who just made it into the light and out of the mummies' reaches.

While in shock, the Egyptologists needed a plan to get the rune column out of the tomb. As mentioned earlier, this was the most important item that needed to be moved. The survivors on hand pondered the question, "Why did the mummy vampires not attack when all of the other stuff was removed?"

The survivors left the scene and wondered how they would kill the monsters inside the tomb. One Egyptologist stated that they could go in with flamethrowers, but that might damage the rune column.

One Egyptologist spoke up and said, "Keep the tomb door open, wrap the rune column in chains, and drag it out into the light where those meddling mummy vampires are defenseless."

Like the Batman signal, a very bright light was brought to the tomb, as was a truck that would pull the rune column onto the truck's bed. This way, they will avoid the creatures at all costs and live to tell the story, hopefully.

The Egyptologists again made it to the tomb and got the mega-light setup. The doors to the tomb were opened, and the light shone into the tomb. The Egyptologists carefully entered the tomb. They walked to get the rune column chained and ready for removal.

The Egyptologists were dumbfounded when they saw that the sarcophagus' were all still open, but the vampire mummies were nowhere in sight. Regardless, at the moment, no one spoke because the rune column needed to be chained.

The disappearance of the mummy vampires was never determined as to where they disappeared. The leading theory, so to speak, was that the creatures turned to dust after being" summoned" and could not live in the tomb after being brought back to life by some strange means.

The Egyptologists quickly chained up the rune column, it was dragged to the truck, the tomb doors were closed, and the team sped off, never to return to that cursed tomb. They were happy that they retrieved the rune column and even happier that they still drew breath.

The 40-foot tall (12.3m) and 20-foot wide (6.2m) rune column will be taken to Greece after a quick stop in Cairo so Egyptologists could take pictures of every rune on the rune column. After two weeks in Cairo, the rune column was transported to Thessaloniki, Greece.

This was the site of the best scientists in the world to study the rune column since the Greeks had 1000's of pages of runes and their meanings meant in Latin. The codex covered just about every rune on the column.

It took the Greek scientists weeks to decipher the rune column, one rune at a time. What they found was captivating. They completely deciphered the hundreds of runes on the column, which they found fascinating.

A complete technology recipe, so to speak, was hidden within the runes. This presumably enabled Humanity to build instruments that could detect anything outside the universe.

This will change everything when the technology was built, tested, and implemented. Everyone at the time had no clue how important this beyond the universe detection system will impact not just our home planet but every other life harboring planet out in the cosmos.

As the Greeks were combing over the runes on the column, it started to shake a bit. Before the Greeks knew it, a small area opened up. This exposed a "hole" in the column where a shiny silver cogwheel was retrieved from inside the column. There was a clay tablet next to the cogwheel, which was deciphered.

The tablet gave specific instructions on how and where to use the cogwheel. The tablet explained a sealed room in the depths of the largest pyramid at Giza. This was where a great machine will be found, and once activated, will trigger the start of the steps being taken to detect anything outside the universe.

A group of seasoned explorers made their way to the catacombs below the pyramid with the cogwheel in hand. Just as the runes stated, a room with an indention in the door could fit a cogwheel. An explorer placed the cogwheel in the indention, and it glowed a deep, crimson red.

The cogwheel continued to light up as the door opened a bit, letting the explorers know they had gained access to the room. They could not wait to see what was inside.

They took the cogwheel off the door and entered the room. The lanterns showed that there was a great machine inside the room. This was something of which was never seen for thousands of years.

The center of the great machine (which was nonoperational) indented the cogwheel. This was exactly where the explorers placed it. The machine started to work once again like something out of a movie. The gears were turning as a loud noise rang out from above.

The explorers knew their work was done, so they exited the pyramid. They walked out of the grand pyramid and were met with what they thought was the night, but it looked more like daytime. It was not long before the explorers found out why it "seemed" like daytime.

They turned around, faced the pyramid, and made an astonishing discovery: The large pyramid was now shooting a perfect stream of electricity up to the sky. As the electricity shot up through the atmosphere, it was so bright it was now daytime during the night.

While looking up at the night sky, the explorers noted that this needed to happen to detect what was beyond our universe. Like magic, the Exosphere (the highest point of the atmosphere) turned green. This made Earth a "green" planet in seconds due to its interaction with the great electricity stream.

Scientists sampled the electricity being emitted from the Giza pyramid and found a "shocking" discovery: the electricity emitted from the pyramid had its charge flipped, and every electron was positively charged now.

The explorers rendezvoused with the Greek scientists who immediately contacted the World Space Project (international NASA), who got to work on seeing what was happening outside the universe. The labs' telescopes could now see through the sky and see directly outside of the universe.

With a violent jolt, everything in the lab shifted. There were earthquakes of 6.9 magnitudes. That happened in more than half the countries worldwide. Humanity had not known what triggered such a monstrosity of earthquakes to occur, all at the same time.

The World Space Project noted that the earthquakes were triggered due to singularities or hearts of black holes universe-wide having exploded. When this occurred, the black holes at the center of every galaxy had their singularities go supernova.

Then they exploded in an ultraviolent array of smoke, light, and dust. Tremendous explosions caused damage to billions and billions of planets, some of which may have harbored life.

While the earthquakes were happening, the World Space Project was celebrating its ability to see beyond the confines of the cosmos. The scientists built a computer program that showed, in infrared, everything that was beyond our universe.

But then the celebration ended when a scientist detected a stupendously large object whose trajectory would hit Earth in the next month or so, and there was no way that the future calamity could be prevented.

From what the scientists could initially detect, many bubble universes were floating in a lighted area outside our universe. Each bubble detected was a separate universe, and there were 1000s of universal bubbles floating around in the place outside space and time.

It was amazing to see such a thing, and some scientists were brought to tears because they could see what no human had ever seen before. It was a very flattering moment for all scientists on hand to see what existed beyond our universe.

Everything was tears and beers until the scientists spotted something outside of the very ominous universe. It was headed our way at speeds that could not even be calculated.

From the object's looks, it appeared to be a gigantic "green" hole, zooming right towards Earth. It was larger than our entire universe. The scientists had no clue what would happen when this gargantuan green hole collided with our universe.

The scientists' party ended abruptly when they discovered that the black hole explosions caused tears that ripped through spacetime. Think of this situation as a hole in an inflatable bed, and the universe was the "air" that was depleting and exiting the cosmos through all 150 billion tears through spacetime.

To be blunt, the gravity was escaping through the spacetime tears so fast that the universe was starting to deflate and deflate quickly. And like that, the Earth started to be sucked through the universe: destination the black hole's tear in spacetime.

Now people could jump five feet in the air as the gravitational depletion was messing with the physics on Earth. As our solar system drew closer to the black hole, streetlights at night shined upwards, guaranteeing that we were headed for a possibly grisly demise.

What was important was the "green" hole on the outside of the universe was still headed straight towards us. It was set to hit us in exactly 17 days now. The distance to the tear in spacetime from the exploded black hole was 18 days (approximately). There would have to be a miracle for Earth to be saved from being sucked through the tear that the black hole caused.

The Earth was about to be sucked into the gravity hole when something peculiar happened. Everything turned green, and like that, the Earth sped up towards the gravity hole at extreme speeds. Earth was no more than 200 miles (322 km) from the gravity hole at this point.

It was known that the green hole swallowed the whole uni-verse, and none of the detection equipment worked anymore. This was because the green hole had consumed the universe and Humanity questioned whether or not it would be able to thrive any longer.

Like that, everyone on Earth became weak with exhaustion and fell to the floor right where they stood. The population had not known that the "green" was a nerve gas designed to put the universe to sleep.

Very few Humans were still awake when Earth entered the gravity hole and disappeared from existence. There was no longer any trace of Earth anywhere in the cosmos.

This would be a sad ending if Humanity did not wake up on Earth on the day before the tomb was discovered. For rea-sons unknown, every planet miraculously ended up back in its spot where it was before the singularity supernovae explosions happened.

This placed all of Humanity alive and well with no killer black or green holes insight. Many people would tell you that everything on Earth seemed new.

What Humanity knew was that the green hole was actually a "universal reset cloud" which swallowed our universe to save Earth and all other planets from being sucked out of the grav-ity hole and into the unknown.

We will most likely never see the outside of the universe again. This was not a problem because, in Humanity's view, they had no knowledge of anything that happened at all. Earth's population was happy with the outcome after having the scare of their lives...even if they had no knowledge of what atrocities had occurred.

THE END

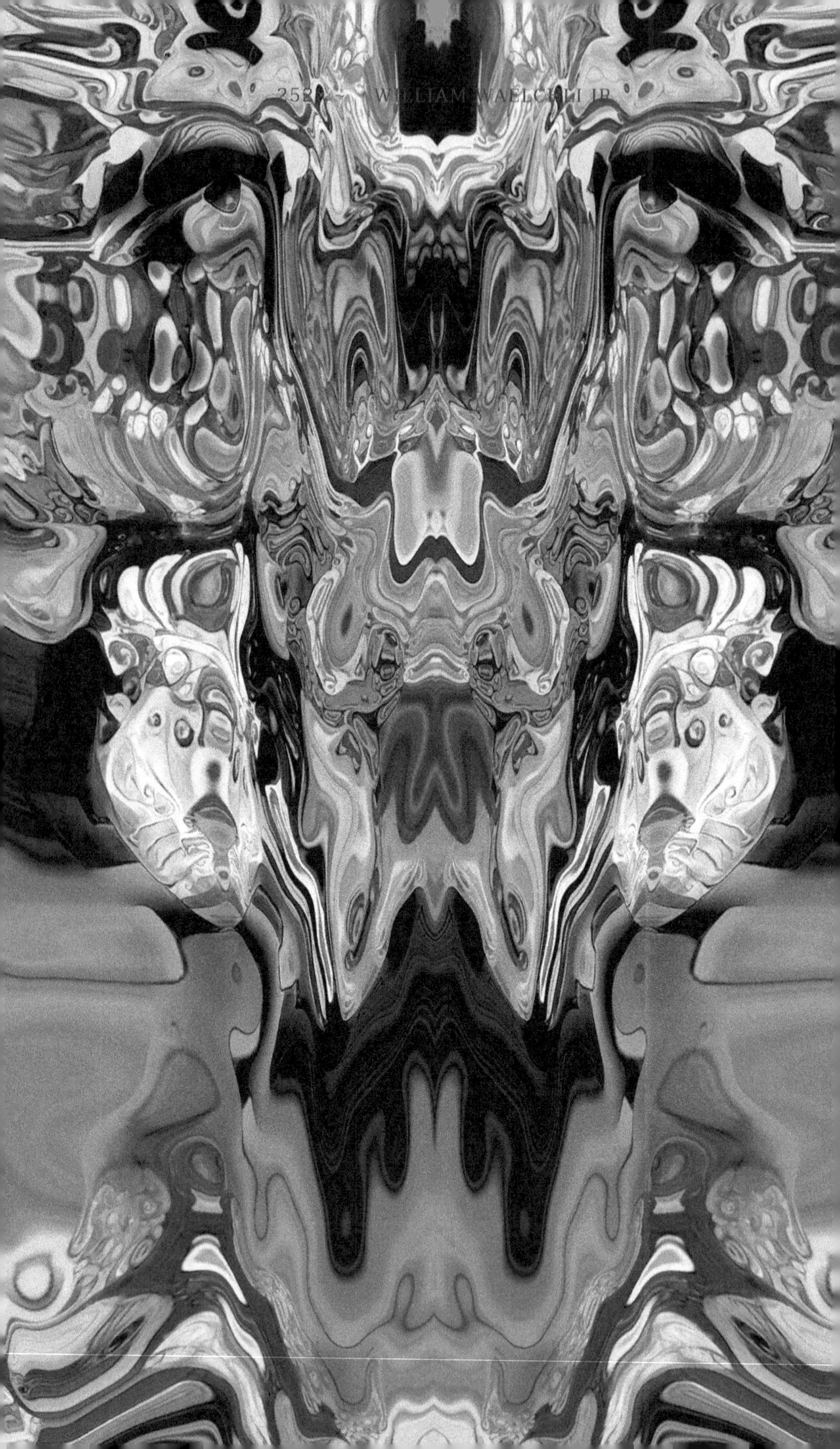

"An Inquiry Concerning the Possible Abolishment of Aging" - or - "Cosmically Condemned"

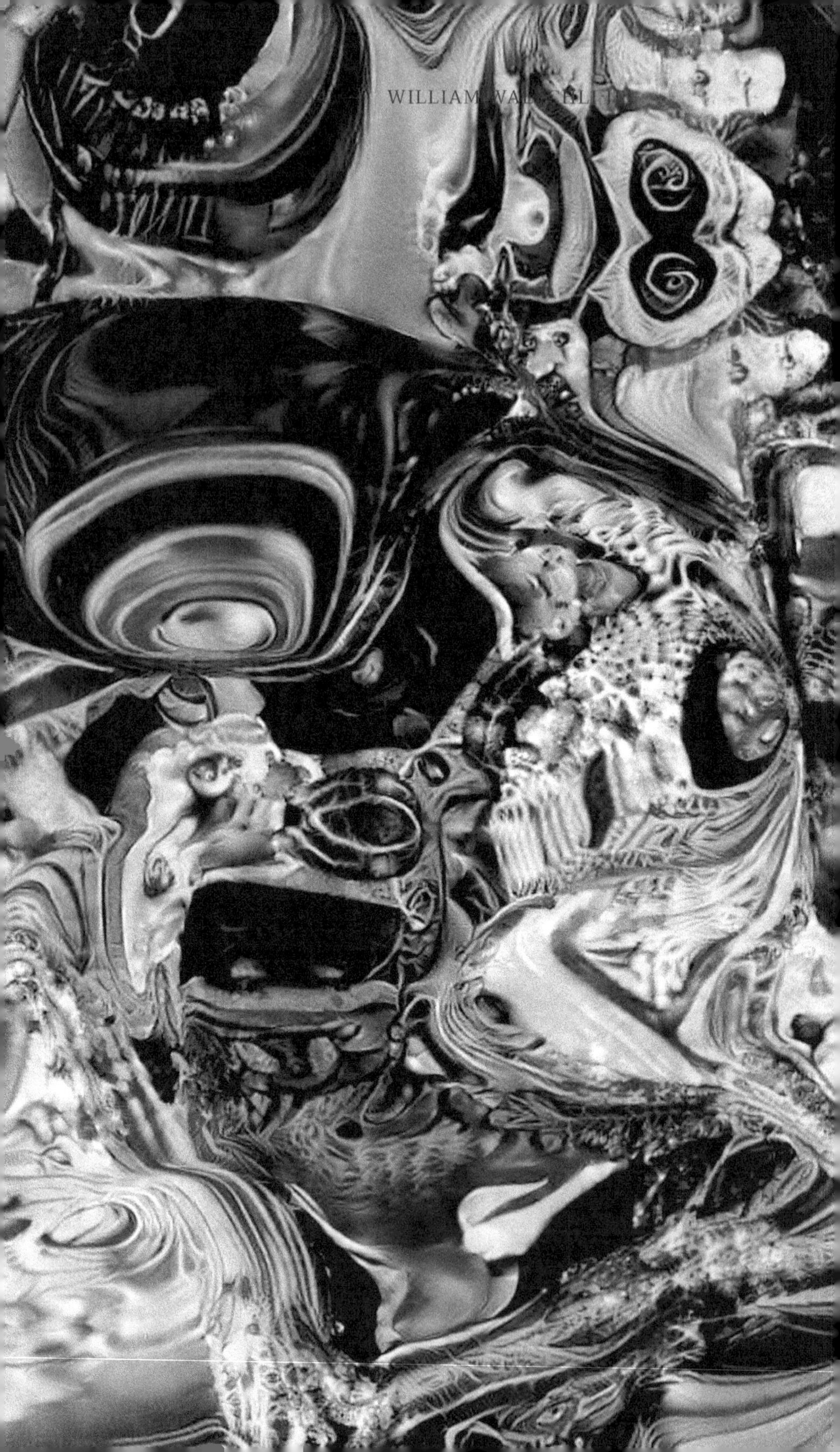
WILLIAM WALLACE

In the future, there existed a great computer known as The Collective Conscience. The Collective Conscience was a great quantum computer spanning many city blocks in size. It ran on light and housed a copy of every person's mind in a backup existing within the colossal supercomputers comprising The Collective Conscience.

The Collective Conscience acted as Humanity's doctor. It was a marvel of modern technology. Without it, Humanity would have no way to look over every person's mental faculties by wirelessly monitoring all levels. If anything ailed you, no matter the disease, the artificial intelligence in the Collective Conscience would mend the body through therapeutic ways.

The Collective Conscience connected wirelessly to the "micro-chip" inserted in all living persons and wirelessly sent informa-tion to Humanity having improved their wellness along with a whole host of features. Its advanced artificial intelligence was an awe-inspiring technological achievement for Humanity.

This guaranteed that Humanity would have its health and mind safe from would-be terrorists who may harm the remark-able Collective Conscience.

There had been thousands of serial killers worldwide working in a pyramid scheme-like hierarchy, where money ruled above all else. The "Say 10" Sadists sect ran murder rings in most major cities across Earth.

They had murdered well over half of a million people aged 21 – 82 in the previous decade at their height. People were paid in United States dollars for the heads of famous people and anyone whom a higher-up told them to dispose of.

The entire sect comprised more than 46,000 serial killers. The "Say 10" existed worldwide. However, it was not too long before the sect became infiltrated. It was only a matter of time before the many serial killers' consciousnesses changed forever, Humanity had hoped.

Nearly every serial killer in the "Say 10" sadists were brought to justice. The "kingpin" of the murder ring was a man named 'Boris." Something significantly "cutting edge" happened when the sadists had their court appearances in jurisdictions spanning the globe.

A new type of "punishment" was created to cure people of the sick and twisted individuals who had taken one life or more. The punishment was to change all 57,997 serial killers' minds using the Collective Conscience. Scientists swapped all of the 'Say 10' Sadists' consciousnesses with a pre-made consciousness of an average person who may be an insurance agent or something of that nature, as an example.

Their new consciousness removed all malicious intent out of the mind of the serial killers by giving them a new consciousness and clearing them of all of the repulsive shit serial killers think about and do.

The courts did this new method of punishment to each and every person alive who took a life. Each person in prison was set free once hooked up to the Collective Conscience and given a new mind/consciousness.

Elsewhere in the world, there was a rare earth element known as Xyquma (ZY-Q-MA), which powered the Collective

Conscience. Unfortunately, this element was running out, and scientists were freaking out. Without any Xyquma, the Collective Conscience may stop running and cause widespread chaos or its shutting down may spell danger for all of Humanity. Imagine if their mind's got stripped?

A race of extraterrestrials 100,000 strong landed their spacecraft strategically all over Earth. The extraterrestrials stated they were here to take all of a particular rare earth element used to keep the main computers on their planet running. Earth had an abundance of this particular element.

Oddly enough, the beings were some race that came from a planet with generous amounts of that rare earth element mentioned earlier, Xyquma, as the beings were "made" from it.

For some very rare reason, Humanity became homicidal. It destroyed all of the extraterrestrials in many strange and inhumane ways and anything else you can think of to end the life of an extraterrestrial.

Humanity made an extraterrestrial bounty for who could return the most heads to their governments until 100,000 heads existed somewhere in the government buildings across the world.

On each of the alien ships, all 996 of them, was a treasure-trove of Xyquma needed to run the Collective Conscience. Humanity now had enough to run the Collective Conscience for the next 812 years.

The alien bodies lay dying and strewn about across the Earths' once beautiful landscapes. Humanity now had a guilty conscience about what they had done to save their own hides. What would you do if you needed a computer that controlled every physical activity in the entire body?

Once some of the new Xyquma was fed into the Collective Conscience, something quite odd happened... It didn't explode or anything spectacular; instead, it attacked artificial intelligence in some bizarre way.

Then every criminal who had a consciousness swap for the last 50 years, the original, homicidal consciousness returned to the criminals, and the criminals grinned, knowing there was a lot of "game" out there now.

Now all the murderers who were legally given a consciousness swap, suddenly got their criminal mind returned to them through a glitch in the Collective Conscience once the alien Xyquma entered the Collective Consciousness. It completely replaced the old "regular" conscience. It was as if someone turned the channel on the television, as the regular persons became serial killers once again.

Now there are tens of thousands of murderers running around all over the planet, and quite frankly, there's no way to stop them. The artificial intelligence destroyed the records that would tell what criminal went with what conscience. So there would be no way to tell who was a school teacher and who was a mass murderer.

Now, something had to happen, and believe it or not; Humanity had a way out of this debacle. Humanity, except for the thousands of serial killers, were teleported to a planet known as Schisma.

Schisma was a planet discovered by Humanity over 500 years ago. The discovery of this planet in our galaxy caused the acceleration in space technologies and terraforming techniques. Although very little terraforming had to be done because the planet was discovered, it was a virgin Earth.

Terraforming was simply the process of making planets more Earth-like. All of Humanity arrived on Schisma and noted that they got there on the exact day which scientists announced that they had done the incredible, the amazing, and possibly the insane... the scientists had discovered immortality.

All that had to be done was transfer signals from the Collective Conscience on Schisma to all ten billion persons who transmitted DNA waves to each human's microchip. This was where it will change the cells of each Human through trans-differentiation.

Transdifferentiation was when cells heal themselves automatically and do this repeatedly, creating an immortal body.

And no sooner did Humanity get zapped with immortality, the same alien race touched down on the electrified planet. The term electrified planet meant that the planet had an Electrosphere.

Think of the sky as electricity, and there you can envision an Electrosphere. The electricity was used to power everything on Scisma, and everything that needed electricity was drawn wirelessly from the atmosphere.

Remember when the sky was electricity? Not soon after Humanity had left, something hellishly horrible happened that was bestowed upon the extraterrestrials. Well, the electric sky started to fall on every alien on Schisma.

As the electric sky started to descend towards the ground, where thousands of the extraterrestrials cried out in horror. Their running did nothing as the electric sky was due to hit the ground...any...second...now...

The sky fell so far that it penetrated the ground while electrifying the entire extraterrestrial race of beings. It was like being in a room where the ceiling was electricity. It lowered until the current passed through the 'aliens.'

As the sky fell, the extraterrestrials knew they were thwarted and that the Earthlings had somehow done them in. When they became electrocuted, they knew Humanity had won. The extraterrestrials assumed Humanity, who built the Electrosphere, had rigged the sky to fall.

Back on Earth, the Collective Conscience was still running in standby mode, as every person was re-established within the massive computer upon their teleportation back to Earth.

As a scientist noticed a threat coming towards Earth, he became inquisitive because what he saw through the telescope was something that Humanity never observed. The scientists were confident that the objects would not hit Earth, and it will only be a flyby of sorts.

Immortal Humanity learned that a magnetar was coming towards the Earth. Scientists are more scared than excited because they will get to observe what this massive and dense magnetar was really about.

A magnetar was a neutron star with an impressively strong

magnetic field. They fly throughout the cosmos in no particular direction.

Scientists were confident that nothing would happen to the Earth because it's just like a giant magnet flying through the cosmos. What could happen? Well...

The first magnetar will be crossing Earth close, within 1 million miles. The second will come in even closer at 50,000 miles from Earth.

The second magnetar was discovered shortly after the first. This did not make Humanity fret in anyway as they were unstoppable now that they were all immortal.

Magnetars were never observed before, and scientists didn't know what would happen when they flew by. The worst-case scenario was that Earth may wobble a bit, then go right back on its rotation... so physics would tell us...

The first magnetar zipped by Earth. All the lights went out. Every single cell phone worldwide, by the billions, malfunctioned. At first, no one knew what happened, but scientists knew.

Not to mention that the Collective Conscience was shut down like a seedy club. This sent a wi-fi signal so strong to the microchips that it overloaded the electricity in everyone's brain. This caused every person alive, except the criminals, to be unable to move any longer because the now-defunct Collective Conscience had control of everyone's body.

Did you ever drop a powerful magnet on a computer disk only to find out that nothing exists on the disk anymore? Think of Earth as that disk. The magnetar, with its super impressive magnetic field, had...

Of course, Humanity was not freaking out as bad as when the second magnetar passed, thousands of miles closer. All Humanity could do was hope that the second magnetar would not wreak any havoc on Earth.

The Earth started to shake uncontrollably, like a top that was about to stop spinning. Before Humanity knew it, gravity threw the Earth off its orbit due to the immense power of the magnetar.

Now Humanity had to look forward to Earth spiraling out of the solar system towards Mars. The worst part was that the Earth was moving so quickly that it was iced over within some time of being off its orbit.

Most of the people on Earth were thinking about Karma and how it really did them in this time. It was bad enough that they killed the hundred thousand extraterrestrials on Earth, but what about what happened on Schisma with the Electrosphere?

The Electrosphere had a glitch that caused the entire thing to "swallow" Schisma, with all the extraterrestrials on it. Karma was not pissed about that one, because quite frankly, Humanity was not responsible for that folly.

This was some cosmic payback for what happened to those extraterrestrials so that Humanity could run the Collective Conscience.

So what was the blood price for doing such a heinous act as Humanity committed? Try drifting in space endlessly on an ice cube with miles and miles of ice above your head, and your heart will beat forever, and the hypothermia will get exponentially worse.

Not to mention the pain of one thousand bullets that will never stop stinging, as the ice never cracks. Too bad the same could not be said about Humanity. They definitely cracked.

THE END

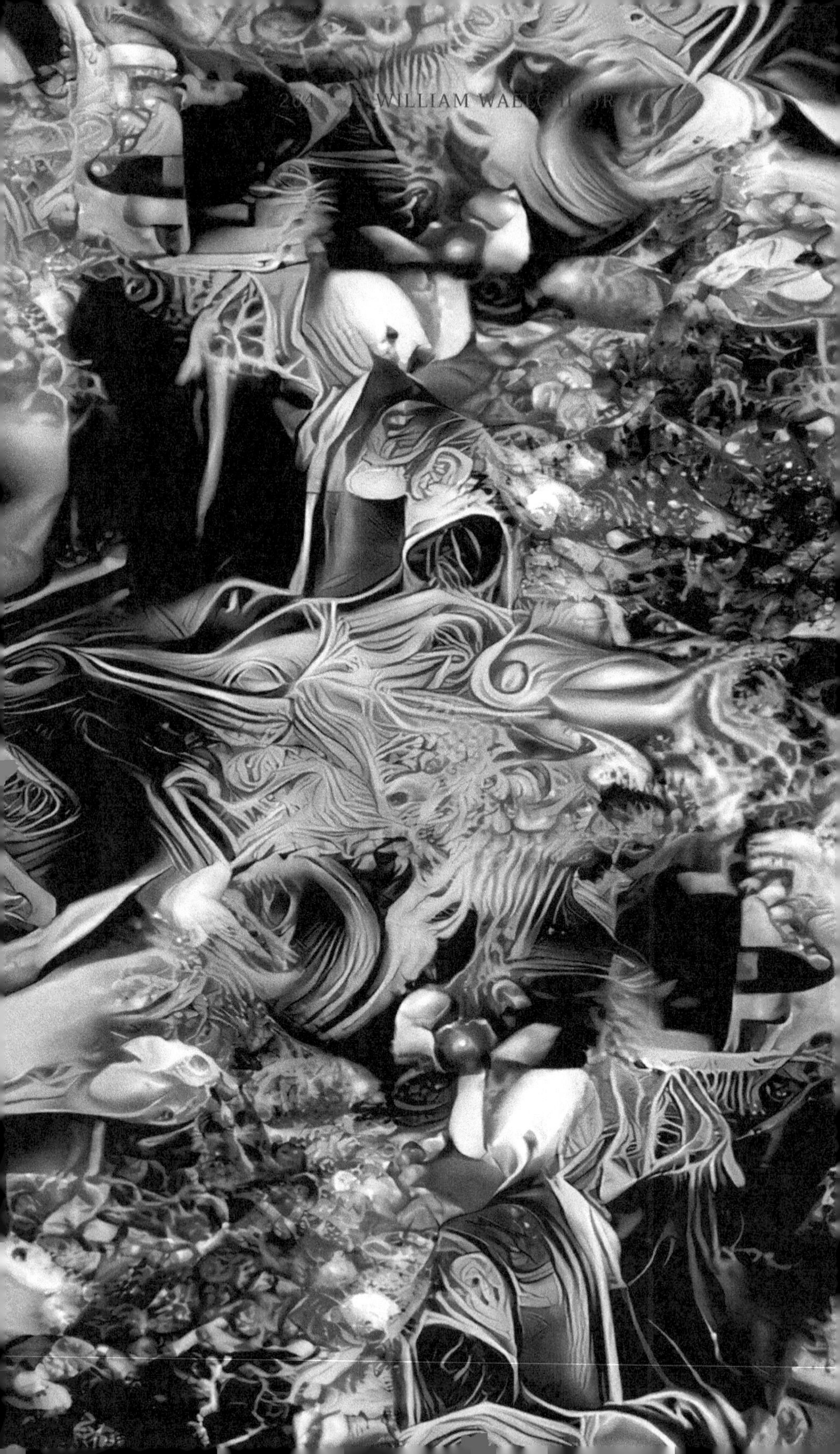

Chapter 25

"Evacuation from the Center of the Mind"– or -"Over Population Earth: Could You Live a Fulfilling Life Knowing the Exact Day You Will Die?"

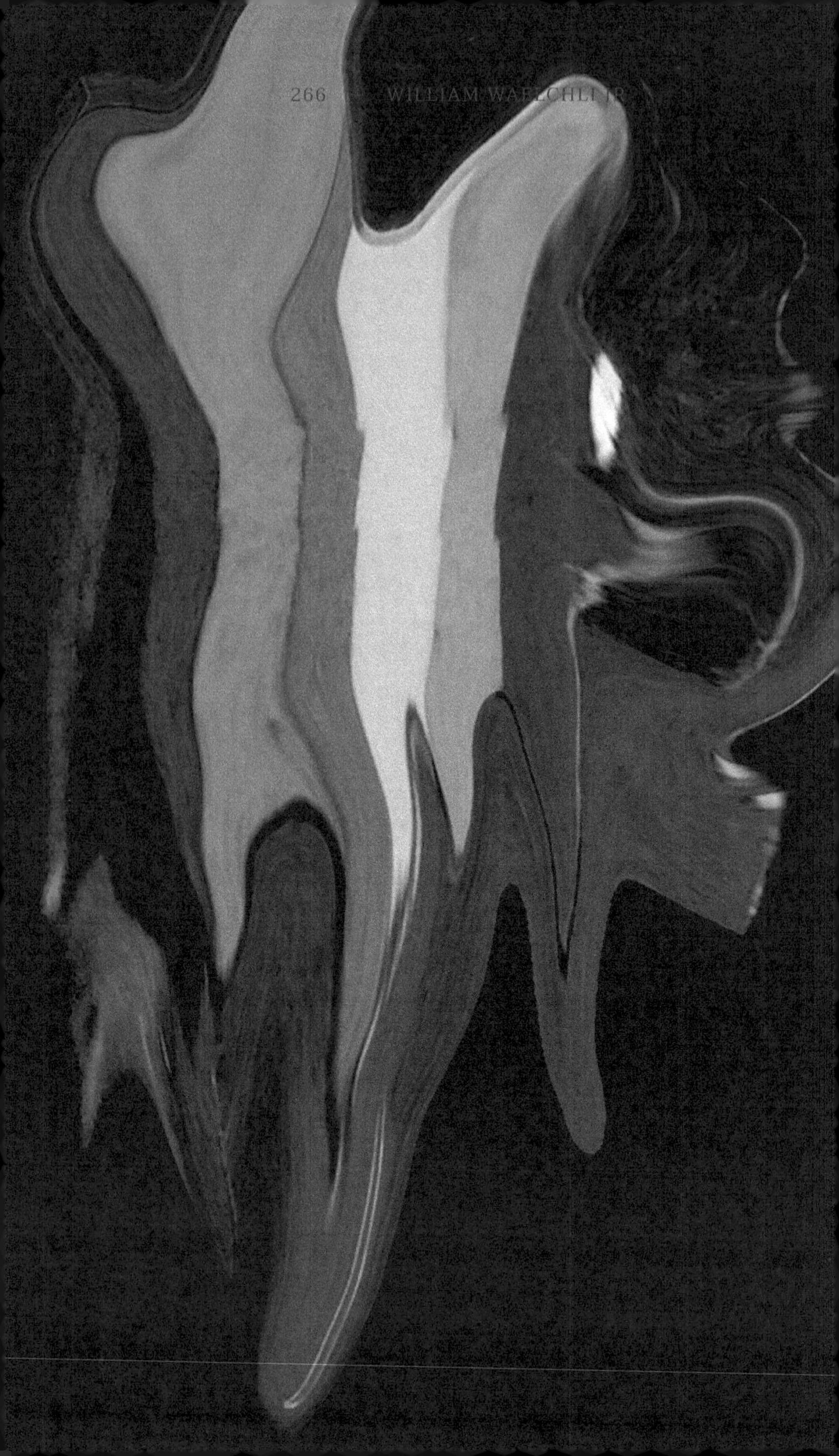

Welcome to planet Earth. It is the year 2444, where there are serious overpopulation issues. These issues are affecting how we live our lives, and these issues have affected every man, woman, and child across the billions and billions of persons on Humanity's only planet.

There was a major change in Humanity's way of birthing new babies. We had to rewind the clock to the year 2222, when a "nuclear cloud" penetrated Earth and every person in the population. Do not worry. Nobody died. Everyone was safe except for the long-term effects of that so-called "nuclear cloud."

Before the side effects are explained, it must be clarified what this cloud actually was and where it came from. Scientists spotted the cloud near Mars, where it penetrated the entire planet. No Martian lives were lost, but their evolution became a bit weirder.

The cloud originated somewhere outside the solar system, where some sort of extraterrestrial laser cannon must have wiped out an alien planet, and the dust and smoke leftover was what penetrated Mars and Earth.

Why must this all be explained? Because it altered all of the baby males who were born, it made for some very different ways of birthing babies forever. After a generation, something very odd happened: baby boys and eventually men developed a complex body system enabling them to give birth through cesarean child delivery.

Male births changed the population of Earth as time passed and forced Earth to be taken to its space limitations with a planet-wide population of just over 20 billion persons. It was a challenge to go anywhere without fighting crowds.

The Global Government introduced the not so bad sounding "Dreamlab" for the management planet's population. Population management was not popular with ANYBODY on the planet when it was initiated just 40 years ago.

Population management worked when a baby was birthed into the world. They were, of course, issued an official birth certificate from the hospital and a Death Date issued by Dreamlab.

Think about that for a bit. People are born now knowing exactly when they will die. The "Die on Date" changed global thinking and made people more caring and humble, knowing that they will only spend a total of 60 years or just under 22,000 days on the planet before persons will humanely perish without any pain.

The death date loomed over every person's head their whole lives. Humanity thought about their impending death date every day, trying to enjoy the time they were "allowed" to be on the Earth. It made the ages 50 – 59 especially trying times knowing those persons are nearing an impending death.

The ever so ominous Dreamlab was where the Time Police took every 60 year old. Do not even try to run, as the Time Police will find you. These Time Police use a "DNA Radar," which, when Dreamlab technicians fed a person's DNA information into it, will show and track runners anywhere on Earth.

The DNA Radar can read the DNA signature of every person on Earth at any location. All Humans knew the DNA Radar would locate them, and the Time Police would track them down if they ran. As a punishment for running, the dream process of eliminating the runners will occur much faster than those persons who were honest and turned themselves in.

The Dreamlab in each country was a wonder of modern technologies in consciousness intrusion where the process to end life began. The Dreamlab was a marvel of modern technologies used to create the "Death Dreams."

There was a Dreamlab in every country globally. Most existed in a skyscraper, where on every floor were advanced computer systems that enabled the soon-to-pass 60-year-olds to have their lives end prematurely. It was about time that the process of the untimely deaths was explained.

The fateful 60-year-old patients were hooked up to advanced computer systems that tap into the patient's consciousness and manipulate their minds in ways that seemed completely innocent, yet the undertones of this process were far more sinister.

The computers tapped the patients' memory reserve. The consciousness was then "altered" to show the memory bank information in the form of a lucid dream induced by Dreamlab. The patient then viewed their long-term memory, where the 60-year-old traveled through a life-like display of what happened in their lifetimes.

Not knowing that they are actually in a dream, the four to twelve-hour dreams continue until the conclusion or crashing crescendo as it is known around Dreamlab. The patient then entered a cave with a light at the other end, and the Death Dream "concluded."

The patient walked through the cave in the dream, and just as they entered the light at the end of the tunnel, a chemical cocktail was intravenously administered, causing the 60-year-olds to quickly pass on in a very humane and gentle fashion utilizing dreams.

What if there was interference in the dream? Just a thought...

This brings us to a delightful and prominent 59-year-old woman named Jill Nobleton. She was a former world chancellor, which she was the president of the world from the ages of 20 – 30 years. Her term was over 30 years ago, and she was crucial in passing the legislation that brought Dreamlab into existence.

She was a hard woman but fair in dealing with the issues that plagued Humanity. Now that her birthday was fast approaching, she naively thought that she would not have to be removed from Humanity by having the Death Dream since she was the person who presided over its implementation.

Millions of persons have lost their lives directly or indirectly because of Jill and her having caused the Dreamlabs to rise, and she was going to run if the Time Police found her. Before too long, she reached her birthday and verified with her paperwork as to when he alleged death day was. As she was going through her paperwork, she received a knock at the door of her mansion.

She checked the peephole and saw the Time Police were here to take her to the Dreamlab, where the minutes of her life would tick down to her impending death. She thought about running, but she knew they used DNA Radar, which would find her in no time. She had second thoughts about becoming a "runner."

She kindly let in the time police, who were thrilled they did not have to pursue her. The one officer thanked her and made the ominous request that Jill had thought about since Dreamlab was established: "You're coming with us to Dreamlab. Please do not put up a struggle."

Jill did not know how to act because the legislation she had instated caused the endings of millions of lives on a global scale. Now that the time has caught up with her, and her hours are numbered, she wondered about her own fate.

Her entire face was wet from tears as she was handcuffed and marched out of her home. At this point, Jill had the sobering thought that she would "never see home again."

Things were about to get real as the Time Police drove Jill to nobody ever wanted to enter the skyscraper. This skyscraper was Dreamlabs' American headquarters in downtown Washington DC.

It dominated the skyline, reminding anyone who noticed that when they turn 60 or their "die on date," they too will have their lives abruptly stopped in that stupid tall building.

Speaking of stupid tall buildings, Jill was escorted into the Dreamlab, where she was meant with a not-so-happy nurse, who welcomed her to Dreamlab and, most likely sarcastically, welcomed her to the conclusion of her successful "run" on Earth.

It's funny how Jill once controlled Earth (to a certain extent), and now what she allowed through her legislation has come full circle, and Jill was not liking it.

The nurse took Jill to the 60th floor of the skyscraper and took her to a private room where Jill had to wear one of those annoying gowns that seemed like it had three armholes.

She eventually put on the gown and obsessively thought about what exactly was going to happen in this unforgiving place that was designed to end the lives of anybody who reached their "die on date."

The room she was in was an unassuming place that included a computer, a few cabinets, and a water bed. Jill knew in her mind that this was the last place she would ever visit, knowing that the computer would wirelessly connect to her brain's microchip enabling the "Death Dream" that will humanely (she hoped) erase her from the Earth's 20 billion + population.

A doctor with a strong British accent entered the small room where she met Jill and thanked her for enabling the population controlling Dreamlab to have been established. Jill frighteningly thanked her and boldly stated.

"Let's do this thing." The Dreamlab technicians then fitted her with many annoying sticky things that left residue all over her skin. She then thought, "I won't be taking those things off anyways because I will no longer draw breath."

Jill lay down on the bed. After a lengthy prayer, she could not open her eyes anymore as she was now connected through her brain microchip to the computer, which wirelessly communicated with Jill's brain, causing her to fall fast asleep. As luck would have it, she was not dead yet.

Jill entered a "familiar" dream drawn from her long-term memory where the "death dream" showed her memories in stunning clarity, as she knew she dreamed a little dream. She yearned for being in the Dreamatrix. In all seriousness, the Dreamatrix would be a vacation, not the life-ending Dreamlab. The Dreamatrix is covered in the second book to this companion saga of the "Untamed Cosmos."

Jill was unaware that the computer's microchip caused all the stored DMT in her spine to release. DMT is a drug made in the brain's pineal gland at the center of the brain. It was believed that DMT assisted the living with their dreams, causing all dreams. Now that Jill was flooded with DMT, it was now a wonder as to what Jill's dream would include...

Jill dreamed of her birth and childhood, showing her imagery from her childhood, where she, in her dream, sobbed, knowing that this was experiencing her past and she will never go back to that point in her life. Next was her teenage years, where she studied politics and hoped she would become a world chancellor being the top government official presiding over the entire planet.

Next, the dream showed her early twenties and her winning the global election and crowning her as World Chancellor leading up to her inauguration and becoming the "top dog" in world politics. Memories of her reign flooded her death dream as she walked through the dream not knowing what to expect next...

The next wave of memories was from her retirement or post-retirement days, where she became a visual artist enabling her to express herself as an artist and not a major political figure who was essential in establishing Dreamlab. She was aware that karma had caught up with her, and now she was reaching the end of her quite fulfilling life.

In the dream, she came to a round, red door. This was when Jill started to panic erratically. Jill knew what this red door was and where it led to.

She opened the door and reached the cave's death path, where at the end of the tunnel, there was a smidgen of light that would flood the dreamer with light while advancing through the cave.

At this point, the intravenous on Jill was supposed to inject Jill with a potent poison called Dreamethyltryptamine. Dreamethyltryptamine is a chemical that ended the death dream. It ends the lives of every person watching their death dream as well. It was the most humane way that existed to cause the conclusion of each sixty-year-old person's life.

This was Jill's dream now, and minutes before Jill would be bathed in light and poisoned and ended her existence, something off the wall occurred in her dream: What appeared to be two ghosts of sorts appeared in front of her. "Come with me if you want to preserve your consciousness and continue your life elsewhere in the cosmos."

Jill knew her death dream was about to conclude, and she knew that The Dreamlab Technicians would soon administer the poison. She was unaware of any "ghosts" of sorts who offered help and an exit from the dream where the preservation of the mind existed.

At first, the ghostly beings seemed unapproachable as they appeared to be holograms. Both of the ghostly beings explained to Jill, while in the cave of her death dream, that they are multiple dimensional beings who save *most* persons from their impending deaths.

They Appeared to be about 5 feet tall and wearing flowing white robes. What scared Jill was that they had faces that appeared to as beings from a DMT trip. Strangely enough, their heads were television screens. They dawned on the face of the Heavenly Son as they led Jill further into the cave. They both instructed her to close her eyes and not look at the light as it would trigger the poison into her body.

They confessed to Jill that they are "The Dream Hackers" who reside on a faraway planet known as Conscientia (CON-CHENT-UH), where they will take Jill's conscience and transfer it to this mysterious planet where she may live in a pure conscious state once her conscience exits her body.

The Dream Hackers guided Jill further into the light, where a purple light shone on her. It was at this point where the two Dream Hackers guided her into the purple light as they explained, "Each atom in your body includes an electron that has a negative charge and includes the consciousness or mind of each 60-year old that is about to reach their demise."

Jill and both Dream Hackers entered the purple light avoiding the white light. As she walked into the purple light, the Dream Hackers reversed the charge of her electrons, which removed Jill's consciousnesses from her body.

The reverse-charged electrons enabled her to have her consciousness beamed across the universe to Planet Conscientia, where she may live out her days. That was unless something drastic happened...

THE END

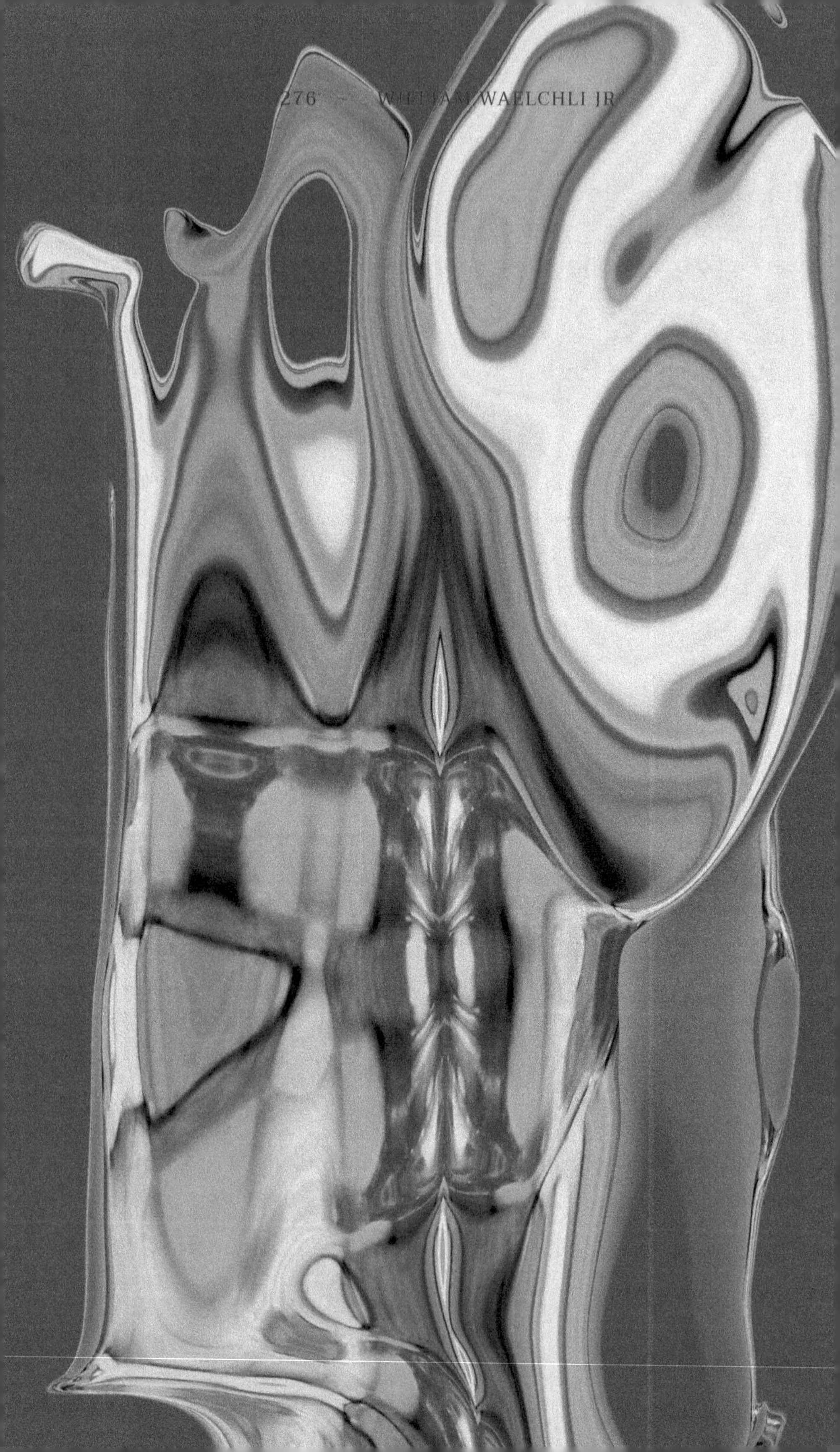

Chapter 26

"Electrickery" -or- "Post Conceptualization of Atomic Manipulation"

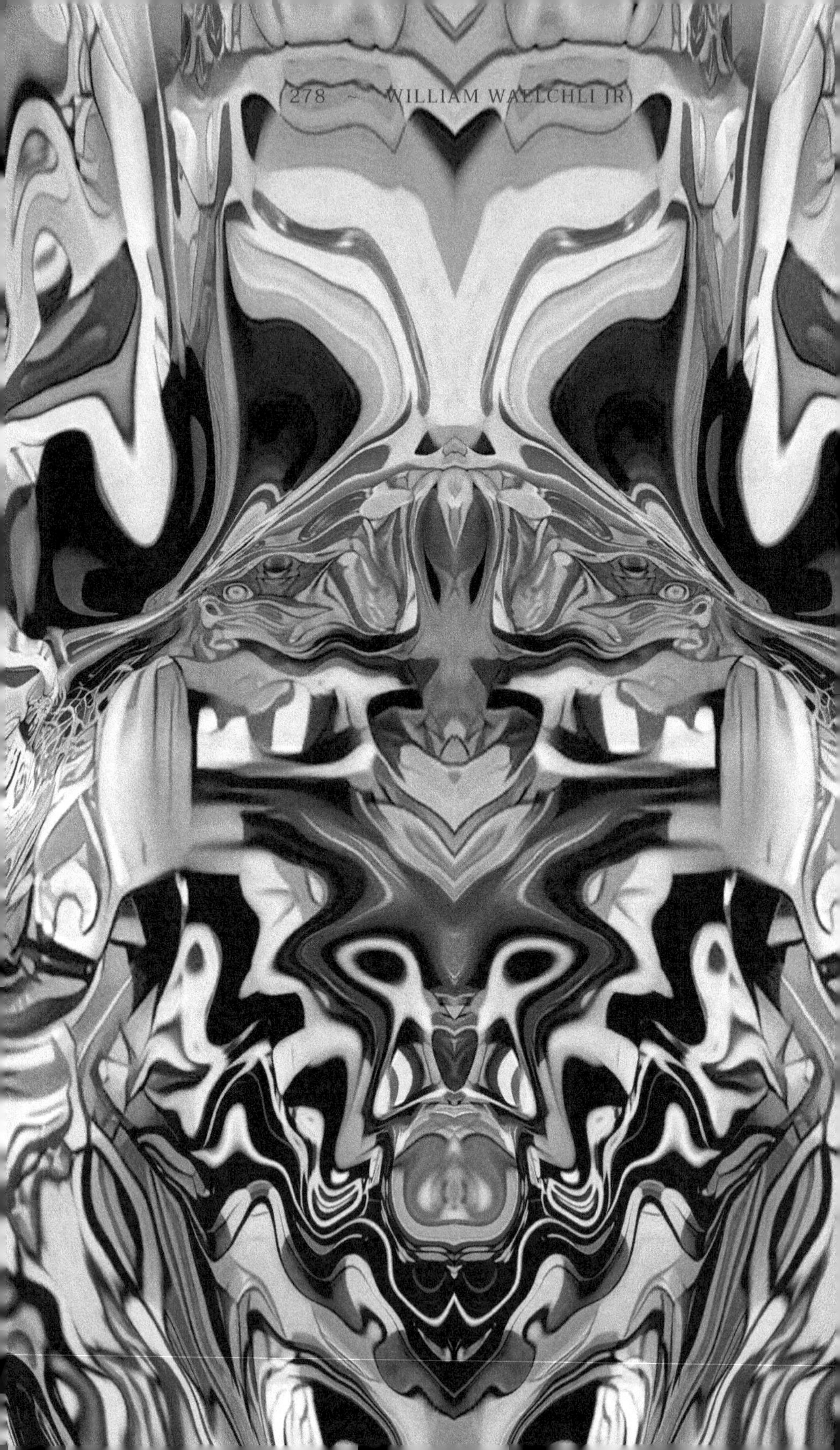

In the year 2477, Humanity had achieved a feat so far ahead of their time; it stuns them at their willingness to push technology beyond its limits for the better part of Humanity.

Humanity became a Type 2 civilization on the Kardashev Scale. Type 2 is defined as: "The Kardashev scale is a method of measuring a civilization's level of technological advancement based on the amount of energy they can harness from Earth (Type 1), The Solar System (Type 2), and the Galaxy (Type 3)."

In so many words, we can now harness the electricity from the entire Solar System. What we do with this new technology will reclassify Humanity as the recently coined term Post-humanity.

This means that Humanity will move far above and beyond what they once were in the past.

The planets and moons had gravity-controlled obelisks connected to electricity, enveloping every planet and moon in raw electrical power. This enabled Earth to harness all of the electricity in the Solar System.

The "Electrolisks," floated in the atmosphere of every planetary body and moon in the Solar System. Other Electrolisks were on the ground to harness all electricity of lunar and planetary bodies' that included the Sun. These Electrolisks will soon be electrified, enabling god-like control of electricity.

By connecting the electricity of all celestial bodies in the solar system, Earth could beam back the electricity of every moon and planet to Earth for use in a near-infinite powered electrified atmosphere. In a way, Scientists will soon discuss 3D printing of particular objects...

Read on to see what the scientists have planned for the future precisely.

By this point, every machine was wireless since it runs off the air, which contains electricity courtesy of the electrified atmosphere (Electrosphere). Humanity called it "E-Fi" for "Electronic Fidelity.

Atmospheric electricity is the study of electrical charges in the Earth's atmosphere. The movement between the Earth's surface, the atmosphere, and the ionosphere are known as the global atmospheric electrical circuit. This fundamental process enabled Humanity to create Electrospheres on every moon and planet across the solar system.

This global atmospheric electrical circuit was expanded when the solar system's atmospheres were electrified and beamed back to Earth.

Energy "mining" of the Sun was done by absorbing nitrogen and helium atoms and stripping them of their protons and neutrons, replacing them with gravitons and neutrinos, respectively, as mentioned earlier.

Gravitons were the atomic particle of gravity. The remaining part, the electron, would then be transferred to the atmosphere as electricity. Neutrinos are rumored to move faster than light, enabling the electricity mining of the Sun.

Scientists atomically set out to copy Earth and the Sun through the use of gratoms. These are synthetic atoms created by scientists. They consisted of a Neutrino (for speed), an electron (as charge), and a graviton (used for replication).

Constructing the Earth and the Sun gratom by gratom was the next step in achieving Posthumanity. This is why "3D-Printing was mentioned earlier.

The high amount of electricity being beamed back from every part of the solar system was just enough raw electrical power needed to create duplicate Earth's and Suns.

With a mixture of gravity and electricity, it was possible to create a duplicate copy of Earth for every man and woman aged 16 and older. Humanity would also travel to any of the Earths they so chose in real-time, instantaneously.

It will become a daily occurrence for Humanity to visit their family's Earth to see what different occurrences had happened and see how they were doing, especially since they control their own planet Earth now.

Since everything had been electrically charged and connected, scientists beamed the electricity from all the planets, moons, and the Sun to create the duplicate Earth's and Sun by releasing a beam out of the South Pole or bottom of the original Earth.

In simple terms, Earth's and Sun's were 3D printed then gravitationally moved around on a ring to make room for another ring of Earth's with a Sun above the newly created planetary ring.

"Paradise Portal" opened beneath the Earth, and a new Earth materialized below the original Earth. The creation of the Earth all occurred instantaneously because gratoms move at light speed.

Since the new planets are composed of gratoms, the Earth created new versions of itself for all persons 16 and over, and anybody who reached 16 years will be gifted their very own copy of Planet Earth to control as they see fit.

A ring of 2,000,000 Earths with a central Sun was made below the first ring of planets. This process repeated for 4000 rings. This completed the "Cosmic Column" and included a copy of Earth for everyone over 16 years of age.

Every Earth's and Suns' creation was formed within a few months; all 8 billion planets were created in a column that stretched billions of miles below the original Earth.

As time passed, the column of earthen rings will grow, and the column will increase so long that it may flirt with near infinity over time.

Before Scientists transferred anybody to the rings, Humanity went to sleep on the original Earth, once the duplicate Earth's were all in place but was not on their Earth yet.

The next day, upon awakening, Humanity was now on its own Earth in the Cosmic Column. They can do whatever they please with the planet. It is operated similarly to a video game that is played by making decisions and seeing their outcomes.

It must be stated that each Earth had a regular population like the original Earth.

Before *"Star Wars"* fans ask, there was no way to "Alderaan" any of the Earth's by making them explode just like Princess

Leia's home planet did in the original *Star Wars (A New Hope)* film from back in 1977.

Each person became the World Chancellor of their very own planet, being the permanent head of the global government, making all decisions impacting the outcome on any particular day on their very own version/copy of Earth.

If the president was not concerned about governmental matters, it could run itself. Still, it was highly advised that they pay attention to it and make decisions accordingly.

The Earth owner must heed this warning: Do not go too long without checking up on the government, or it may jeopardize the planet.

While under the influence of a gratomical structure, all humans' atoms are now made of electrons, gravitons, and neutrinos (a particle that may move at light speed).

This atomic structure enabled Humanity to travel between any Earth's, in any ring, anywhere. It was also desirable that they could time travel by going back to any period in Earth's history.

Unfortunately, for the Future-heads, travel into the future was impossible, as scientists "could not get the math right."

The Cosmic Column and their respective Suns as a whole became known as "Undique Utopia" (or UU), meaning "everywhere and nowhere" in Latin.

Humanity was now free of the burdens of 9-5 lives and can now control an entire planet since they permanently hold the World Chancellor title as head of the global government.

With the structure of the planets composed strictly of gratoms, the Earth can "heal itself" by transferring the gratoms back in time to a past state where the damaged part of the Earth was not damaged.

Periodically, the cranial computer included in each Human had received notifications in a soothing voice about things that affect all of Undique Utopia and usually need immediate attention.

One morning, everyone woke up to horrific news. Somehow, the Sun's atomic restructuring went awry as it was learned that the Sun's might burn off their electrons. Upon releasing their electrons, they will follow the path of least resistance. Quite simply, every planet may be electrocuted once the electrons are released.

It seemed that the "Alderaan" scenario might happen, and all eight billion Earth's will explode in a barrage of dirt, stellar shit, and burnt flesh, among other things.

The World Chancellor (or planetary owner) had to inform the planet. What would you tell your population? You could keep it a secret and have them find out later. But angry mobs are not something that anyone wants to deal with.

You could tell them the truth: at any moment, albeit a second or a year, the Suns will release their electrons and send charges so sizeable that it will electrocute the entire column of billions of planets.

After surviving the night without being fried by electricity, a new message came through every World Chancellor's cranial computers. It was not good news again, and maybe even worse than yesterday's news.

"This news will make you wish the situation from the message yesterday already happened." It continued, "The Sun is also in danger of losing its electrons. As you know, what we learned is that it may burn through its neutrinos first before its electrons.

It will accelerate the Sun's life cycle one billion-fold if it does. The Sun's red giant cycle will expand so far that it will engulf and incinerate all Undique Utopia within eight years, including the eight billion Earth's in the Cosmic Column. It was as if the Suns were about to end their existence by their own doing.

Perhaps now we knew why it was a supreme law in Undique Utopia not to10 view the future. Scientists said because of the math? Many humans did not buy that malarkey, but what could they do?

Scientists hypothesized behind closed doors, while back on the original Earth, before the Cosmic Column was created, that the Sun might eventually release its electrons. However, nothing was relayed to the population of the original Earth.

This will end up causing an encompassing shock, destroying all of the approximately 80 quintillion people across the 8 billion + Earth's. As a mind refresher, quintillion is a 1 with eighteen zeroes. So with that said, the population of Undique Utopia is staggering.

It has not been stated what would happen if the Sun decided to strip its gravity, but only neutrinos and electrons will exist in its atomic structure.

Under this scenario, it will cause the Earths to be pulled towards the central Sun, where every planet will burn up, and everyone would perish from dehydration because water gets too hot to drink and will boil off as the planets pull towards the Sun. In the process, it may burn off all the waters in the oceans if the temperature reaches over 225 degrees.

If I were you, I'd make a hot cup of coffee or tea and ponder whether you would like to:

1. Be electrocuted,
2. Get consumed by the Sun when it expands through each Earth or
3. Be slowly pulled towards the central Sun of all planetary rings, having burned up all the planets.

Better douse yourself in suntan lotion because it's getting HOT in here.

THE END

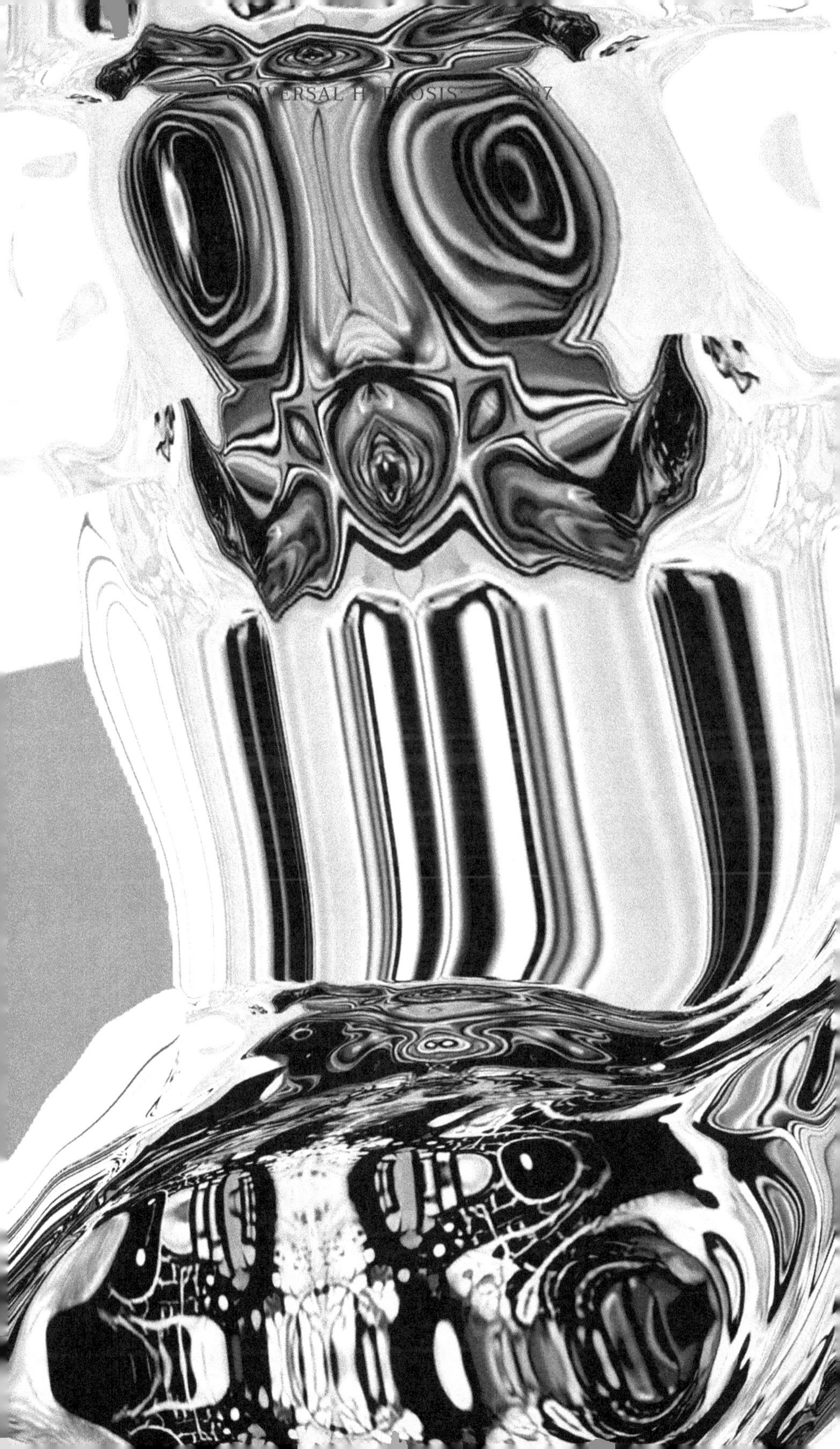
UNIVERSAL HYPNOSIS

Chapter 27

"Chainsaws & Robots"- or – "The Realest Reality TV Show Ever Seen: 'To Free A Killer'"

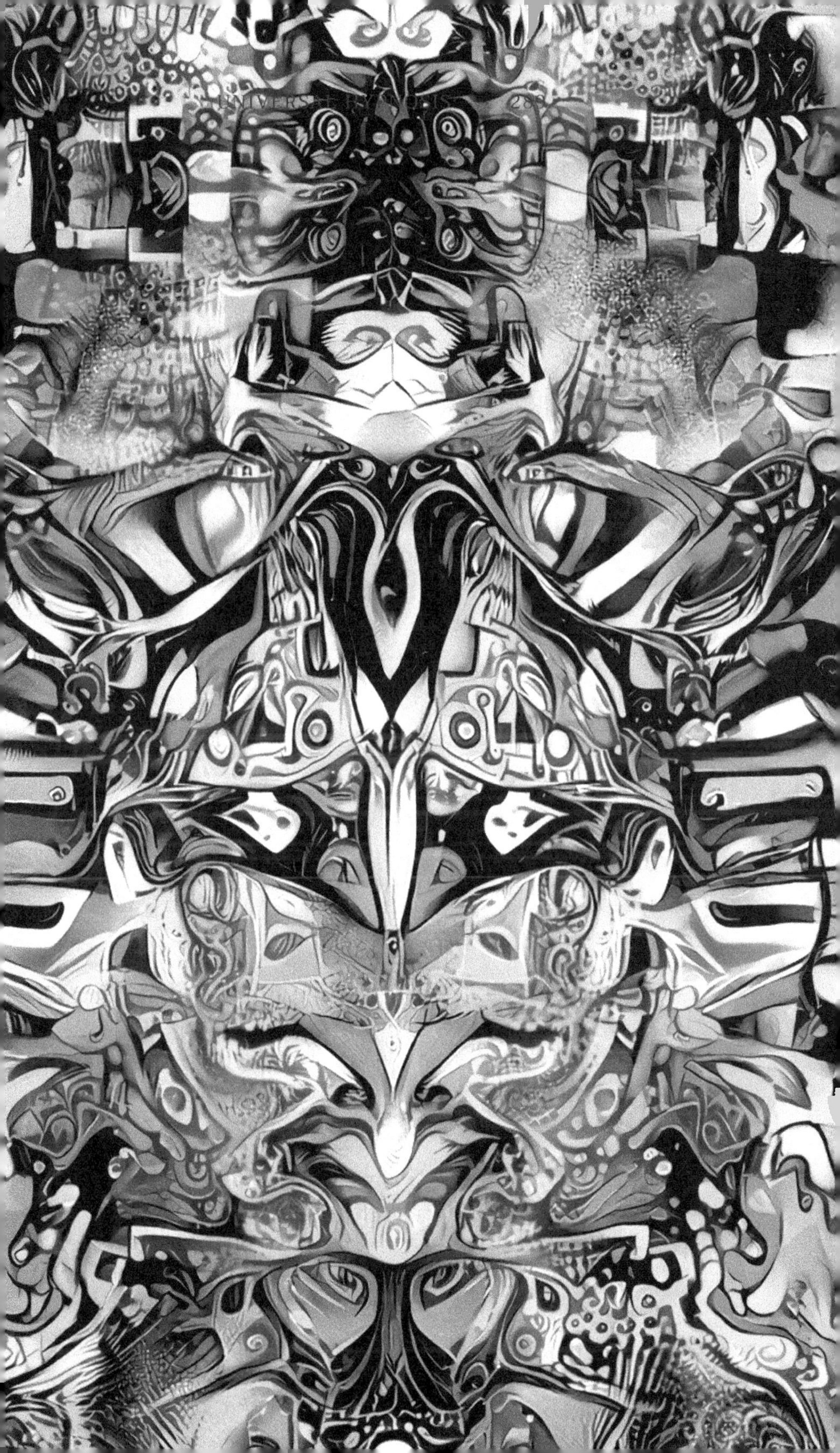

Today, it was thrilling news as a "serial killer sting" resulted in seven suspected serial killers' apprehensions. The crimes of the "Sadistic Seven" were more heinous than any crime scenes ever witnessed.

Due to the results of the 66 persons murdered by the Sadistic Seven, they were deemed to go to court through a "different" system that had been newly instated.

Over time, the Sadistic Seven had all of their trials. The result of all trials was the most dreaded and hopeless sentence that any person could ask for. The courts sent them to "Robot Island."

The sadistic seven were better known as:
1. "Bloody Cocktail," Brendon Mortimer
2. "Drunk on Blood," Roger Unatatis
3. "The Oblong Noose," Roy Mortanious
4. "Drown Them In Blood," Chris Duorum
5. "10 Precise Stabs," Glen Klidleatis
6. "Hung Like A Noose," Marc Sanguine
7. "The Bloody Deluge," Majeeda Delphine

Most grisly of all the serial killers was the "lady" named Majeeda Delphine. Her murders were the worst by far, dominating the heinousness factor over all of her male contemporaries by at least fivefold.

The courts decided that all seven would be cast to an island in the mid-Pacific, previously mentioned, as "Robot Island." The "7" had taken place in a televised reality show where the seven serial killers will compete against each other until only one person reigns supreme over their former contemporaries and competitors.

Once the last person stands, it was stated that they would be able to go back to their hometown, where they will be given somewhat full freedom to live their lives as they see fit. They will then be on house arrest for the remainder of their lives.

The island included a 200 feet (1 Meter) high active volcano where an advanced maze was situated in the caldera. The maze walls were made from mirrors, making it extra difficult to evade the foes that lurk in the maze. Inside this distorted maze was where many homicidal robots lurked. They were known as "The Sawbots."

These devious machines had many ways to end someone's existence if they were not in full-on survival mode.

These are the defensive weaponry that all of the robots in the maze have:
1. A short-range laser on their shoulders that can shoot with pinpoint accuracy
2. A slot on their chests that shoots saw blades out at incredible speeds
3. Chainsaws for hands with articulation that enabled the chainsaws to move in many directions, making them lethal.

These "Chainsaw Robots," as they were popularly known, could only be defeated with only one weapon. Known as the "Lazar," this laser was an anti-electricity gun that subdued robots in the maze and rendered them completely defenseless.

Each person sentenced to the robot maze was given a high-power flashlight and a Lazar to incapacitate the homicidal robots in hopes of escaping with their lives.

What if the former serial killers could successfully complete the maze? In that case, they are given passage home when the crew leaves for home in the future. Although to this date, at present, no one has ever escaped during previous visits to the menacing Robot Island.

It came time for the sadistic seven to leave for the island. They arrived at the uninviting tropical island to partake in the televised reality show entitled "To Free A Killer."

The Sadistic Seven went through six challenges until only one killer stood victorious. That winner will, as previously stated, win passage back to society.

The "contestants" walked in front of a makeshift studio, where the show's host, Darren McKinley, came out from behind a partition and welcomed the Sadistic Seven, and laid out the show's rules.

The first challenge was called the "Crocodile Long Jump." Each person had to long jump over crocodiles. The long jump was done by standing still and jumping forward as far as possible.

The very first person to attempt the crocodile long jump was Majeeda. She had no problem making the jump across the rabid and very hungry crocodiles below.

It came down to Roy and Roger. Roger was brave enough to go next. He slipped and fell face-first into the crocodile pit, about to be the meal of the hungry crocodiles.

Roger managed to stand up, and while thinking of his many victims, a crocodile bit him on his neck as a whistling sound rang out.

The crocodile wrangler came in and pulled the crocodile off of Roger. Little did the audience know, but all of these crocodiles had no teeth. The creators of the crazed Reality TV show did it this way to guarantee that the loser would have to go to the robot maze.

Some of the cast of the show took Roger to the top of the active volcano within the hour, where he entered the robot maze. The maze was built inside the volcano's caldera, which was next to impossible to escape.

Roger was given his Lazar (anti-electricity gun) and a flashlight. He was forcefully placed into the maze where the homicidal chainsaw robots lurked.

It wasn't soon before long that the shrieking of a nearby robot could be heard, and before Roger even knew it, a saw blade flew at his head and slammed into it about four inches deep. We can only hope that the immense pain felt by Roger could never had been equal to the pain he put his innocent victims through.

He lost his mind due to blood loss and fell flat on his face, causing the saw blade to slit his head right in two with its impact on the ground.

Five challenges later, and after the robot maze had consumed all but two of the "7", the pool of seven came down to two persons who were eager to find out what the final challenge was.

The two persons left were the heroine of sorts, "The Bloody Deluge" Majeeda Delphine, and the "10 Precise Stabs" Glen Kloriatus. They will be pitted against each other to attempt to find a harmless robot somewhere on the island and bring back its motherboard or brain of sorts to the host. Winning the show will cement the serial killer's win and enable the lucky person to gain passage back to society.

Upon starting the challenge, Majeeda and Glen went in opposite directions, where they searched the island for the elusive robot. Majeeda came to a clearing where she saw blinking red dots in the distance...robot!

She started to run in the direction of the lights, as she noticed that the lights had gone out, and there was nothing in the distance that could be seen. Nonetheless, she ran and found the robot, where Glen first saw it and was currently dismantling it.

Glen and Majeeda had a past and knew each other quite well. Glen tried something out of the blue: He swung the motherboard at Majeeda, but she ducked and grabbed the motherboard from Glen and smashed the motherboard over his head.

Upon striking the ground, Majeeda proceeded to kick Glen so hard in the head that his neck snapped.

Triumphant, Majeeda trekked back to the makeshift studio. Once there, she showed the bloody motherboard to the host, who then announced Majeeda as the winner of this grotesque and scary Reality TV show known as "To Free A Killer."

Majeeda was playfully given a Lazar and a flashlight. The Reality TV show's host, Darren McKinley, joyfully told her that she could board the boat back to society as all her crimes were now absolved.

"Take me back to California where my heart-sick family awaits. I did everything required, and now I want to see my family damn it!" Majeeda snarled as she did not want to spend even one more minute on Robot Island.

Majeeda got on the somewhat large boat: Destination California. After several hours and being completely disoriented by the boat ride, Majeeda saw land in the distance. She started to get overjoyed, knowing that she would see her family again and go right back into society.

She held a dark secret, though; she knew that she would kill again, even if it were in years to come. She made up her mind that the thrill she received from killing was something she needed to remain herself.

The boat docked on a random island, not California, where the boat had to make a pit stop.

Majeeda was pissed and wanted them to leave at once. She walked off the ship and went to chew out the captain, only to her surprise; everyone had already gotten back on the boat.

She did a power walk toward the steps of the boat. Before she knew it, The Captain put up the steps, and the boat started to leave the island. All she heard from the boat was the show's host, yelling, "Welcome to the REAL Robot Island."

As Majeeda pondered what the captain had just said, she started to tremble from her towering anxiety. She was now on the real Robot Island and had no escape from the horrors that lurk in this small but deadly wooded place.

She started to hear some kind of white noise in the air as she turned around...

Seven different types of homicidal robots were charging towards her. She thought first about the Lazar that could have subdued these robots had it not been for her throwing it away in angst.

As the robots made their way towards her, she ran into the ocean. She only hoped that the homicidal robots could not swim...

THE END

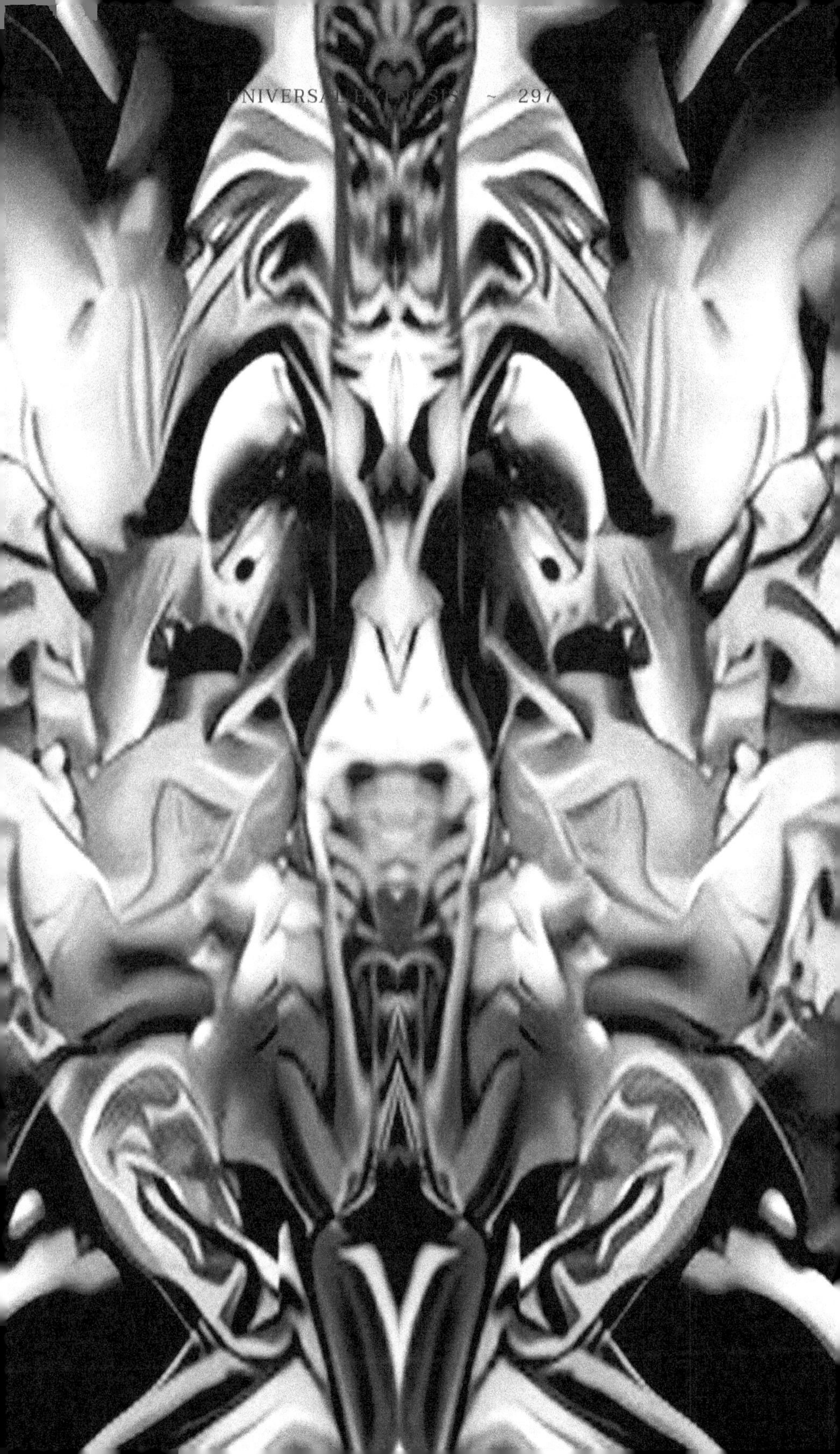

"Invasion of the Resource Snatchers!" -or- "Trippin' Earth" -or- "The Only Good Purploh Is A Dead Purploh!"

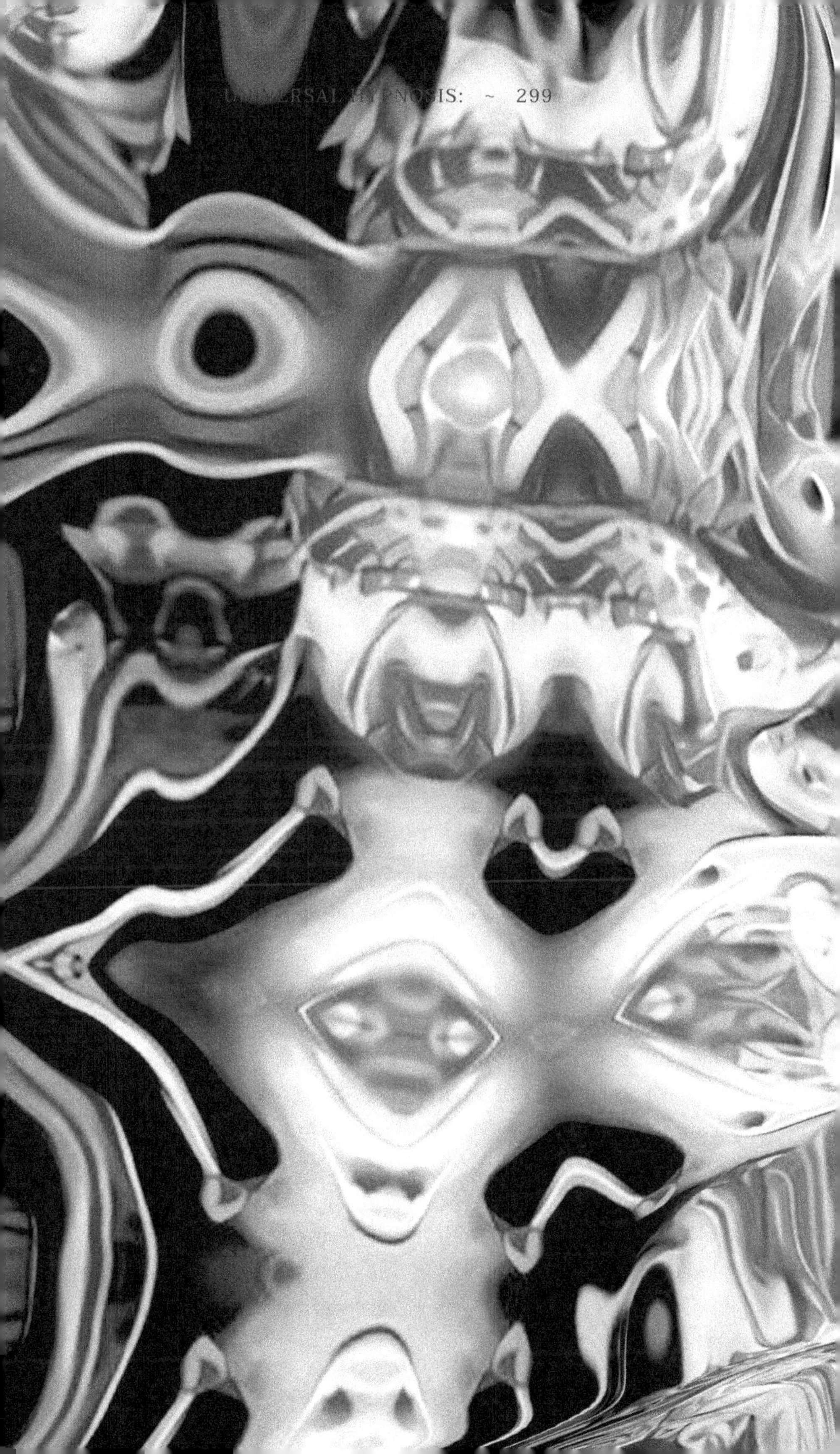
UNIVERSAL HYPNOSIS: ~ 299

The year is 2099, and Humanity survived the technological singularity by becoming "friends" with robotkind. Acclimating to a world filled with robots was no easy feat. Over time Humanity did it with the prize of having controlled the robots how they saw fit.

The technological singularity is defined as "a theoretical future in which technological growth becomes uncontrollable and irreversible. The singularity will have results in unforeseeable/ unpredictable changes to human civilization."

The evolution of robotics had reached its pinnacle. Rarely did a robot go faulty and need significant repairs. The robots' structure was flexible, just like Humans, and they all had civil rights, just like their Human controllers.

Now, of course, some Humans, over half, had become cyborgs by being fitted with everything imaginable as it relates to "Robo" upgrading.

For example, the electronic eye became an early craze that allowed the Internet to appear in the vision, almost like virtual reality.

A harmonious state existed between Humanity and their robot brethren. Morale planet-wide was higher than it had been for as long as anyone could remember due to this positive relationship between humans and machines, among other things.

Robots now operated all of the flying taxis. Also, most retail jobs were given to robots, along with countless other simple jobs. Engineers, for example, were not replaced.

Nothing would negatively sway our robotic brethren to go homicidal and start wiping out the population.

Just a thought...

On a mild day in mid-July, astronomers noticed some sort of pink "cloud" approaching Earth. The astronomers had no idea what it was or where it came from but knew Earth's destination. Scientists knew that it came from somewhere out in the untamed cosmos. Upon closer scientific inspection, it was figured out what the cloud was composed of...

Lysergic Acid Diethylamide (LSD) or Acid was the main part of this pink cloud with other gasses, none of which seemed to be of any relevance to Humanity. They also noticed that everything found in the great cloud was non-toxic, thus poses no dire threat to Humanity.

Let's ponder the previous sentences for a bit. A pink cloud approached the planet composed of enough LSD to have everybody in the entire population, Trip for an exceptionally long time...possibly permanently. Let that one set in for a while...

The Psychonauts (persons who regularly use psychedelic drugs, including but not limited to LSD) were very excited for the pink cloud to hit Earth so they could see what it does to the entire population. They wanted to experience Humanity's negative and positive repercussions when they collectively joined the "Incredible Global Trip."

In other parts of the world, things were about to get very psychedelic...

In Chapinero, Bogota, Colombia, a man, Jonathan Ospina, sat down for the evening to enjoy his favorite television program. Please note that Jonathan is not a Psychonaut and has never touched any drugs besides aspirin.

He looked over at his window and took notice of the fantastic evening sky. He had never seen the sky so pink before. It was a sight that Jonathan would not soon forget.

Little did he know that this would be a night that would be etched upon his brain until the day his Soul exited Earth. As he watched the sunset, pink smoke came into the room and engulfed his entire home.

Humanity learned the hard way that the pink cloud can move through structures, pretty much anything ever built, and the cloud can penetrate through, leaving not a single person safe from the pink cloud and the inevitability of being under LSD's psychedelic grasp.

Like a snap of the fingers, the man entered an extremely potent Trip. Where space bent around him, and millions of colors beckoned him.

This Trip also happened to over 98% of persons across Earth. The remaining two percent worked far below the surface and did not enter a permanent trip. They were either pissed or ecstatic that they were not tripping...

Jonathan had never experienced a body load like this before, ever...Jonathan was tripping so hard that he had to go to the hospital. He left his apartment building, which was only five blocks from the hospital.

While he was halfway out of the front building door, someone handed a newborn puppy to someone through the door as he was walking out of it. Jonathan made eye contact with the puppy and felt a different presence come over him.

He looked up the road and saw all kinds of signposts telling him to turn right, but were the signposts real or just a figment of his imagination?

People were outside their homes and were tripping too. It was actually kind of cool because it appeared that they were having a blast in their newfound psychedelic state.

But Jonathan was not doing well with his acclimation to being so LSDevious. So he rounded the corner and walked up two blocks, missing his turn.

This predicament prevented him from having a quick passage to the hospital. He reached the intersection of the next block up. Like that, Halloween-type music started playing loud enough for everyone outside to hear. Its source was unknown.

Psychedelic lights started to flash off the buildings of red and blue hues. The lights were blinking hypnotically with the music. The Trip was unlike anything Jonathan had ever experienced. It was very overwhelming for a non-psychonaut.

He thought that somehow his point of view got switched with the puppies when he exited the building. This was the only thing he could believe because he had no idea that LSD had taken over him and was now on a permanent trip.

The cars were speeding by him at breakneck speeds, squealing their tires, and doing donuts in the streets. Jonathan walked down a hill towards the hospital and had a grand idea: "Why don't I direct this traffic, so no one gets struck by these speeding cars?"

He stood in the middle of the street and attempted to direct traffic as the speeding cars came towards him, then somehow or another, moved around him without hitting him.

A policeman beckoned to Jonathan and wanted to know what he was doing. "I need an emergency room." He said. The policeman placed Jonathan in his squad car and drove him to the emergency room.

Jonathan entered and noticed that all the walls were "breathing" or moving in and out. He further described it as being "not of this world." He was called and sat down in an inconspicuous room within a half-hour.

Jonathan looked over at a poster on the wall; the poster was spinning and changing colors. Remember, he never did LSD and became overwhelmed, not knowing what was in that damned pink cloud. He was in the best place for himself. Maybe the tripping doctors could remove the LSD from his system?

The nurse brought in a little wooden table on wheels to place his belongings on. Before Jonathan knew it, the table started to sway as if water was just under the surface. This baffled Jonathan, although he felt quite entertained at the same time.

The nurse brought in an IV and hooked it up to Jonathan. He turned white like the moon and was under the impression that the IV would replace all of his blood with new blood. It did not.

That was nothing compared to what happened next...the nurse brought in an unassuming turkey sandwich where Jonathan took a single bite.

He, for reasons unknown, peeked under the bread of his turkey sandwich. It was...ALIVE ...with three pale white tentacled creatures that were in motion. Their tentacles beckoned to him as he observed what these strange creatures were doing.

The turkey sandwich was a living-breathing macrocosm of life. On the right third of the sandwich was a pale white tentacled creature. It had no features whatsoever and had four giant tentacles that were rhythmically moving. Its body was about an inch across, with its tentacles being a good three inches long.

Also, what was presumed to be female creatures were going up a conveyor belt type hill to the "male" creature just described. The male gave "food" to the female creatures, which then went down the conveyor belt to babies at the bottom, who were just being born while breaking through their egg sacs.

He did not take another bite. Jonathan managed to get a bit of sleep, which was well needed as could be imagined. Perhaps he dreamed about having tentacles? He awoke to the doctor, telling him it was time to leave.

He left the hospital but still felt very similar to the way he did last night. It was Sunday, and the chapel was open behind the hospital. Jonathan had never been in it and was excited to see what was inside.

It was a magnificent chapel with sky-blue ceilings and grand statues. Mesmerizing stained glass windows over ten feet high adorned the walls.

Jonathan took note that the children in the stained glass windows would dance whenever the band would play music. It was a sight that he would never forget, along with everything else he witnessed the previous night.

Now that Jonathan's Trip had been explained, it can be admitted that this Trip happened many years ago to the author when half a milligram (500 ugs) of synthetic LSD (1P-LSD) was ingested (this is a rather large dose). This Trip was accurately and factually stated, just as it occurred to the author on 16 August 2016.

Across the planet, Humanity fell under the LSD spell as their sight became "Liquid Visions," and they experienced unforgettable trips that will most likely never end.

It must be explained that the trips were about 8 out of 10 and everyone worldwide still had some sort of grasp on reality. From what was gathered, pink elephants were stopping traffic in many locales... Leprechauns must have been out in droves due to all the "rainbows" seen by the tripping population.

In Buenos Aires, Argentina, an engineer, who oversaw the robots at a Fortune 500 company, noted that she overheard two robots conversing quietly.

One said that the pink cloud was not just LSD when it penetrated the entire planet; it also altered all robots' sentient nature, causing them to possibly go homicidal in the worst-case scenario.

The consciousnesses of all robots had been somehow manipulated, and they were slowly and horrifically evolving.

The engineer (a closet psychonaut) phoned her superior and informed them of the possible incoming global genocide. Without the robots' knowledge, governments worldwide set out to thwart the robot's plan for planetary peril.

On a random day in October, it was reported that a gang of robots went berserk and attacked several guards at Buckingham Palace.

England stated that it would cut its electricity temporarily to stop the robots, England cut its power, and the robots fell to the ground, defeated. The world followed and "paused" electricity.

It took only minutes, and every robot fell in place and was no longer a threat to Humanity. It was enforced that every robot would be dismantled and recycled immediately.

So with that, every robot worldwide was recycled. It was difficult to imagine how much of a chore this was while under LSD's guise.

Many sculptures were built by molding the surplus of the robots together. Many other creative ways were thought up to use the overabundance of obsolete robots.

They had been defeated in their sick game that was a bit sad since the robots had no violent intentions until the pink "consciousness" cloud penetrated Earth.

The robots' motives were not their fault since their circuitry was reprogrammed to become homicidal, and they followed their internal orders.

In time, all robots were disconnected from their internal power sources, and the electrical grids worldwide came alive again.

Apparently, "someone" out in space did not like that we were not defeated by the robots. This could or could not spell doom for Humanity.

It was hypothesized that the cloud was sent to render Humanity mindless so that extraterrestrials could take over Earth due to the massive amounts of LSD everybody ingested.

It looked like our extraterrestrial neighbors didn't know that we humans could handle copious amounts of LSD, and Humanity was far from mindless.

The Earth now appeared more vibrant and friendly. Now, millions of colors can be seen, no matter where the population walked on Earth.

Astronomers noted that through their great telescopes, they observed that some sort of spacecraft headed towards Earth.

It was moving very fast, and it was not alone. There were so many other spacecraft that it was a chore to count them.

Nobody bothered.

A few days later, the strange spacecraft started landing on Earth. They were orange triangular ships that were at least 1000 feet long. In simpler terms, the spacecraft were over three football fields long.

The humans, with their new psychedelic haze, were ready for anything. It was believed that the massive amounts of LSD consumed by Humanity convinced us we were better at war for some strange reason. Humanity was ready for the fight and was prepared to do whatever was needed to protect and keep Mother Earth our own.

It was reported worldwide that the large spacecraft landed in every country, with multiple spacecraft landing in the larger countries.

In the United States, nine ships landed precisely in each direction on the compass, including one in its center. It was strange that none of the spacecraft doors opened upon landing. It was as if there was nobody aboard.

This gave us enough time to get each country's military worldwide to surround the ships and wait for them to open the doors.

By now, everyone outfitted with a firearm was trigger-happy, and being under LSD's guise made all persons want to destroy their share of these extraterrestrial interrupters.

For all we knew, the ships were empty...Until the doors, all at once and on, every spacecraft flew open. Before the bum rush, each spacecraft had a "general" who made a speech:

"We are here for your resources and will destroy every human who gets in our way from absorbing this planet's resources." "It is not our intention to destroy you, but quite frankly, we have no use for you people. Enjoy your Trip."

Hairy purple humanoids, about four feet tall, bum-rushed all the militaries all over Earth.

They had purple skin, yellow hair, and blue eyes. They had long, coarse hair on their heads that were mohawks. They had medieval-style shields and beautifully crafted swords, which appeared to be platinum.

The short "Purploh's" (as their nomenclature became) were mighty fighters and were somewhat powerful. One thing they were good at was sneaking.

An unsuspecting person could be walking through the park doing their thing when BANG! A sword penetrates them through their heart from behind.

This was the current state of Earth, and although our planet had the numbers, the Purploh's had the agility and other abilities that were too many to mention.

It cannot even be stated what it was like to partake in a war while the humans' minds permanently tripped on good ole' LSD.

It is painless due to LSD tricking the brain into believing that pain is nonexistent. It took out the fear factor of war and caused the militaries to barge right in and fight for our planet.

We would be damned if some extraterrestrial race would wipe us clean off the map and exploit the resources of our Mother Earth. We could not let that happen now or at any time in the planet's future.

After countless purploh casualties, Humanity looked like they were winning, although it was hard to call victory with the Purploh's that came out of the 300 - 400 ships. We knew that the war was not over as long as those vile creatures walked our planet.

After 14 months of grueling combat, the idiots left in their ships and launched into the sky, hopefully never to return again. Eventually, the ships all left the planet, and we declared victory!

There is the story of the last living purploh being seen. This story, beyond the shadow of a doubt, must be told.

While interrogating the last surviving Purploh, it said, "There will be a wave of our masters who will come to Earth because too much of our blood was spilled."

This is the direct result of the Purploh's losing the war with Humanity. "I'm not going to lie; they would have made you wish that we wiped you guys out." These were the last words of the final living purploh.

The last living purploh laughed in a maniacal-like tone until it stole its sword back from the interrogator and jammed it thru its heart. The soldier went back to headquarters and told her superiors what the last purploh said.

We checked the skies, and nothing was headed our way. After some months, the world became more stable, and things were getting even better than before the Trip.

We missed the robots, but they had to be discarded as they were recycled. But then the day came: one thousand space-craft, lengthier and more massive than the Purploh's ships, were headed towards Earth. All at once, the spacecraft landed all across Earth. Just like the last time, the doors did not open.

We took note that the exit doors on the craft were all at least fifty feet high, telling Humanity that they would not be fighting any four-foot-tall extraterrestrials this time around.

Then it happened, the doors descended, and Humanity's new adversary: forty-foot tall cyborg-ape cyclops's were now seen worldwide.

Every last one of them was a super-advanced technologi-cal marvel. The "Cyborgorillas" was an evolutionary leap light years beyond our former robots.

At first glance, the soaring cyborgs appeared indestructible.

We noted that we could run really fast in our LSD-influenced bodies now.

To explain what ensued after this would cause a lottery power ball winner to become depressed, so the story must end here.

The End

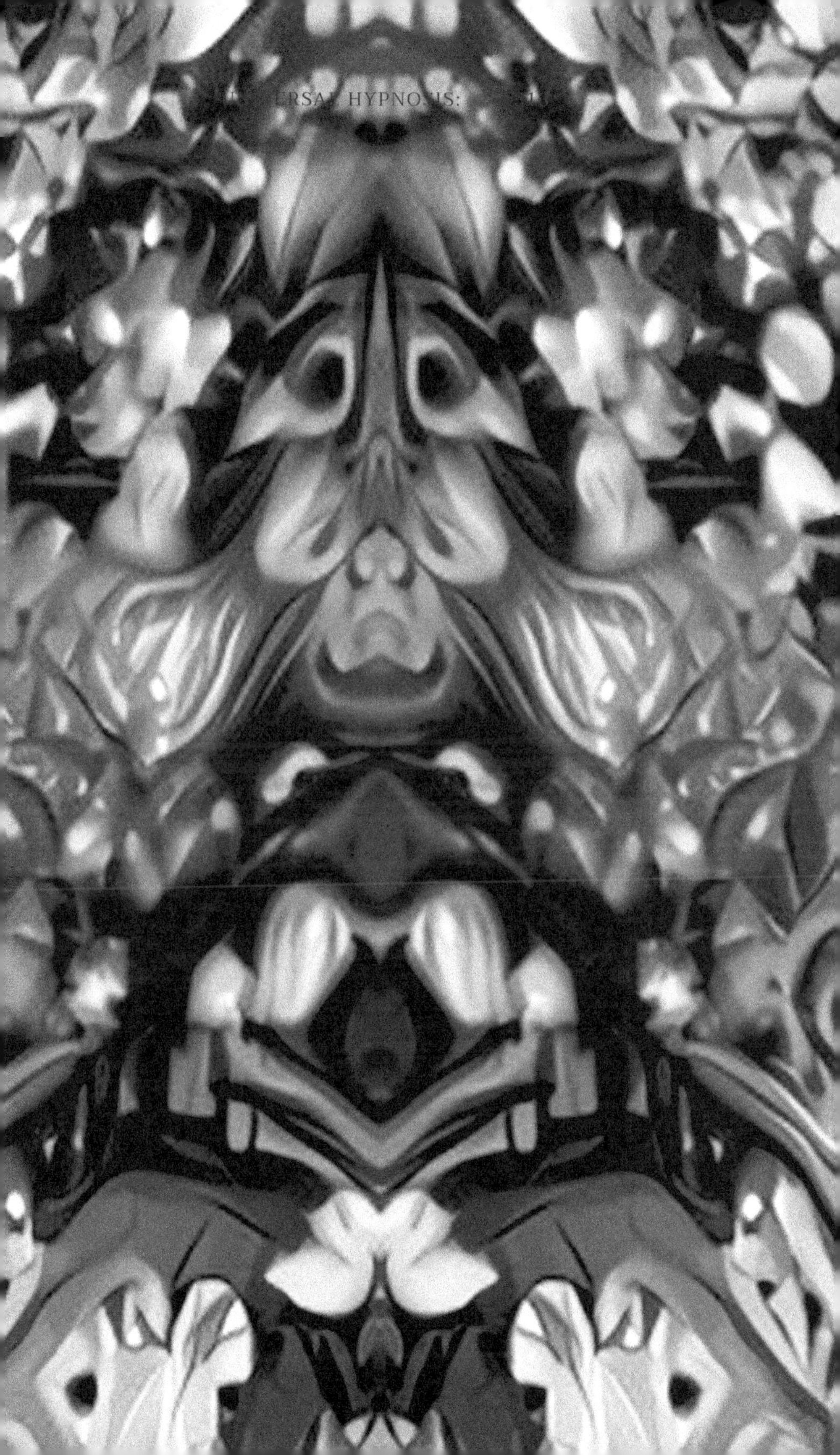
UNIVERSAL HYPNOSIS:

"How to Colonize the Moon: A Treaty to Conquer Space, Finally" - or - "Civilization or Colonization: The Choice May Not Be Yours"

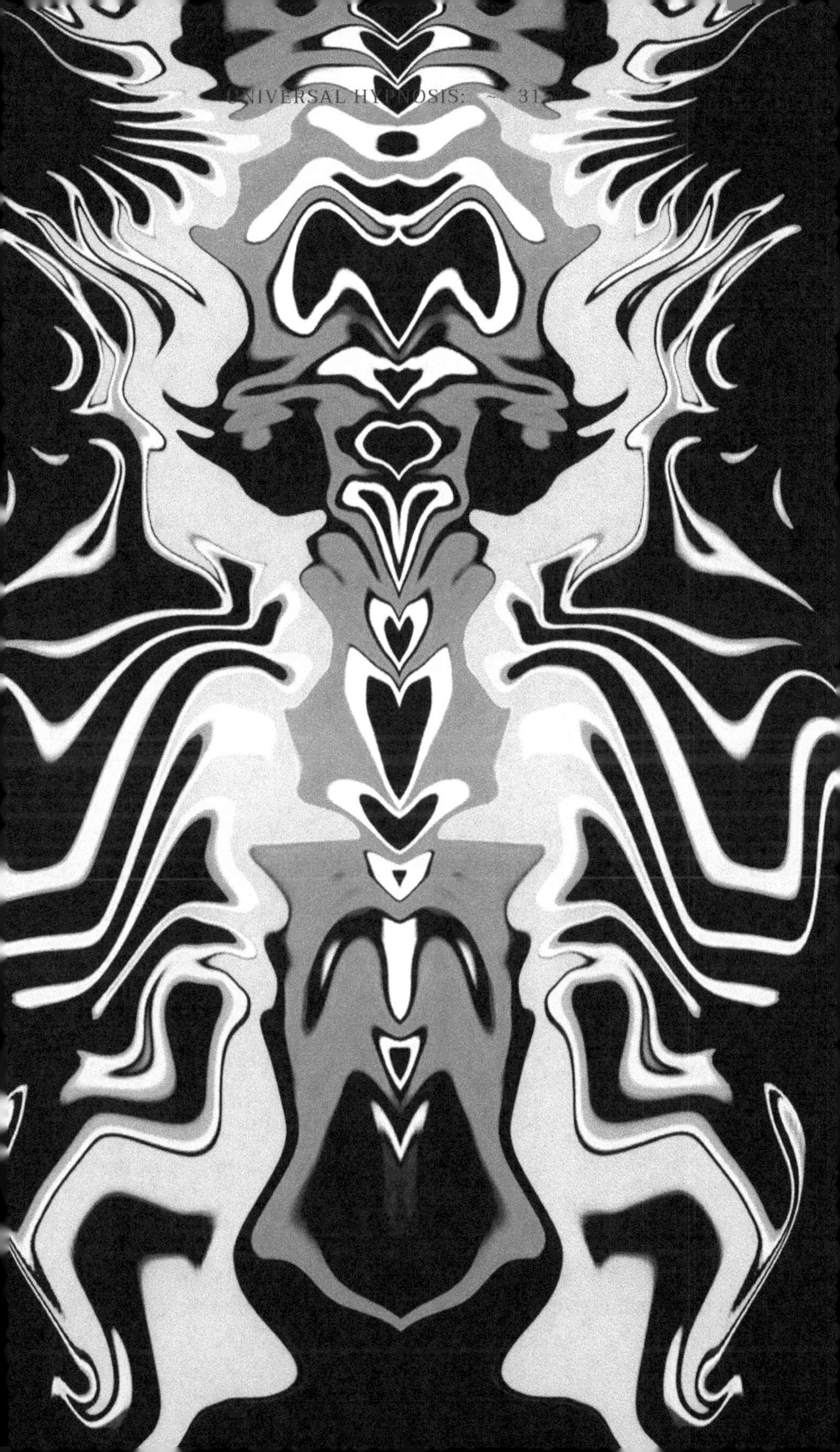

UNIVERSAL HYPNOSIS: ~   315

Humanity recently inked a treaty to colonize the Moon, where each country had to sign the treaty or else it was null and void. The last country had signed it, making the Moon Colonization a future reality.

The world rejoiced, having learned that the colonization of our lunar neighbor would soon become a reality. Most of Humanity was giddy, knowing that they would soon walk the Moon like many other astronauts before them.

Engineers and scientists will construct obelisks and electrify them using a sizeable electromagnetic bomb, which will create an artificial atmosphere. This electrifying of atmospheres had all worked on small-scale experiments.

The electromagnetic bomb was needed since once dropped on the Moon. It would "light up" the obelisks, which would cause the Electrosphere to be created.

The creation of Electrospheres worked by having electrified the argon in the atmosphere, which will cause the electrical charge from the obelisks, covering the entire Moon in useful electricity.

Once Engineers and scientists built the obelisks, not soon after, citizens will live on the Moon in three-month intervals.

Humanity was in peace as our most significant efforts put forth had now paid off. What a wonderful time for humans to be alive!

The obelisks needed to be built, also a space elevator needed to be installed, and some other buildings had to be erected on the lunar surface before the first civilians could set foot on the Moon.

The day arrived, where the world watched the shuttle's launch that would haul the 50-ton (45.36 tonnes) electromagnetic bomb to the Moon.

The seasoned astronauts came to the platform and waved to everyone watching, knowing that Humanity would begin our colonization of space.

The astronauts entered the spacecraft and fired up the engines.

It launched beautifully, but tragedy struck when about three miles off the ground. An electrical fire started when the electromagnetic bomb was disconnected from its power source on the ground since no one cared to disconnect it. This will change the world right before Humanity's eyes.

The disconnection of the bomb's power source caused a major electric spark that was so powerful that it was evident that things would get worse.

The rear of the shuttle caught fire. The fire caused a mini-explosion, regretfully disconnecting the shuttle's electromagnetic bomb, which caused the 100,000 (90.79 tonnes)-pound bomb to had plummeted towards the ground.

As luck would have it, the astronauts were safe...or did I speak too soon?

The world watched in utter terror as the electromagnetic bomb plummeted miles to the ground and ignited, sending a lightning-like shockwave over the entire Earth, which had halted all electronic functions and scrambled every person's thoughts like an egg.

Immediately upon the bomb's detonation, civilization changed or pretty much halted. This is also not just a temporary thing. When it was stressed that all of Humanity's brains were scrambled like eggs, there was no sensationalism or sarcasm in that statement.

If the state of affairs on the planet improved, there might be help for Humanity, but they were basically zombies with no appetite for now. Although maybe they wanted to start eating brains since they had no brains themselves – at least one that worked.

Now that the electrical grids were wiped out and the Internet was a thing of the past, all other electronic functions ceased.

What helped create light at night were the global brush fires, which were now in over 100 countries. After some time, all the while, the fires spread and spread since Humanity no longer had the intellectual capabilities of rectifying the situation.

Humanity could not hold its biological functions now.

It was not out of the ordinary to had seen a perfectly fine-looking man, and a look at his behind revealed more skid marks than Talladega Superspeedway. The man would have cleaned up any other day after himself, but now his brain is mush along with the rest of Humanity's brains.

When the shockwave penetrated Earth, it altered everyone's way of thinking by causing their synapses to fire much faster. There will be more on this subject a little later. Before too long, the brain developed a mental cocktail of depression, schizophrenia, Amnesia, and the dreaded psychosis, with a dash of mania.

Once the shockwave penetrated everyone, the "erosion of consciousness" destroyed what the mind once was down to a primitive nature unable to comprehend in any discernible fashion the world around them.

The number of thoughts a Human has in one day is around 60,000 – 80,000. This equates to approximately one thought per second—synapses or thoughts fire at 268 mph.

With the brain's strange electrically induced state, it had sped up thought processes to slightly over 5,000 miles per hour. Now the number of thoughts is nearly 1.4 million in 24 hours.

Now Humanity was having thoughts, not at the old rate of 1 per second; they were nearly 1000 per minute or 15 per second. This sped up the minds of all Humanity to be faster than the Autobahn.

This is not necessarily a good thing... There were so many thoughts that no one could sleep anymore or concentrate on any task due to the overwhelming state of never having clarity in their minds.

Lifeless people wandered around as best they could, emitting random noises, and their feelings inside were incomprehensible. Humanity needed a way out, which may not be possible under the present circumstances. Nothing electrical worked anymore, either. The Internet blacked out, and the world went dark. Social media died...just like the mind.

The social media models probably starved since they didn't get likes on their selfies anymore. They were clueless over how to live now. They found out the stone-cold hard way that was looking "good" meant nothing in the current state of affairs.

In retrospect, the models should have spent more time in the library than in the gym, which may have made their chances of survival better than a lab rat. Suddenly and without warning, the population started getting migraines. Their heads pulsated as if their brains were spinning in their heads.

Shortly after, most person's eyes caught fire. Brains became flammable due to the unimaginable electrical synapses firing in the brain. Thus, an electrical fire in the brains of Humanity caused their brains to go supernova. They were exploding into an array of red, black, and gray-colored pigments.

Legions of exploding heads resulted in headless people littered everywhere. No one could gauge how much electricity is internal, which would tell us when cranial supernova may occur. Still, Humanity had no way of having known until their eyes burst into flames.

The astronauts who were supposed to transport the electromagnetic bomb to the Moon, yet failed, were not affected by the shockwave and were" normal." They are indirectly responsible for this terrible mess that had altered Humanity and turned them into lifeless shells of their former selves.

The shockwave did not affect all persons on planes that survived their landings. It would be assumed that the persons who were on planes were happy to be still cognizant... they weren't. They were the only sane people left in a world of global insanity brought on by the extremely powerful electro-magnetic bomb.

The sane people spent their time holed up inside their homes, scared at what had transpired and disgusted how quickly Humanity's minds degraded so rapidly.

Once global cranial supernovae occurred (many, many head explosions) worldwide, all non-infected persons roamed the Earth, searching for water and whatever food they could find. That was the only way to survive this new and insane world.

These are the only resources that will keep them alive while walking through a wasteland littered with fallen & headless corpses.

Only several years later, the world is void of any living humans. Animals came out of their hiding places and feasted upon the 10 billion corpses littered throughout the land as the 'Electromagnetic Armageddon Machine' did not as savagely harm their brains.

THE END

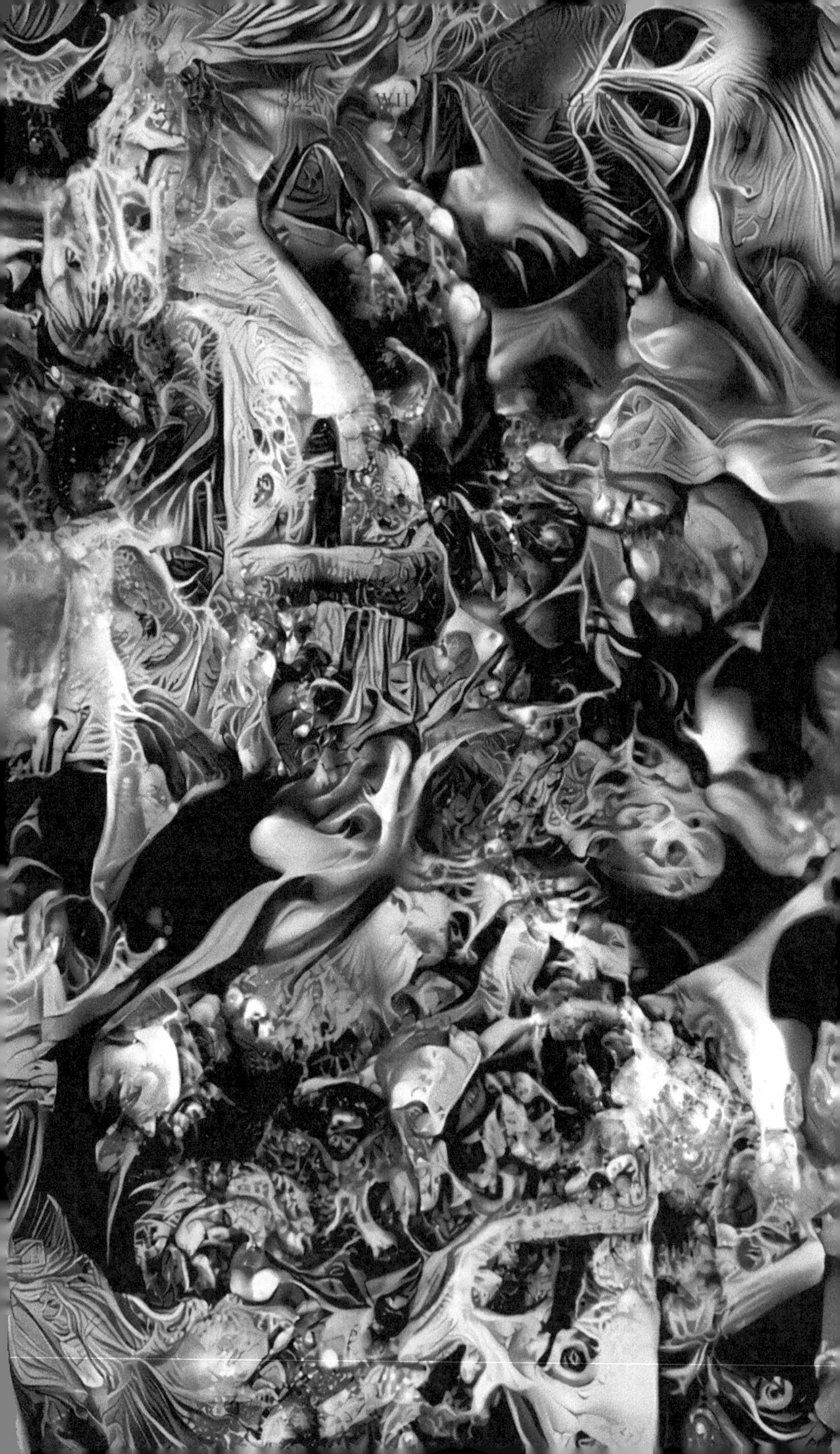

Chapter 30

My Pet Black Hole

UNIVERSAL HYPNOSIS 75

The Earth was not very prosperous in the year 2099. It was the dawn of a new century, and, quite frankly, Humanity was surprised that Earth lasted as long as it had with all the pollution that all humans created.

The problem now is that the global temperature is too cold due to previous Near-Earth-Objects that passed by recently. The global temperature had lasting adverse effects on the planet that may never return to normal.

Some months back, this occurred when a rogue planet zipped by Earth at around 30 million miles per hour, knocking our planet off its orbital path. Earth was not hit very far, only slightly, and still orbited the Sun.

Earth orbited the Sun every 512 days and was not that problematic for Humanity. The good thing about this is that people aged slower, but that wasn't enough.

This new orbital path caused Earth to be a lot cooler. It was not frozen solid as some might think. The planet received approximately 14 percent less sunlight because the Earth was further away from the Sun after the rogue planet violently zipped by it.

Humanity's number one mission was to warm up the planet somehow. Their ultimate survival hoped that warming up the planet might bring Humanity back to a more stable state. Humanity needed to do something about global cooling, and they had to do something quickly if the species was going to survive the sharp decline in temperature.

Scientists spent copious amounts of time formulating a way to increase the planet's temperature. They stated that they could engineer and manufacture a long laser that will release heat from the core that will heat the Earth when scientists shoot the laser into the Earth.

A powerful laser was planned to "cut" a hole halfway through the planet and release heat from the core. The scientists threw around some ideas. They would precisely stop the laser at a length that they chose that equals the exact size that the laser had to shoot underground to expose the core's heat.

The laser took several months to build, and before Humanity knew it, the laser was complete. This single idea may have saved Humanity, causing them to be taken off the endangered species list. The laser had a dial for how far the length of the laser could shoot. There were several notches on the laser that dictated how deep the laser would cut.

The great laser, code-named Tutumlux, which meant "Safe Light," was finished and ready to hit the dirt within a week or two.

The laser was set up at the South Pole (or in Antarctica) and ready to go operational. The time came for the laser to zap the ground and make a circular hole over fifty feet across. They positioned the laser and set it off.

Here it seemed that the laser was, in all actuality, set to the furthest most position, set to go on forever in any direction. The scientists were unaware that it was set at that position. The position of the notch on the laser may prove infinitely lethal. It could even have been terrorism with someone who purposely changed the laser's dial to severely mess up the planet.

Without warning, lava rapidly shot out of the large hole at

daring speeds. The death toll was small due to only the scientists perishing during the colossal eruption. This eruption was on par with the eruption of several supervolcanoes.

The eruption was so loud that people in the north of South America heard it. Initially, no one from the general population was harmed since no one lived near the South Pole. Spewing out of the hole, the lava shot hundreds of feet in the air.

The laser penetrated straight through the planet to the Arctic, precisely on the planet's opposite side, at the North Pole. Again, no one from the population was harmed since the eruption happened far from human civilization.

For twenty-four days, lava spewed out of both holes in the Earth. During that time, no one knew how long the eruptions would last. Eventually, the lava stopped flowing, and scientists could assess the actual damage.

While scientists surveyed the immense damage to the sites, it was noted that some sort of swarm of what appeared to be floating mirrored circles emerged from both holes in the poles in extraordinary numbers, nearly blackening the sky due to their intimidating numbers.

Again, swarms almost blacked out the sky because of how many "circles" were exiting the holes. These circles baffled the surviving scientists, who offered absolutely no explanation for what these circles were. There must have been billions of them exited both holes at both poles.

For weeks they exited the holes. It was such a strange phenomenon to witness what were believed to be "micro" black holes spread across the entire surface of our ailing planet.

The swarm finally stopped exiting from both holes. The strangest bit of it all was that a micro black hole affixed itself 10 inches above each human's head across Earth.

They were not an immediate threat, although no one was happy to have what was believed to be black holes floating above their heads. Still, it was anyone's guess as to what they were.

Looking around, black holes floating above people for no reason made Humanity wonder, "Why did they not annihilate us instantly?" It was a bizarre occurrence that baffled everyone, including those who studied black holes.

The mirrored circles followed everyone around permanently and forever tagged around with everyone across our planet. The micro black holes hung out above each head of Humanity. Perhaps, it can be imagined how uncomfortable it was when someone took a shower, and the water would go into the one side of the black hole but not exit through to the other side.

This fact made Humanity nervous because that proved that they have mouths, and of course, they will get hungry after a while. Earth was in a state of disrepair. We dreamed about other planets we could colonize, although that was impossible since the colonization of other star systems' had not happened yet.

It was but a week later, suddenly and without warning, the micro black holes began to spin above everyone and eventually lowered and swallowed everybody up across Earth. Not a single human existed any longer on our planet.

This act rendered the planet completely "humanless." Talk about "life after people." Before the population knew it, our planet awakened where humans had been brought back to the past. Humanity is in an alternate reality where the rogue planet never existed, and no temperature issues plagued the Earth.

The Earth was on its original orbital path around the Sun. This was the most glorious thing to learn. The "pet" black hole portals each dived into the ground and cut through the dirt and will lie in wait just in case Humanity decides to do something cataclysmic again.

Earth was "reset" to a time in the past as if nothing catastrophic had ever happened.

It seemed that the "portable portals," as they came to be known, were merely a planetary fail-safe that enabled the human race to survive another day.

In time, the Earth prospered way beyond what Humanity thought could happen to our near-pristine Mother Earth.

THE END

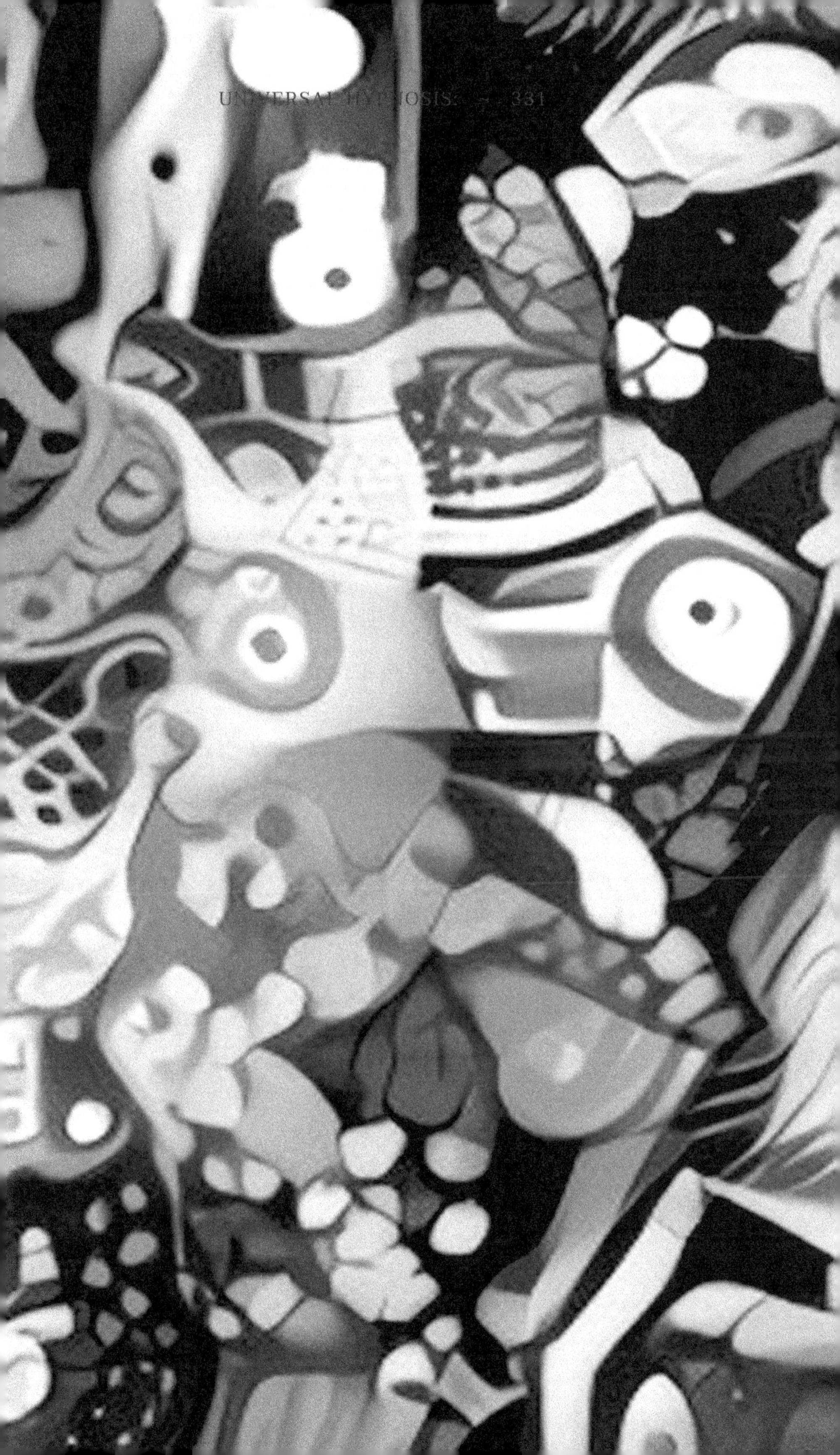

Chapter 31

"Planetary Evolution 101" -or- "Surfing A Magma Wave Beyond The Barriers of Infinity"

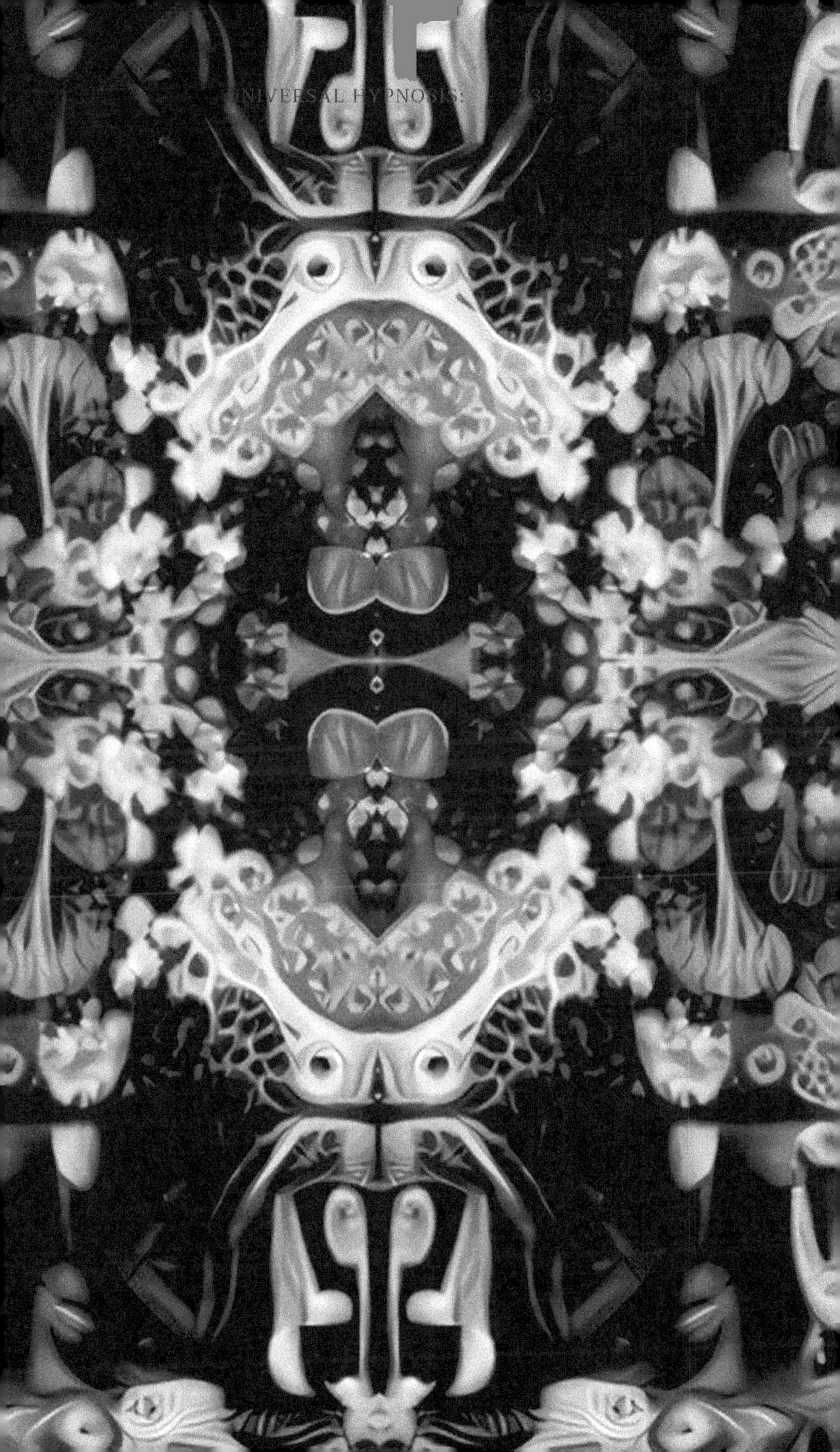
UNIVERSAL HYPNOSIS:

It was many years in the future, and our Earth had an accelerated temperature change. The Earth's average temperature increased by an intimidating amount, and in the hottest locales on our planet, it showed no sign of getting cooler. Humanity could have done nothing to save the ice in the Arctic and Antarctica from having completely melted.

On a positive note, Humanity built up the Arctic and Antarctica, which eased a sizeable amount of congestion in our coastal cities due to the land lost from rising sea levels. With the melting of the Arctic, Antarctica, and all other ice on the planet, sea levels had risen 200 feet (61 meters), swallowing 4.21% of the Earth's crust. Forty percent of households lived near the coast, where the relentless ocean swallowed homes and then the cities.

An example of a popular place to have lived was Greenland, on its virgin fields that were never explored before all of the ice melted. Due to the extreme heat, Humans barely ventured outside anymore as the scorching heat made it too difficult to go where there was no air conditioning. The phrase used to poke fun at the rising temperatures was, "Go outside and melt in a minute." Thankfully this was not an accurate statement.

Scientists sought a solution to the temperature debacle before the planet became inhospitable. They noted that there had been numerous brutal earthquakes near supervolcano sites all over the planet quite recently.

These twenty supervolcanoes might erupt due to the overwhelming amount of seismic activity pretty much encircling them. We tried to safely evacuate all persons who were not harmed by the earthquakes caused by the "awakening" of the twenty supervolcanoes and placed them a safe distance away from the seismic activity.

News agencies worldwide reported that suddenly and without notice, each of the twenty supervolcanoes erupted precisely 65 minutes apart. No one will forget that fateful day of constant eruptions. The supervolcanoes spilled ash hundreds of miles across Earth and spewed lava many miles into the air and even into space.

As much as Humanity could evacuate many from harm, the eruptions were just way too powerful to have saved everyone. Scientists were unsure what could have caused such a catastrophic scenario that ended in scores and scores of lives lost. There had to be answers, so they looked over the core's data collected since 1849.

They went back and checked their very old records concerning the core, which had not been updated for many decades, because why would the core have ever changed? They noted, to their horror, that the very old records showed steady increases in the core's size.

At the time, it was deemed "unnecessary work" to check the core's size. Scientists at the time did not consider it essential to have looked over the core and its ever-changing state. Also, scientists had been inundated over the past several decades and had little time to check it. This was (hopefully) not an excuse and may prove fatal on the most lethal of levels.

Now that it went unnoticed for many decades, the core was measured again. Scientists discovered that it had expanded so far that it was a mere 500 feet (152 meters) below the surface of the land or crust based on technical observations and testing done by the scientists.

To put this into perspective, anywhere anyone walked on Earth, lava was a mere 500 feet (152 meters) beneath where they stood. The damned media people quoted the term "Time Bomb Earth," a very sick and twisted way to describe the state of affairs. This was "the new abnormal," as the media stated many times.

The core kept expanding, and no one knew what would happen, but it could not be a good thing if it reached the surface. The scientific community scrambled to stop its expansion, but it was too late to fix the creeping lava from possibly penetrating the surface.

Climatologists determined that the cause of global warming was the fact that the core was expanding. The core's expansion had caused a dangerous amount of heat below the surface. This somewhat positive revelation for climatologists now answered what made the planet so hot. But who cared? Maybe the climatologists could stop the lava...

Humanity hoped the core never made its way to the surface, but now that the supervolcanoes have all erupted, it was not looking good. In Yellowstone National Park, closed since the supervolcano eruptions, "lava geysers" started to erupt all over the park in high numbers.

Imagine the famous geyser "old faithful," but composed of lava, ten times the size and shooting miles higher. Much higher, like a hundred miles into the atmosphere, sending some of the soot and ash off into space.

The rest of the lava hit the ground, causing fires and an intimidating amount of casualties. This happened as many lava geysers formed on Earth, one after another. The lava geysers erupted in all 229 countries. The lava geysers could be seen within a certain radius anywhere anybody traveled on Earth.

Lava geysers appeared under the oceans, triggering towering tsunamis the size that Earth had never seen before. These wiped out almost every standing building on Earth's coastlines that the creeping oceans had not destroyed since the melting of Earth's ice.

The thick black and acrid smoke from the millions of lava geysers was in danger of blocking out the Sun, but Humanity hoped that would not happen before they could develop technologies to prevent the smoke from engulfing the sky.

As bad as things were getting, Humanity kept holding on because it was believed that Humans would eventually find a way to stop the geysers and not have the Sun blocked from all the harsh smoke. Many persons wished it was an asteroid strike that occurred because that would have been a "faster way to go," as some Humans thought.

Eventually, the earthquakes came. One thousand+ 5.0 or higher earthquakes occurred within six months. Some even reached the 10.2 Richter scale reading, previously thought unreachable. It was surmised that there could not be 10.0 earthquakes. There were, and they crippled entire cities along with the other more minor but still deadly earthquakes.

This dwindled the population of Earth down due to the immense number of casualties lost across the planet. This was unlike anything that had ever been experienced in Earth's 4.5 billion year history.

Then, without warning, the entire Earth began to wobble on its axis, and deafening rumbles sounded out from beneath the Earth. It was as if an enormously powerful earthquake was about to break the planet into two pieces.

Composing all land on Earth, the entire crust gave way and took a pitfall into the core's molten oceans of unforgivable magma. The lava utterly destroyed all that had ever existed, melted the crust into a thick soup-like concoction that was absorbed back into the Earth.

Humanity had perished by having drowned in the core's molten iron lava. Nothing was left of the surface, having been melted by the immense amounts of lava that "consumed" the surface.

This caused the Earth to revert to how it looked 4.5 billion years ago when She was in Her infancy. Humans never knew that Earth used this evolutionary tactic to "renew" Herself every several billion years, and planetary evolution started back from day one.

The life cycle of the planet continued just like it did eons ago. Eventually, Earth will once again be teeming with life. We can only hope that evolution does not make a mistake twice of allowing Humans to once again rise to the top of the food.

THE END

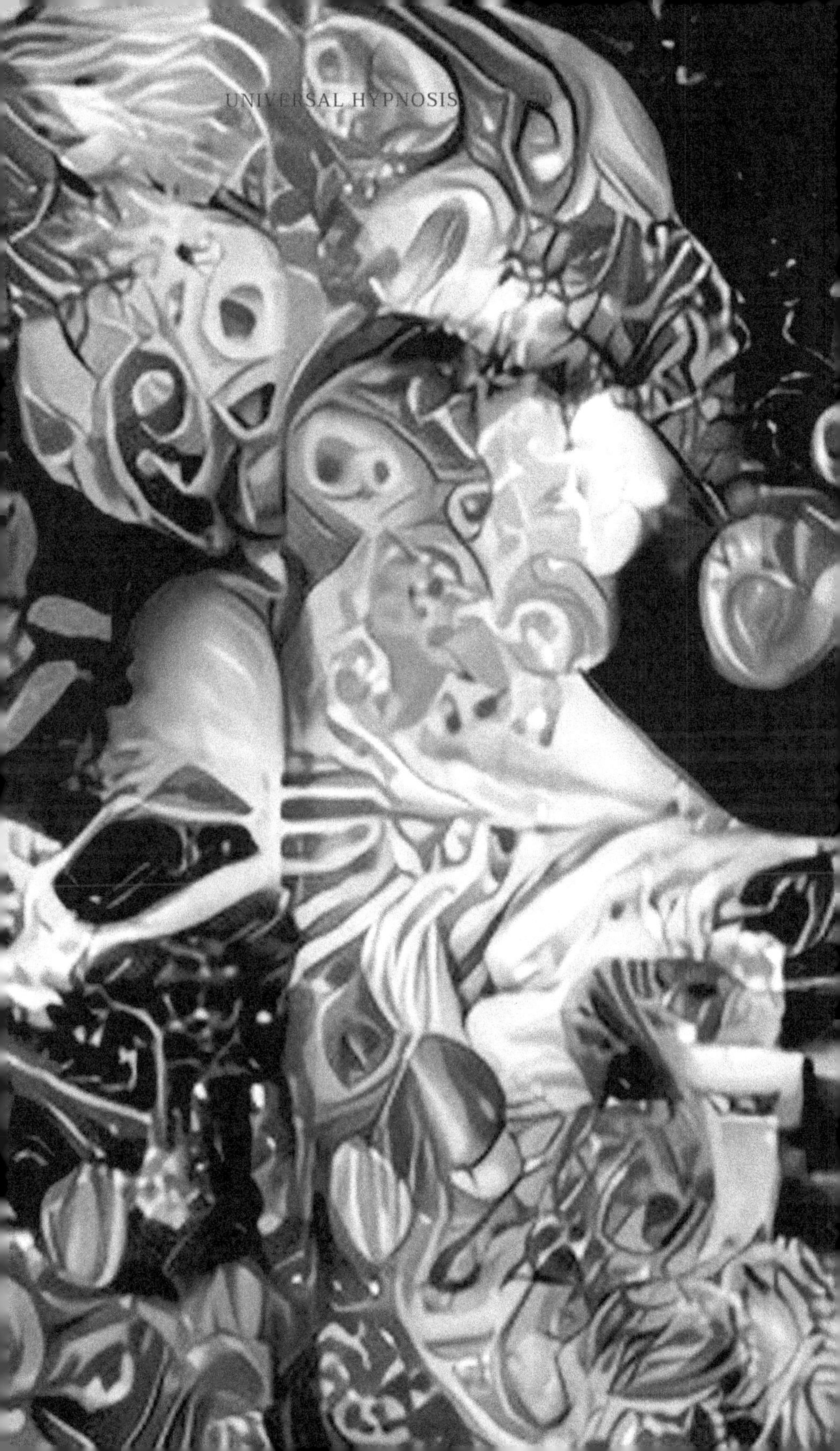
UNIVERSAL HYPNOSIS

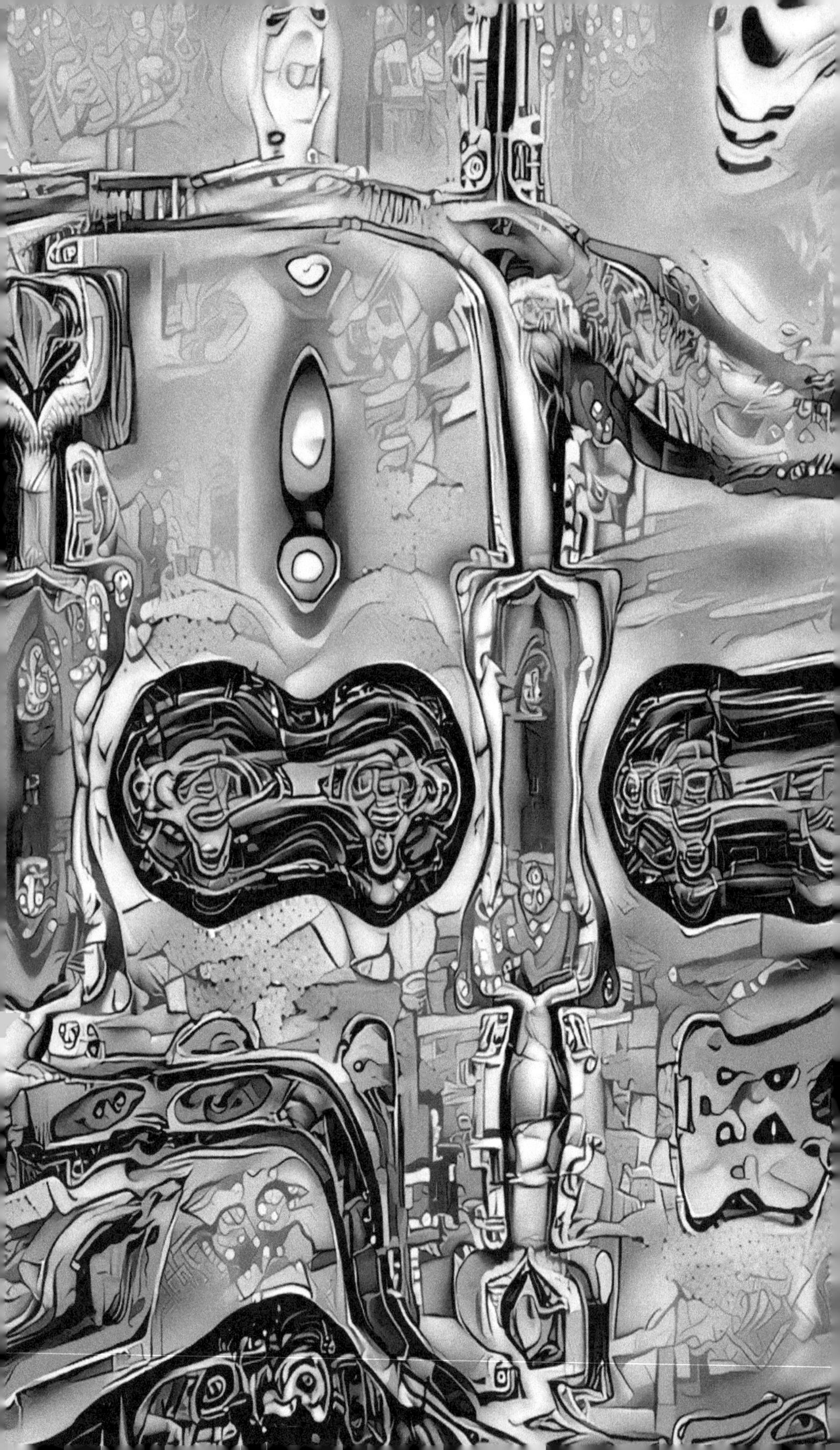

<u>Biography of an Artistic Author:</u>

William has always had a vast imagination for as far back as he can remember. He has always embraced his gift of writing/storytelling and Art, both of which he absolutely loves practicing...

In 1995, William discovered that he had a knack for writing short stories. Fast forward 25 years, and he published his first very short story collection entitled "Cosmic Apocalyptic Phenomena: Morality Tales from the Untamed Cosmos." This book was released in August 2020, which included 40 morality/space tales reminiscent of the classic "<u>Twilight Zone.</u>" Cosmic Apocalyptic Phenomena... was also William's first book to be published, and he would tell you that now being published is nothing short of exhilarating.

William decided to combine the book mentioned above with his new group of short stories and rearranged all 62 stories into two books, composing a saga entitled the "Untamed Cosmos Companion Saga." The saga will be spread across three books, as he still has over 100 story ideas for future very short stories.

As for being an Artist, that all happened in September 2010. William had this life-changing thought (out of the blue) "Why don't I make a photo box and place small clay sculptures into it, take pictures, and then edit them on my computer." This single thought changed his life forever and for the better.

It is a night and day difference in styles when comparing the old (2010) with what the new Art looks like. William has a certain likeness for his earlier work because it defined the creative spirit within him that drives him to create more and more every day. His early designs were all created (nearly 28,000 designs) with just a 13 color palette.

More recently, William started using artificial intelligence in his Art designs, causing the 13 color palette to bloom into millions of colors. The AI caused a new evolution in his Art, opening up new avenues and alleyways that further fuel his mind.

What is fascinating about William making Art designs is that he does not dictate what the completed design will look like; he lets the design show *him* what it looks like. By following this method, editing designs are similar to Christmas because it is never known what the final design will look like until the Art is edited, pieced together, completed, and viewed.

William had another life-changing thought related to a short story he had not completed from 2012. On 13 January 2020, he had a future defining thought: "Why don't I write a story where a fossil of extraterrestrial origin is discovered, rewrites the entire evolutionary record, and an unforgettable adventure ensues."

This thought was critical because it closed the gap between 2012 writing and current writing, curing William's many years' long writer's block. Then on 15 August 2020, he became a published science fiction author penning the book mentioned earlier.

William is working on many different projects, both creative and literary. The third book in this "Untamed Cosmos Companion Saga" is in the research and idea-building stage of the writing process. Once complete, this will be the third entry in the "untamed saga."

Lastly, William is quite the Jokesmith, having written more than 2000 original jokes, which he plans to make into a "Look & Laugh" book composed of his visually stunning designs and his laughter-inducing jokes.

Dated 2-22-22

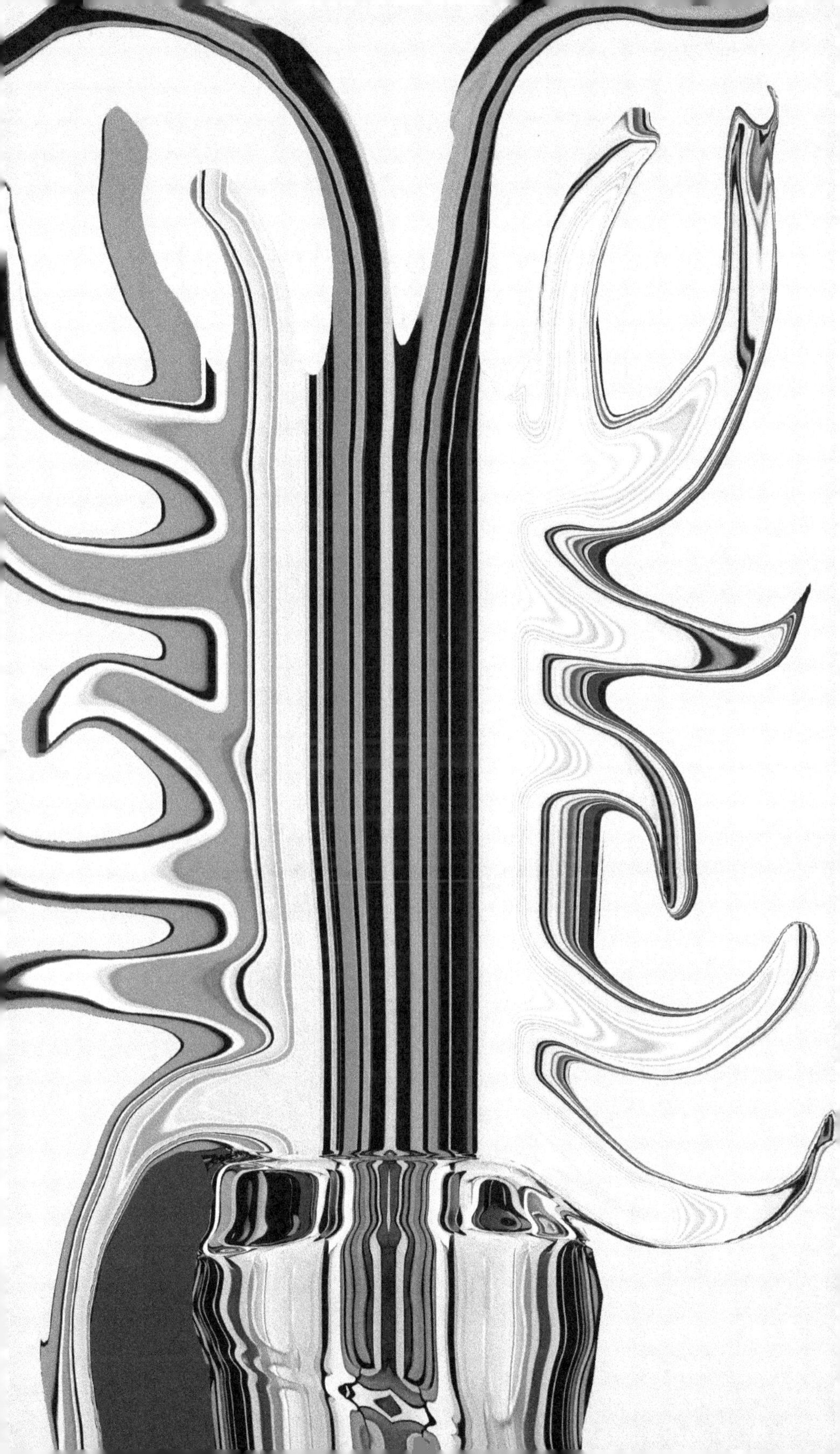

Information About the Illustrations & How to Purchase the Author's Art

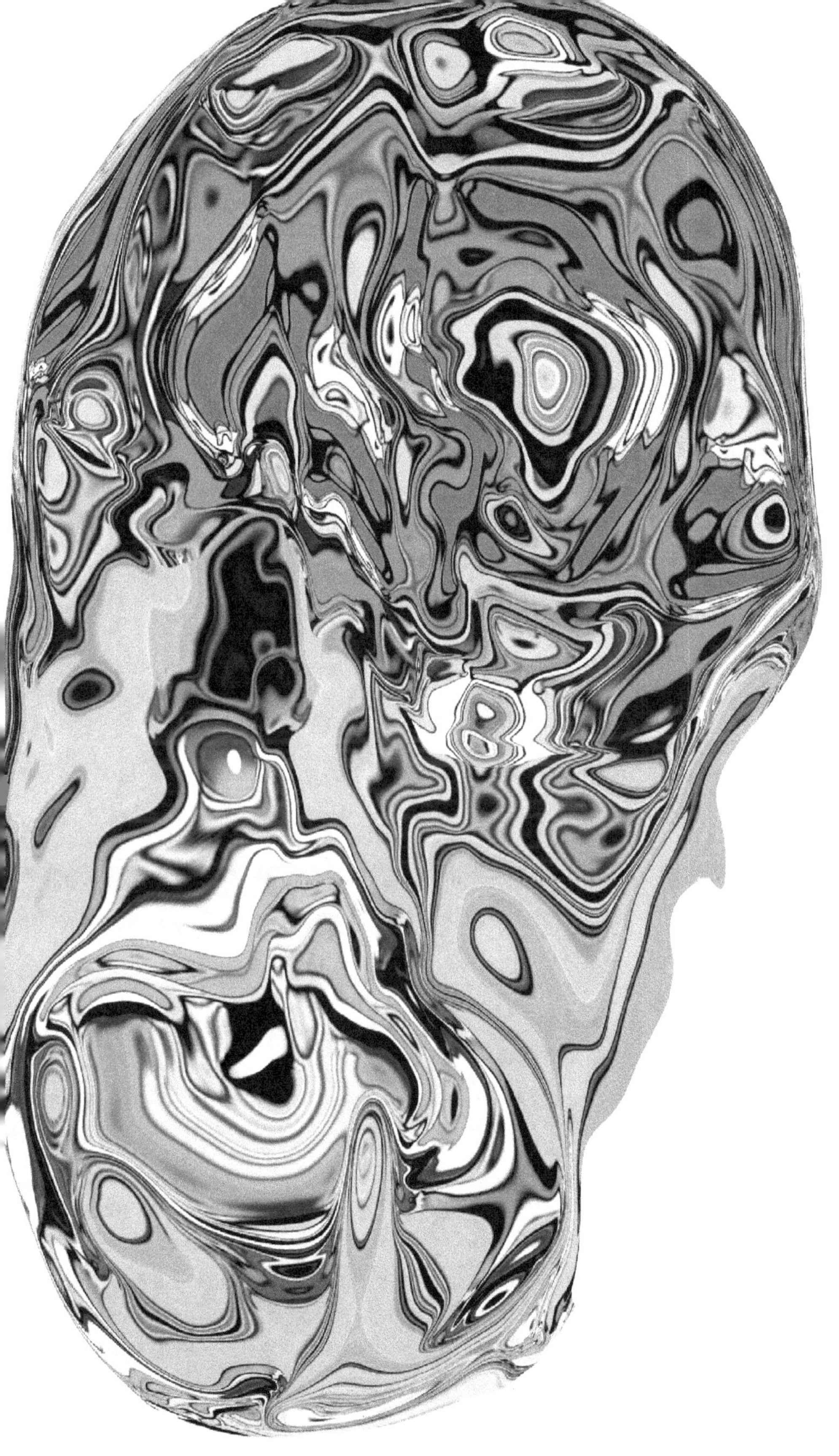

The author created the illustrations in this book, and many others, using micro clay sculptures, photo boxes, and digital manipulations (including artificial intelligence), resulting in the illustrations displayed in this book. Even though they are black and white, the designs are actually full color.

Did you thoroughly enjoy the illustrations throughout this book? Do you want to own your very own piece of <u>Waelchli Art</u>? For Art inquiries about obtaining prints/canvases or anything you wish to have adorned with the author's illustrations, please email Will@8Words.Art.

Please make sure that your email's subject reads "Art Inquiry." You may be the next proud owner of a design(s) from the author's vast collection of wholly original designs.

As of this book's printing in January 2022, the author's 'Psychedelic Design Artchive' includes nearly 50,000 unique & original designs, all of which can be made into many print sizes or printed on canvas or almost anything imaginable. All you need to do is send that initial email to Will@8Words.Art to get things started.

For a suggestions list about what the designs can be placed on, please write and request this list. It can provide the needed push from the reader to the new owner of authentic 'Psyentism' Art.

'Psyentism' is the emerging Art Movement that the author has established after working nonstop for over a decade on his creative craft. Psyentism is a mixture of the words Psychedelic + Science + Schism explaining the division (schism) between pre 21st-century psychedelia and post 20th century digital psychedelia.

The author strongly suggests you send a simple email to Will@8Words.Art with your inquiries and see where the email takes you. Hopefully, it will result in some of these 'Psyentism' designs being acquired by you and adorning anywhere you choose to place them.

These designs also act as conversation pieces and can provide entertainment by looking for different items within the designs of many select works. The Art purchased will spice up your space and improve your way of Life by being captivated by the elaborate & hypnotic works of pure Psyentism.

Lastly, please email Will@8Words.Art with the "ART Inquiry" subject line to possibly own one (or more) of the nearly 50,000 unique designs contained in his Artchive.

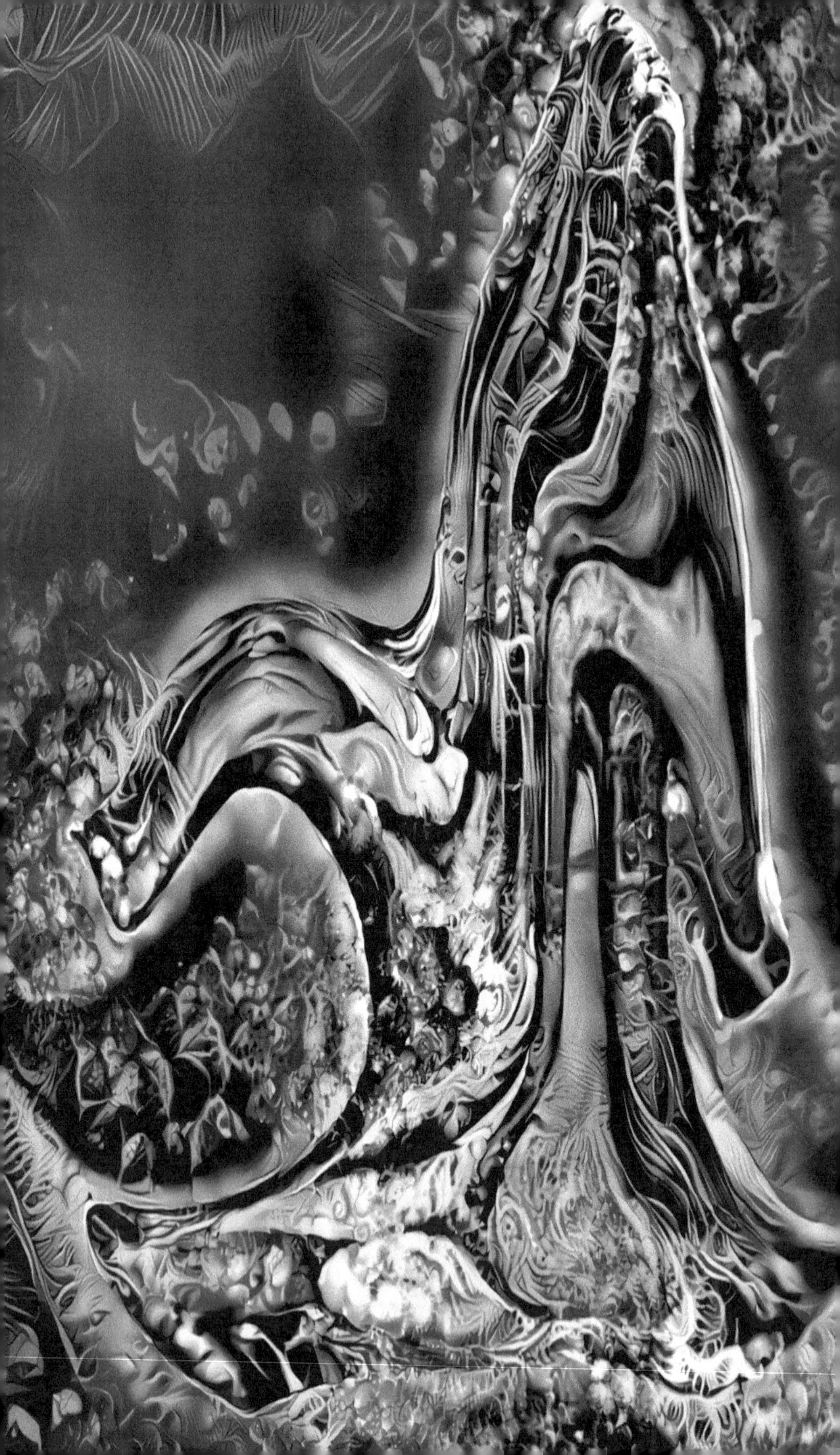

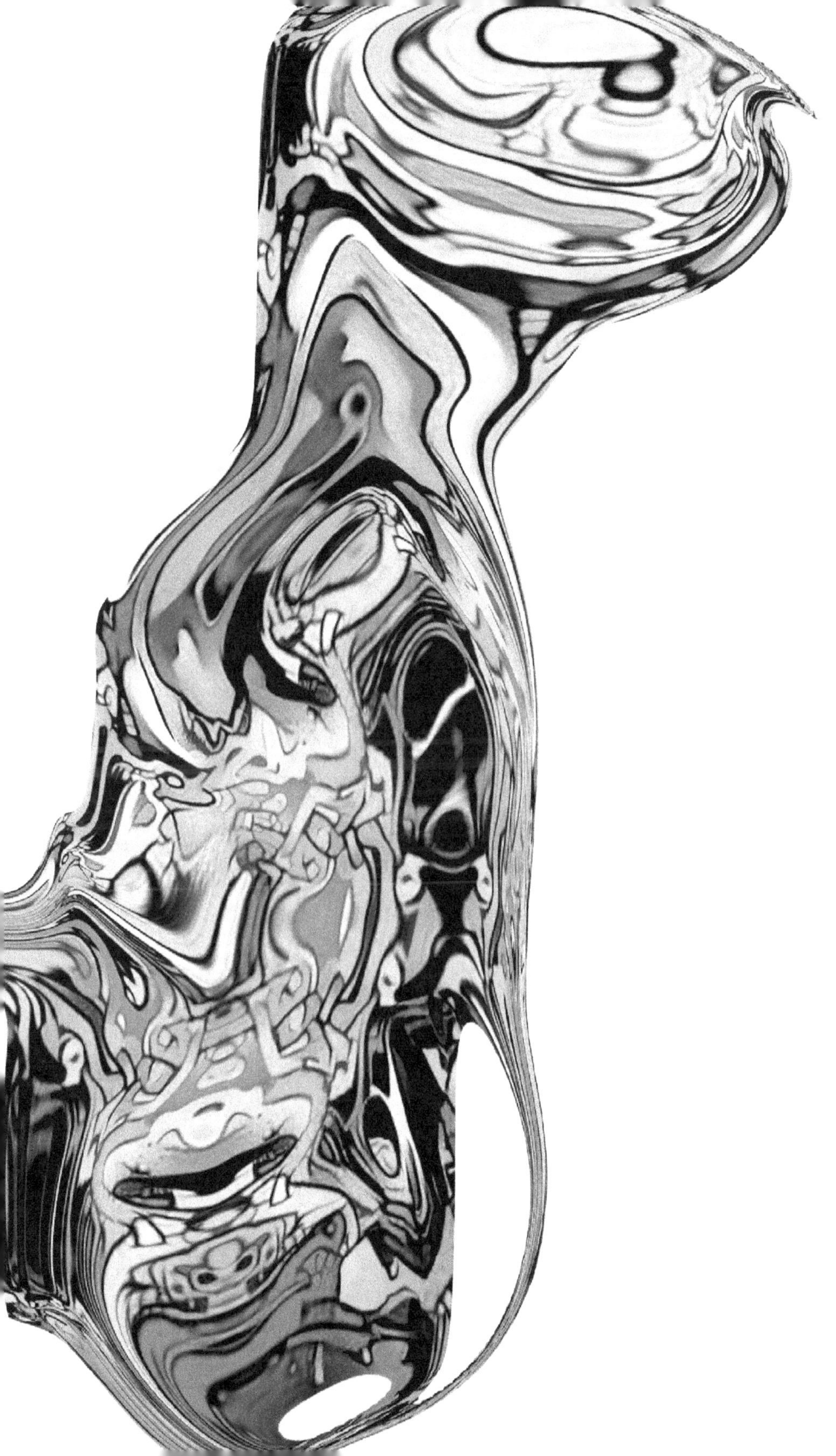

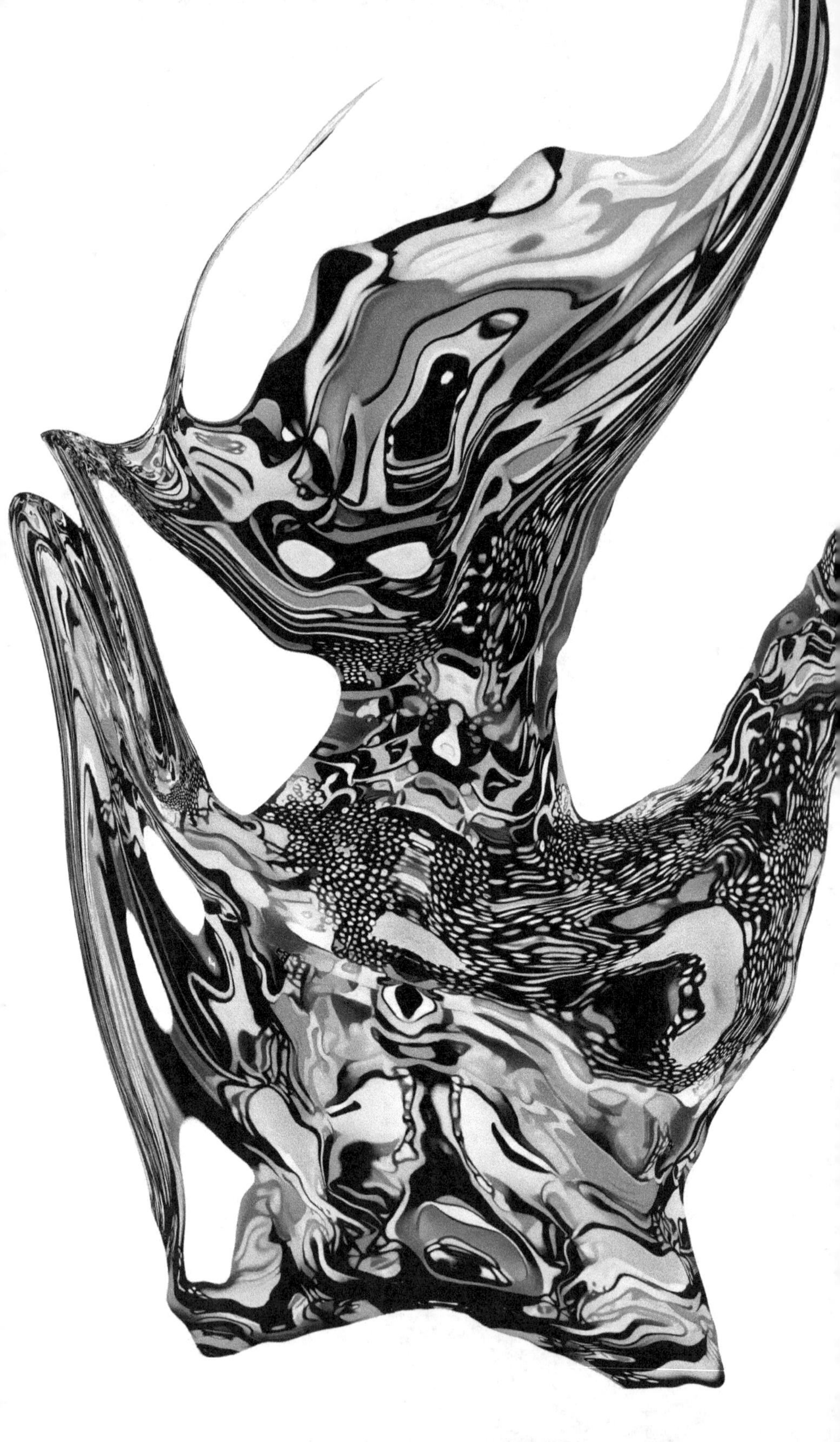

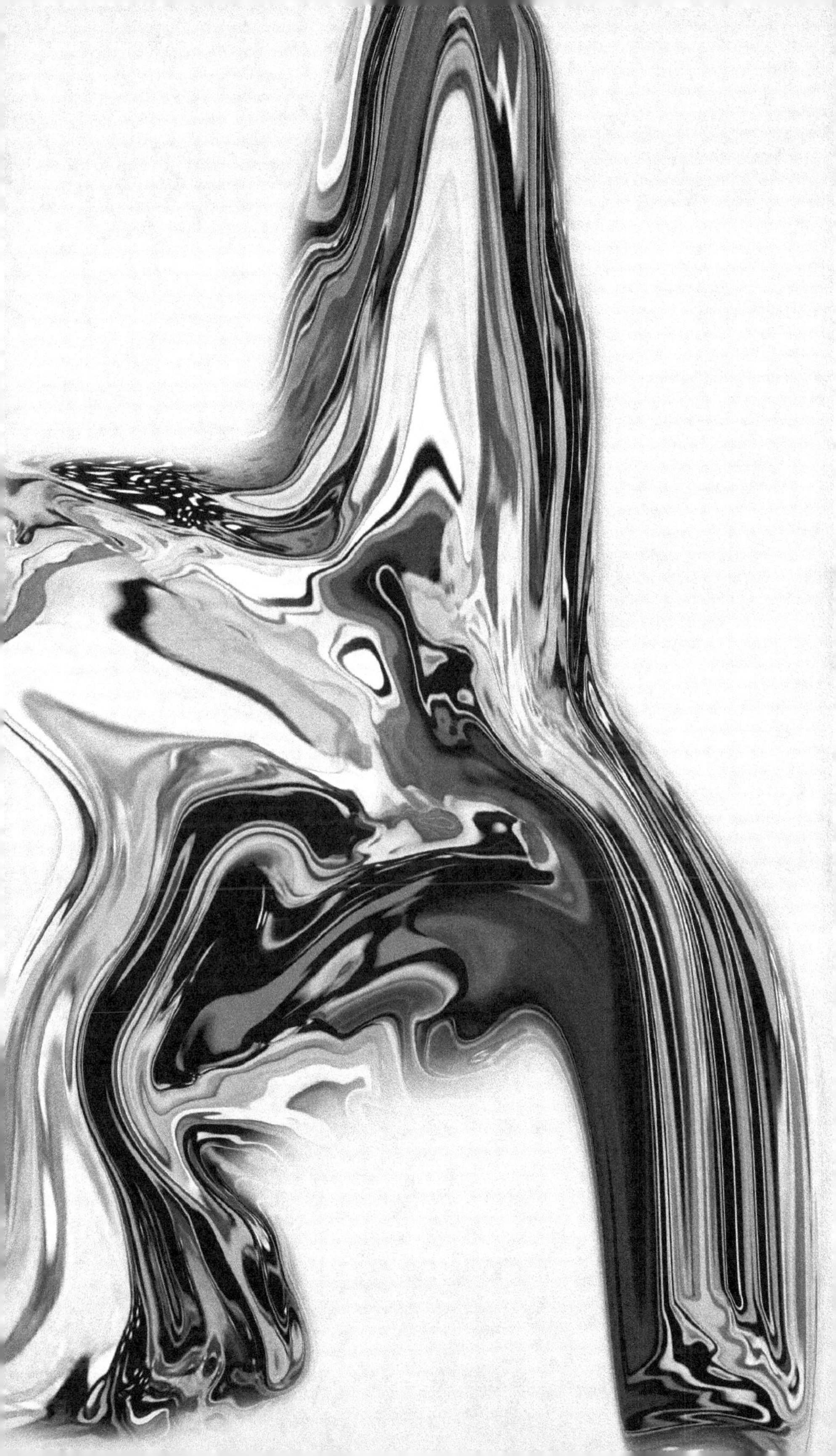

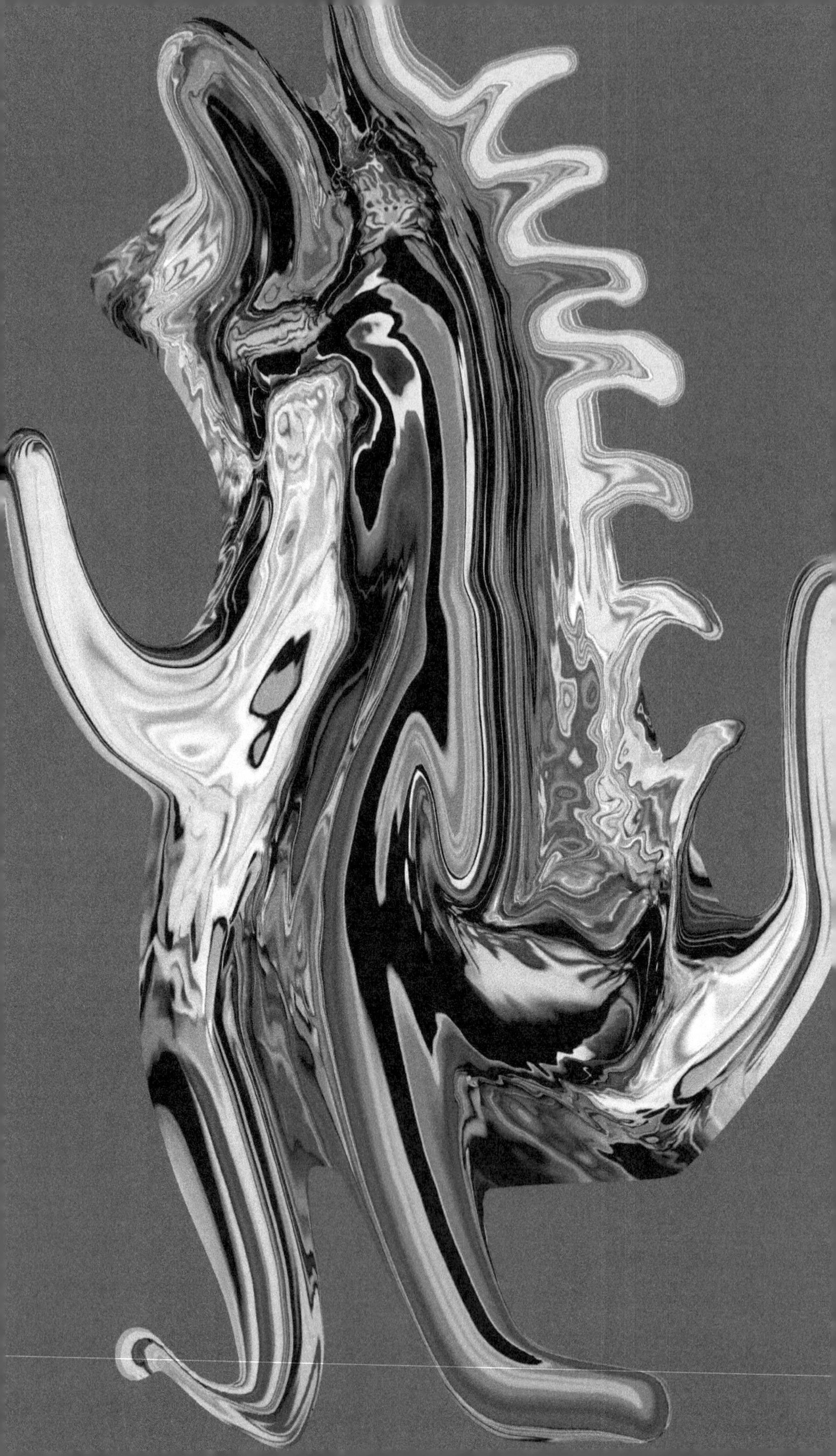

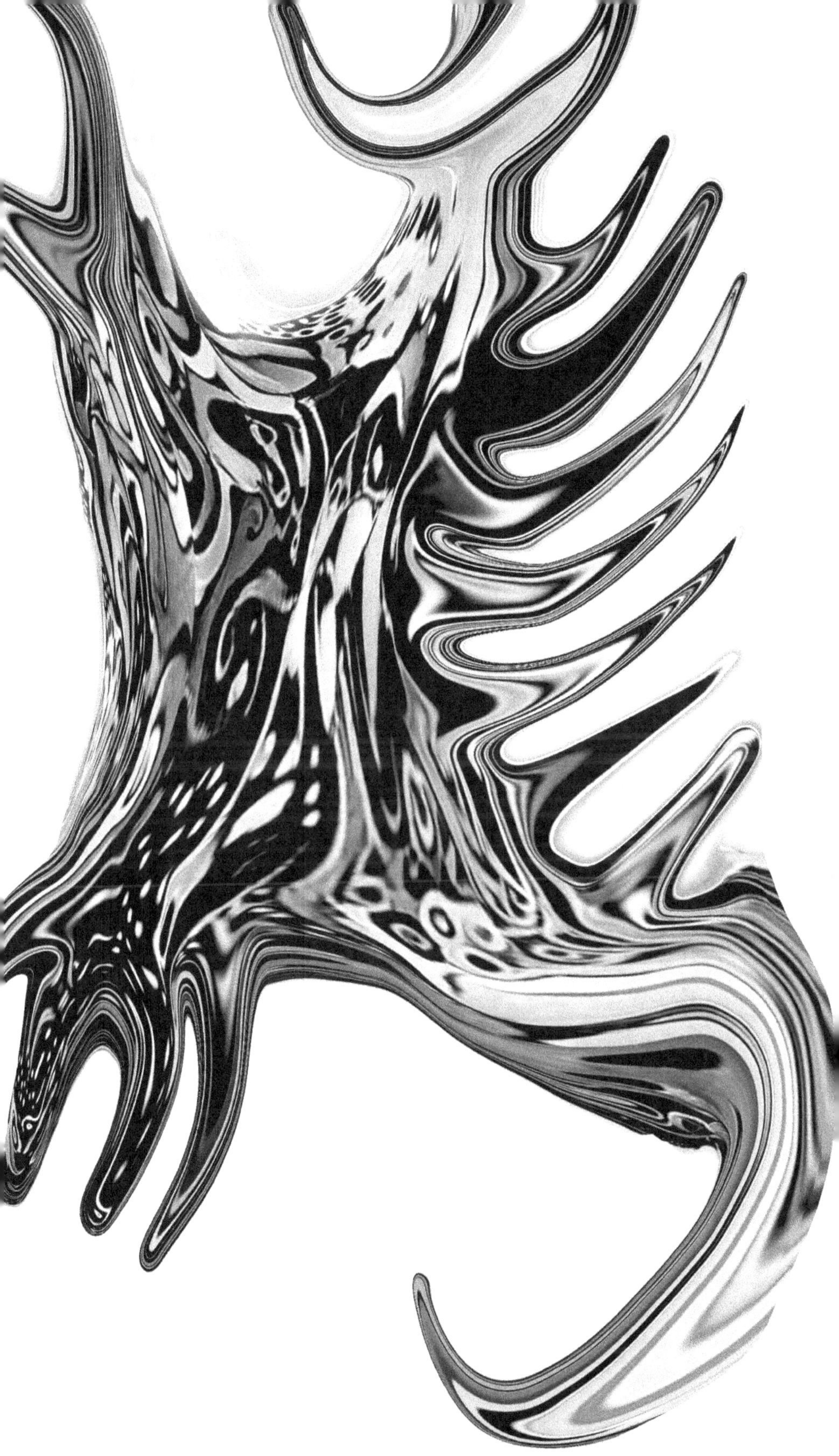

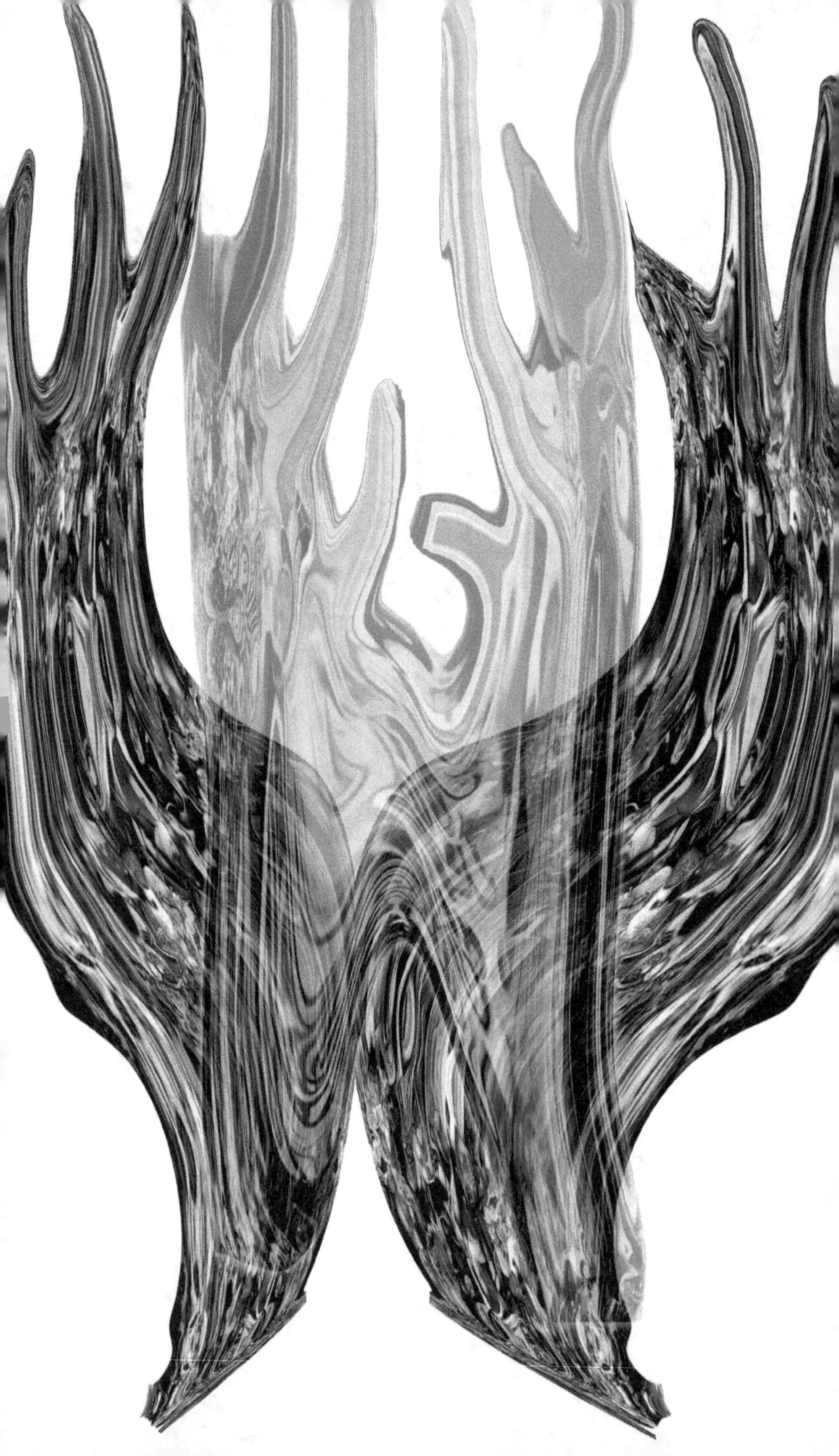

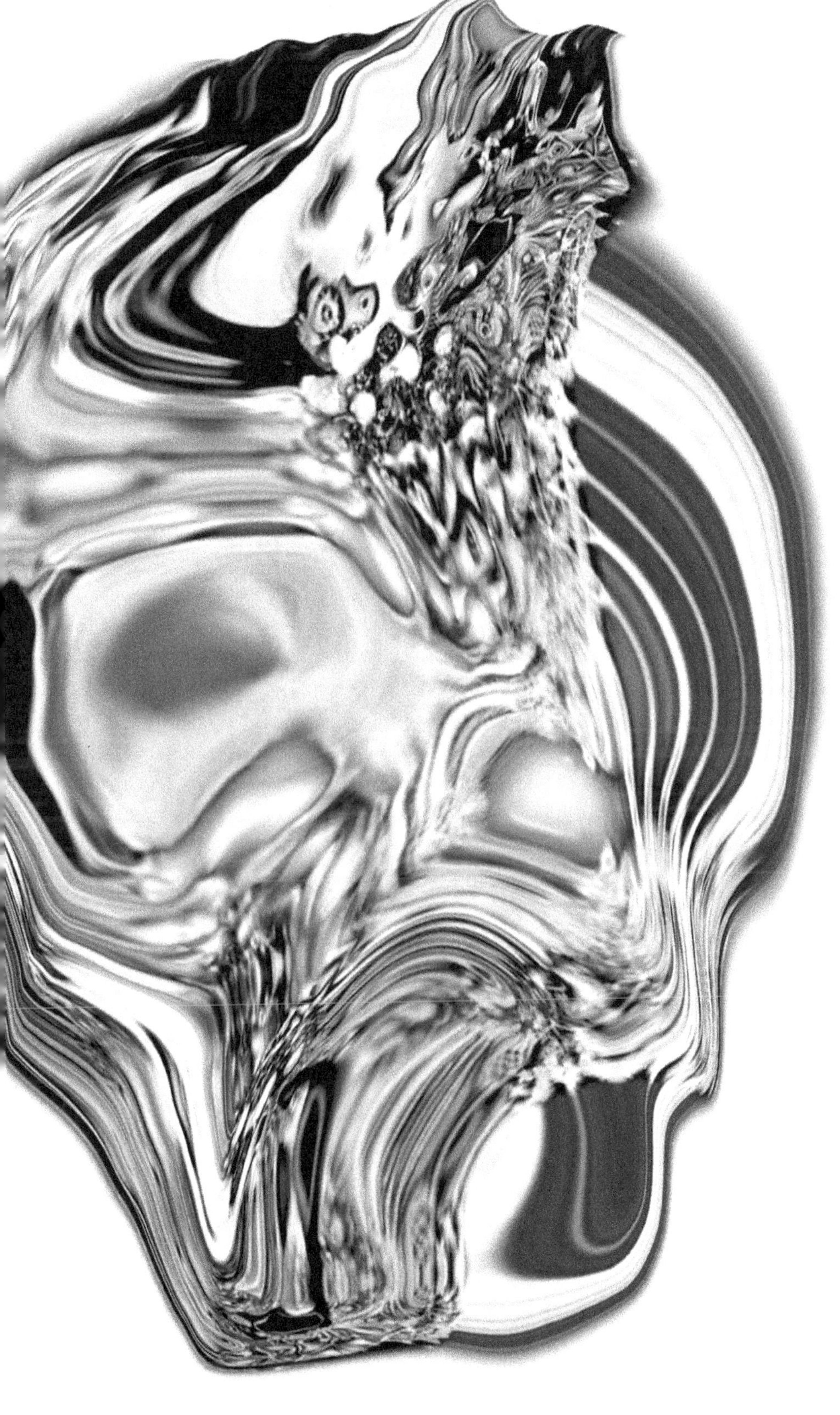

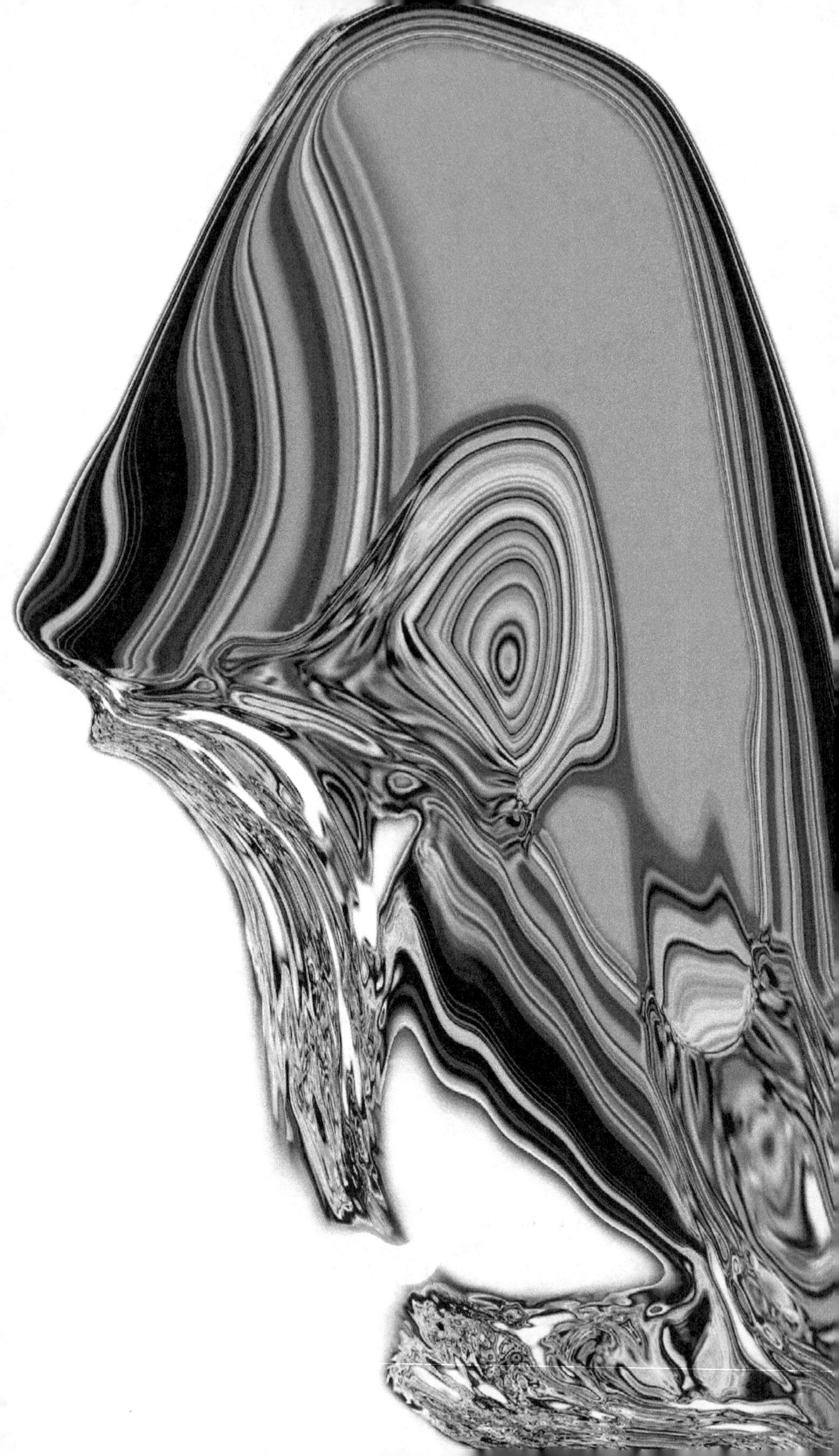

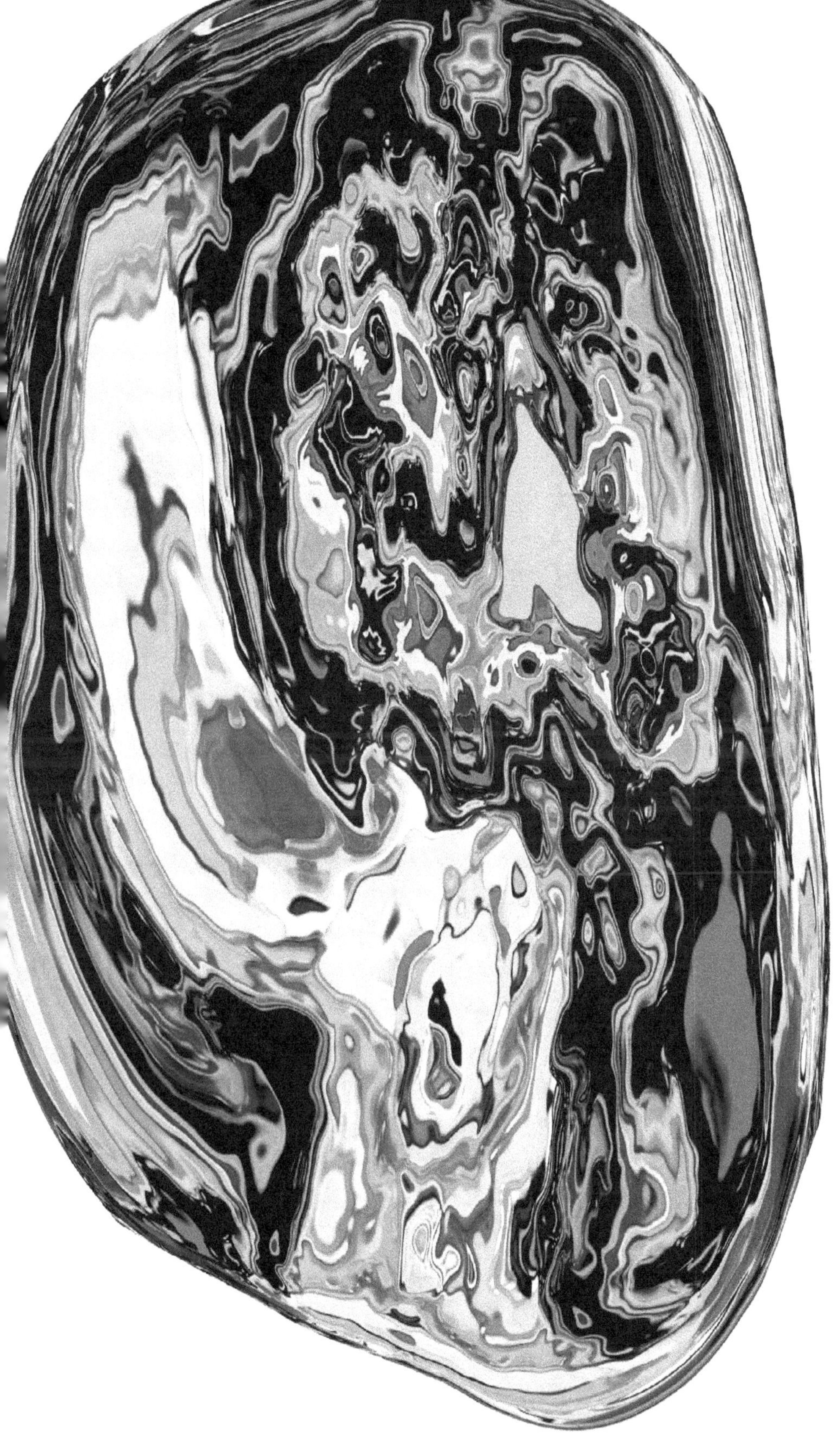

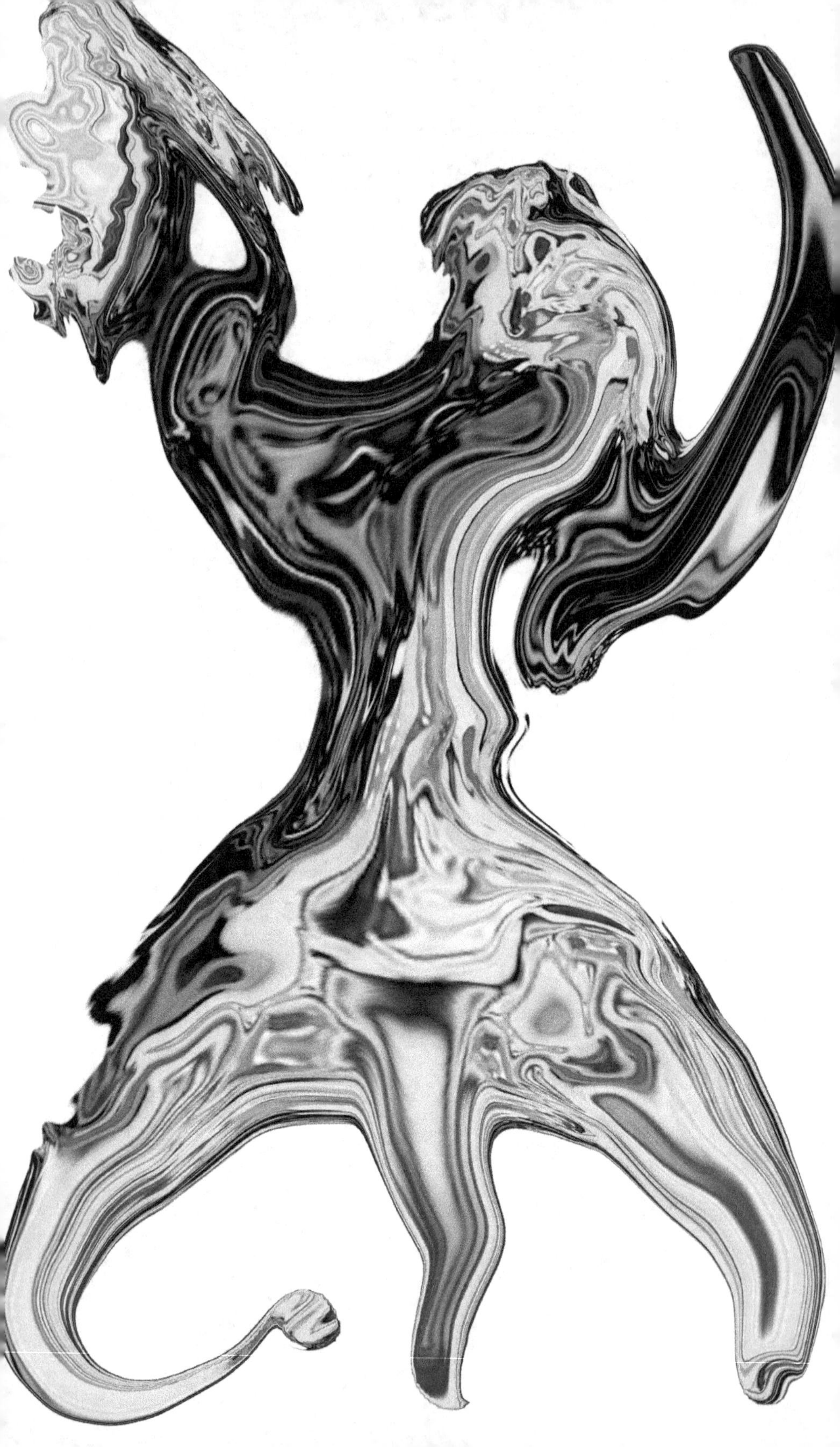

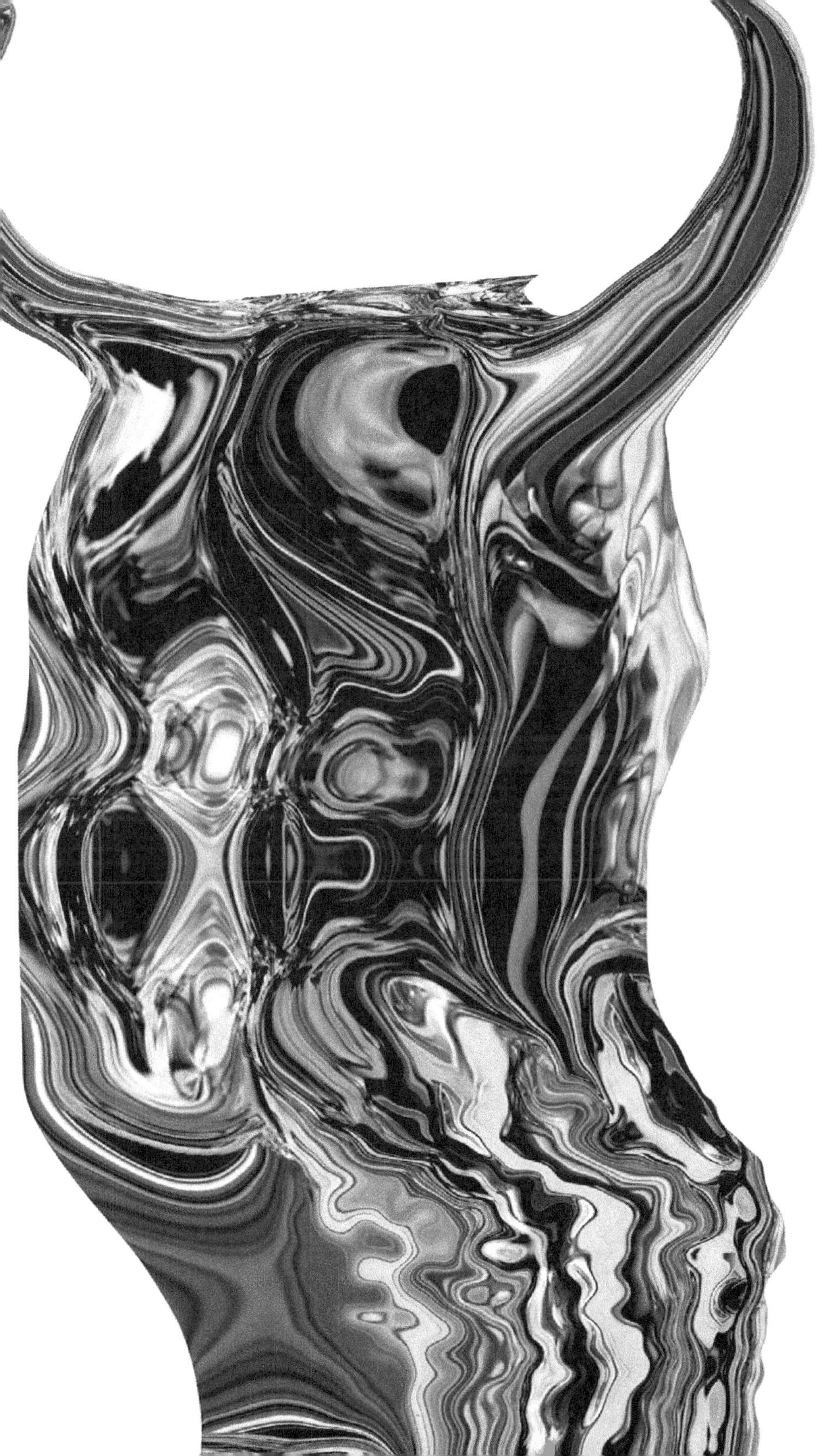

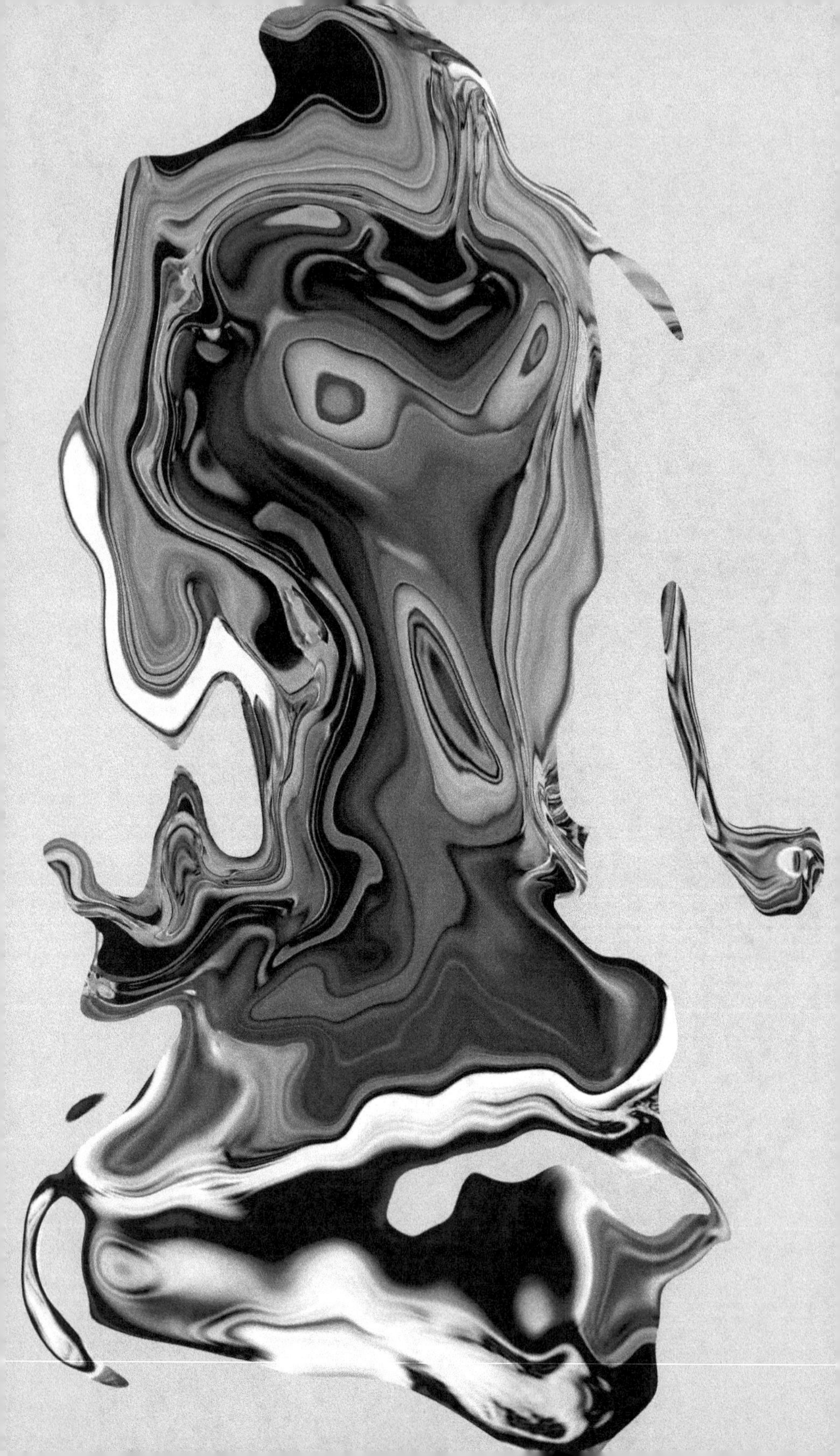

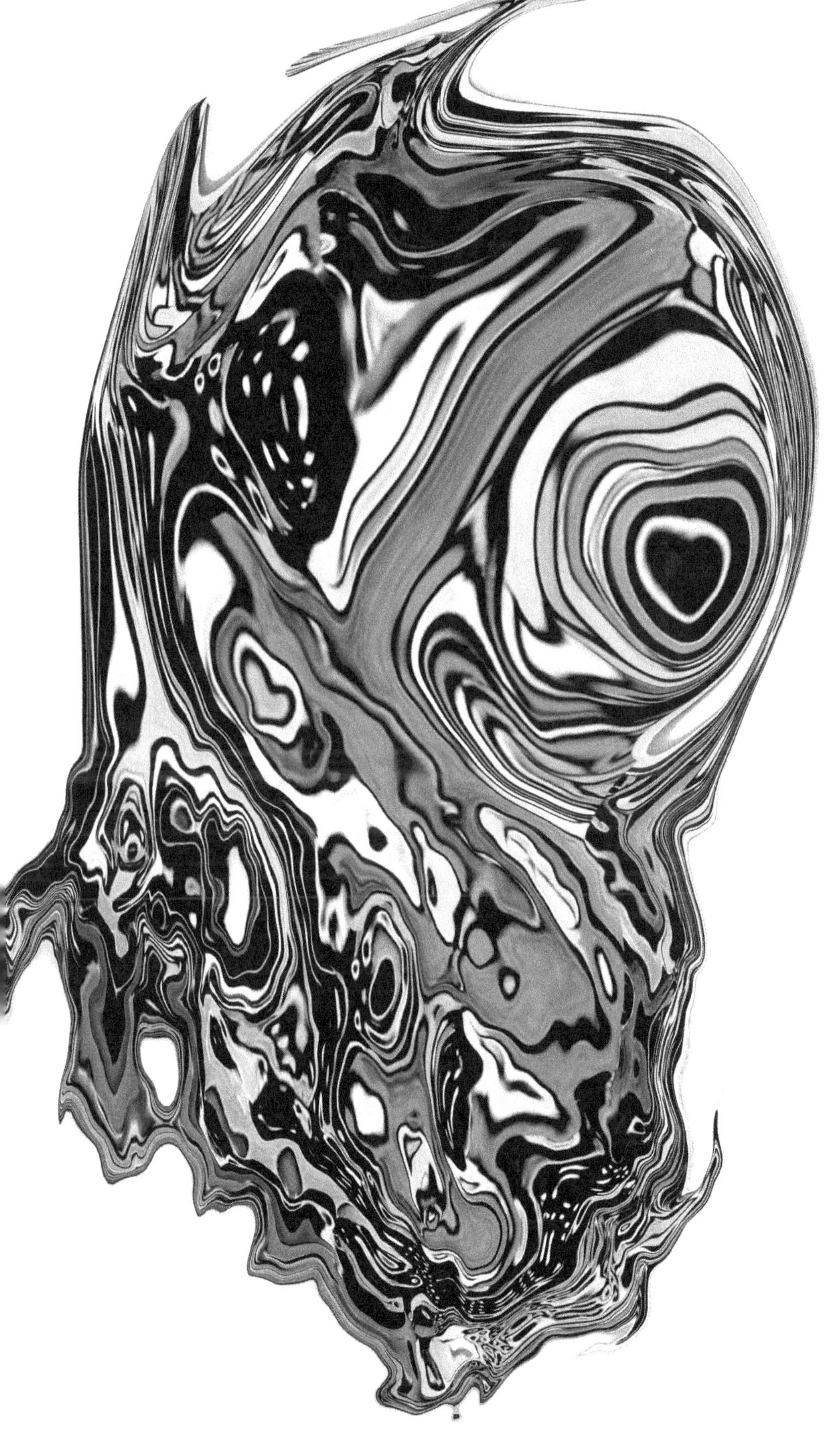

One Last Thing...

363

The author wants to extend a most apocalyptic thanks to you for making it through the chaotic and cosmic calamities that encompassed these "Tales from the Untamed Cosmos."

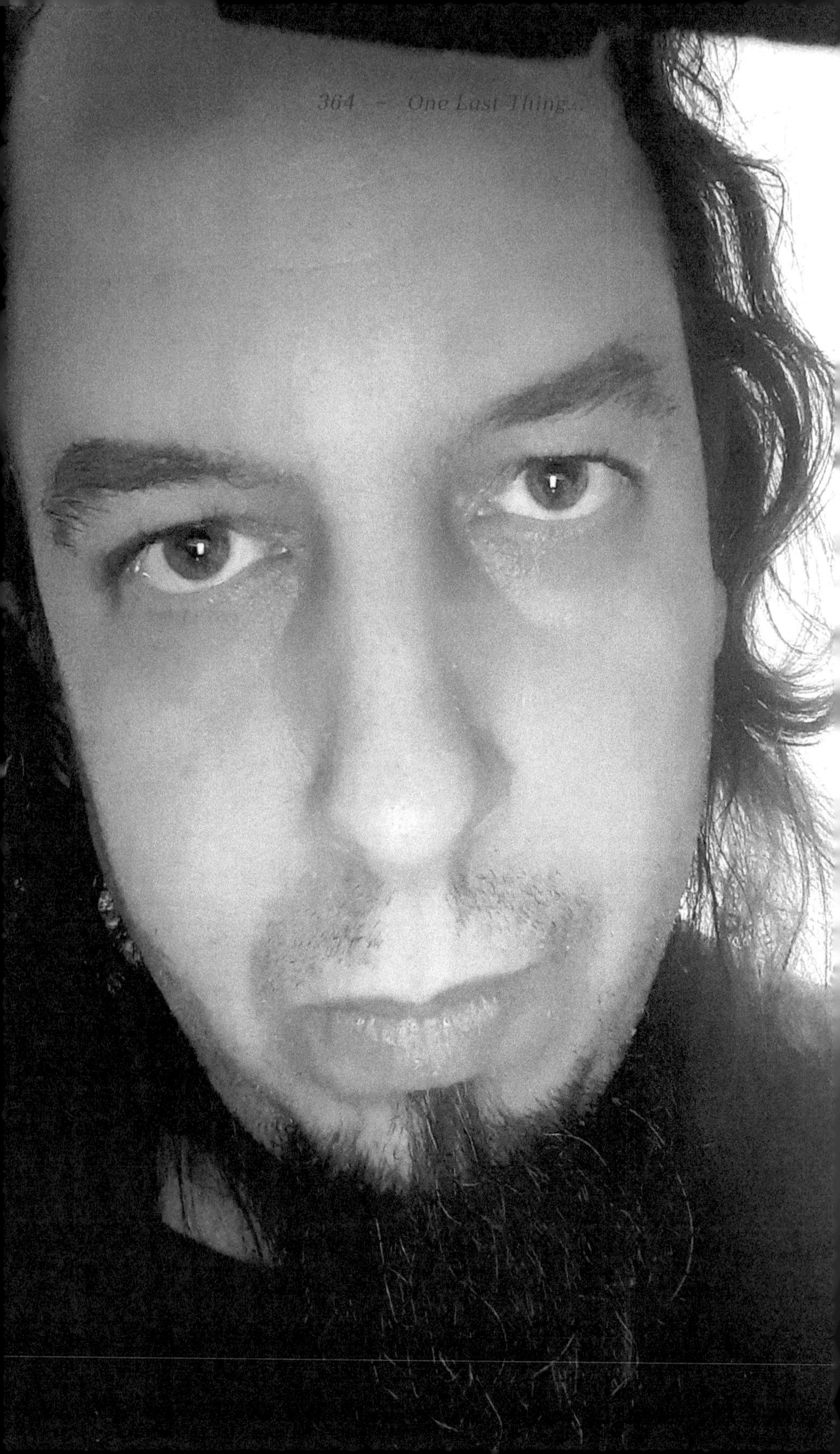

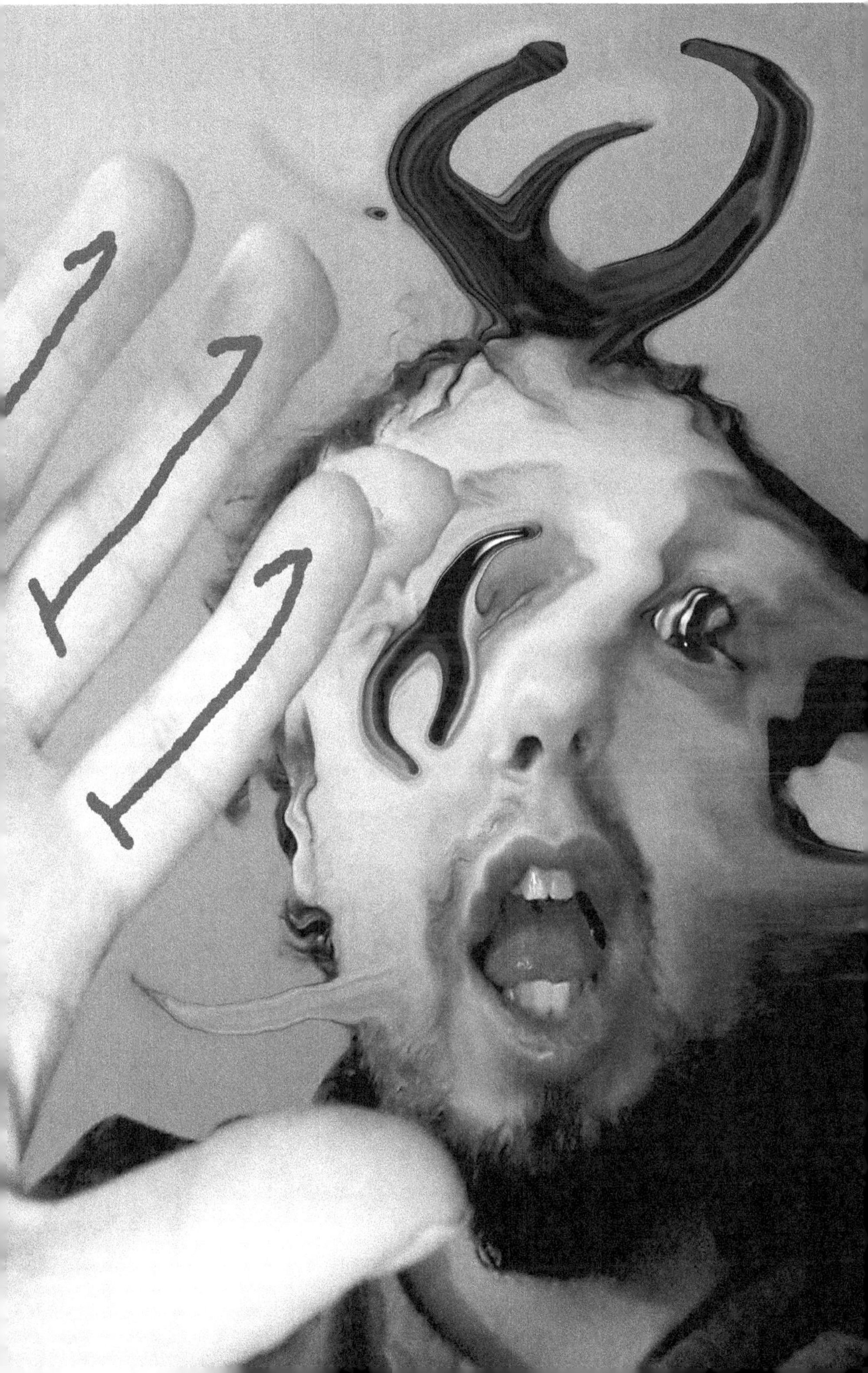
One Last Thing... ~ 365